THE FARMHOUSE KITCHEN

THE FARMHOUSE KITCHEN

MARY NORWAK

WARD LOCK

First published 1975 by Ward Lock
Villiers House, 41/47 Strand, London WC2N 5 JE, England
Reprinted 1979, 1980, 1981

Revised edition 1991

A Cassell imprint

© Text Mary Norwak

British Library Cataloguing in Publication Data
Norwak, Mary, 1929 –
      The Farmhouse Kitchen – rev. ed.
      1. Food: British dishes, – recipes
      I   Title
      641.5941

Typeset by August Filmsetting, Haydock, St Helens
Printed and bound in Great Britain by The Bath Press, Avon

ISBN: 0 7063 6970 X

The publishers would like to thank the following for kindly
supplying colour photographs reproduced in this book:

British Egg Information Service
Meat Promotions Executive
Milk Marketing Board of England and Wales
Sea Fish Industry Authority

CONTENTS

FOREWORD

Old and cherished recipes have survived a long time in country cottages and farmhouses. These dishes were devised by house-wives to feed large hungry hard-working families, often very poor, and accordingly, many of the recipes are very simple and made of the cheapest and most easily available ingredients.

Whole meals were made from mixtures of flour or meal and water or milk; a little flavour might be added with onion, or a tiny piece of cheese, root vegetables or herbs. A few pieces of fruit were turned into a filling pudding with a flour crust or with crumbs of bread. Cakes were plain but sometimes enlivened with a little precious spice or dried fruit.

The pig was the most commonly kept animal, fed on kitchen

scraps, so that pork and smoked pork appear most often in meat recipes. Hens scratched in the yard and ducks swam in the pond, and their eggs and flesh added variety to meals, along with rabbits and game which were trapped or shot, and river fish. In coastal areas, local fish was widely used, but rarely sent inland until mid-Victorian times. What they did have though was properly-hung meat and game, fresh dairy produce and newly-dug vegetables.

I hope that this book helps to recapture the flavour of farm food, and will encourage the use of fresh produce and of home preserves. It may also serve to remind us of regional delicacies and festive foods which gave a little much-needed spice to the quiet and often impoverished lives of our ancestors.

METRIC AND IMPERIAL CONVERSION TABLES

Quantities have been given in Metric and Imperial measurements. Work either in entirely Imperial or in Metric units; do not mix the two. Exact conversion from Imperial to Metric does not usually give very convenient working quantities, so the Metric measurements have been rounded off into 25 gram units, but they are still close enough to ensure successful results.

grams	ounces	ml	Imperial
15	$\frac{1}{2}$	25	1 fl oz
25	1	50	2 fl oz
40	$1\frac{1}{2}$	75	3 fl oz
50	2	100	4 fl oz
65	$2\frac{1}{2}$	150	$\frac{1}{4}$ pint
75	3	175	6 fl oz
90	$3\frac{1}{4}/3\frac{1}{2}$	200	7 fl oz
100	4	250	8 fl oz
150	5	275	9 fl oz
175	6	300	$\frac{1}{2}$ pint
200	7	325	11 fl oz

grams	ounces	ml	Imperial
225	8	350	12 fl oz
250	9	375	13 fl oz
275	10	400	14 fl oz
300	11	450	$\frac{3}{4}$ pint
350	12	475	16 fl oz
375	13	500	17 fl oz
400	14	550	18 fl oz
425	15	575	19 fl oz
450	16 (1 lb)	600	1 pint
575	$1\frac{1}{4}$ lb	750	$1\frac{1}{4}$ pints
675	$1\frac{1}{2}$ lb	900	$1\frac{1}{2}$ pints
900	2 lb	1 litre	$1\frac{3}{4}$ pints
1 kg	$2\frac{1}{4}$ lb	1.1 litres	2 pints

Spoon Measurements

1.25 ml = $\frac{1}{4}$ teaspoon
2.5 ml = $\frac{1}{2}$ teaspoon
5 ml   = 1 teaspoon
15 ml   = 1 tablespoon
All spoon measurements are level.

NOTES ON
FARMHOUSE COOKING

FATS

Butter was an expensive commodity in the past, so lard and dripping were mainly used by country families. Lard was obtained from the cottage pig, and dripping saved from roasting beef, pork or lamb joints.

Lard was obtained by cutting up the surplus pig fat into small pieces and 'rendering' it or 'doing it down' over a low heat. As it melted the fat was poured off until it ceased to give, and this resulted in pure and delicious lard, often flavoured with a sprig of rosemary. Throughout the nineteenth century, country children had lard spread on their bread instead of butter. When the lard had been extracted, there remained crisp crunchy pieces of fat, called, variously, 'scratchings', 'cracklings' or 'fritters'. These were often eaten rolled in salt, or added to a mixture of apples, dried fruit, brown sugar and spice in a delicious pie, or added to a cake mixture.

Dripping, the strained fat recovered after roasting meat, was kept in separate containers, according to whether it came from roast beef, lamb or pork. It was a particular teatime treat when spread on hot toast, but was also a traditional ingredient in puddings and cakes. Before using in recipes, dripping should be clarified.

Clarified dripping Make the dripping hot and pour it into boiling water. Stir it for three or four minutes and leave it to get cold. The impurities will sink to the bottom and should be removed with a knife.

Butter, when it came into general use, was heavily salted. Unsalted butter went rancid very quickly. Today, most recipes (including the ones in this book) expect you to use slightly salted butter or to add a pinch of salt, except when frying or making cakes. For these, use unsalted butter if possible.

FIRES

Many old country recipes specify the use of a bakestone or girdle, or recommend that dishes should stand by the side, or in front of the fire. These methods arose from traditional ways of cooking. Originally food in cottages and farmhouses was cooked on or in front of an open fire. Meat was cooked on a spit set just before the fire, and baked goods could be prepared on a flat suspended girdle or griddle. Meat, bread, pies and cakes were frequently taken to the village bread-oven for cooking, being baked on the floor of the oven when the fire had been lit and removed from it. A similar bread oven was built into larger farmhouses. Early enclosed ranges began to appear at the beginning of the nineteenth century, and these gradually developed with a hotplate at the side on which pans could stand. Subsequently an oven was fitted at the side of a range so that housewives could prepare baked savoury and sweet dishes as we know them today.

SUGAR

Most less wealthy country homes did not have sugar until quite late. When sugar came into general use, it was in the shape of 63 kg/14 lb blocks or 'loaves' which had to be cut or scraped with a sharp knife, and the sugar itself was coarse and granular. It had to be pounded to make it soft and fine, like modern sugar. Today, granulated sugar can be used for many recipes, but caster sugar should be used for cakes and custards.

FLAVOURINGS

Country meals which were often rather plain and monotonous were sometimes varied by the use of liquid flavourings, spices and herbs.

Liquid flavourings Rosewater and orange-flower water were used to flavour creams, sweet cakes and biscuits in the more prosperous households. They are still obtainable today from the chemist and give a subtlety to many sweet dishes.

Robust meat, poultry and game dishes were flavoured with cider, wine or beer. Home-made cider was prepared and used on small farms and in cottages, and home-made wines were also widely used, the sweeter flower wines being particularly popular in sauces. Larger houses had their own brew-houses and ale or richer stout were both drunk and used for cooking. These alcoholic liquids not only flavoured dishes, but also helped to break up tough fibres and give succulence to slow-cooked meats.

Spices A wide range of spices was used for all types of sweet and savoury dishes and for pickles and preserves, but they were too expensive for small farmers or cottage dwellers. Originally they served to disguise the ill-flavour of winter-salted meat, and stale materials, but they became popular in their own right. Ginger was a particular favourite, particularly used in the gingerbread eaten on so many festive occasions. The ground spice was employed and in richer households preserved stem ginger was used. Root ginger was most often used in chutney and pickles, but it needed breaking up with a heavy weight to release its flavour.

Herbs Many of our favourite herbs were introduced by the Romans, including onions, rosemary and parsley, and they have been popular flavourings in this country for nearly two thousand years. About 200 herbs were in common use in medieval times, but the number dwindled to about forty by the mid-nineteenth century, and we only use six or seven regularly today. Country-dwellers made use of such herbs as nettles and sorrel to flavour plain suet puddings, mint to flavour fruit dishes, and cottage geranium leaves to flavour jellies and cakes. Herbs to go with meat were originally chosen from the grazing herbs which the animals had eaten. Thus English lamb, grazed on the marshes, was normally served with mint; the Welsh prefer thyme for their mountain sheep; while Greeks and Italians prefer oregano (a member of the marjoram family) for lamb dishes.

PASTRY AND PIES

Three types of pastry were most commonly used in farmhouse cooking. *Shortcrust pastry* which is a simple mixture of fat, flour and water; *puff pastry* which is a richer mixture of fat and flour; and *hot-water pastry* made with fat, flour and hot water. The latter was used for meat, game and a few fruit pies, and used to be moulded over a wooden shape or over a clenched hand, but is now more commonly cooked inside a metal mould or cake tin.

Huff paste was made as a covering for baking joints of lamb, pork, ham and venison, rather as we use foil today. It was usually made with flour and water, but venison huff paste also contained fat. This paste kept the meat moist, but it was not usually eaten, being discarded into the hen bucket.

Shaping pastry Early pies were rarely baked in special moulds, but were formed into turnovers or pasties which could be baked directly on a bakestone or griddle, or on the floor of a bread oven. When saucers came into general use, old ones were often used for baking little pies, particularly those made with fruit.

Pastry which covers a deep pie needs a tiny edge, and this is best achieved by *knocking-up*. This keeps shortcrust pies neat and decorates them, and it helps richer pastries to rise during cooking by opening up the edges. When the pastry is trimmed off, the knife should be held horizontally and the sides of the pie tapped with a slight upward movement forming a series of shallow cuts. This edge can be *crimped* or pinched between finger and thumb, or it can be *fluted* by holding the pastry lightly with the forefinger and thumb of one hand, pressing the pastry between them with the forefinger of the other hand.

CHAPTER ONE

BREAKFAST

Many farmers have two breakfasts because they start work so early in the morning. A modern farmer may only begin his day, at first light, with a cup of tea and some toast or cereal, and then eat his full breakfast meal about nine o'clock. But in the past, those who had to start the day's work at some distance from their homes would begin it with porridge and then return later to breakfast. Those whose work was nearer home would begin with a hearty breakfast, and come back for 'ten o'clocks'.

Either way, a farm breakfast usually starts with a cereal or porridge. After this comes a cooked dish of two or three 'fries,' such as bacon, eggs, tomatoes, mushrooms and fried potatoes; sometimes there may be kidneys, sausages or fish. In warmer weather, cold ham, brawn or boiled bacon is popular. After this comes plenty of new bread, oatcakes or toast, accompanied by honey or home-made marmalade.

PORRIDGE TO START ON

OATMEAL PORRIDGE

25 ml/1f fl oz cold water
1½ tablespoons coarse oatmeal
1 saltspoon salt

Use the quantities above for each person. Bring the water to the boil and start stirring it while you run the oatmeal in from your hand. Stir very well to prevent lumps forming. Season with the salt, and bring to the boil. Cover with a lid and simmer for thirty minutes.

Serves 1

CROWDY

Fine oatmeal
Salt
Boiling water
Butter
Milk

Crowdy differs from porridge in that it is made from finely-ground meal and no cooking is needed if boiling water is used. For one person, put three tablespoons fine oatmeal into a bowl and add salt to taste. Pour in boiling water and stir briskly until it is as wet as you want it. Leave the crowdy to stand for a minute or two, and it will have swollen. Put a knob of butter in the centre of the bowl.

The crowdy should be eaten by taking a little on a spoon and dipping it into a mug of cold milk.

SAVOURY COOKED DISHES

POTATO HOTCAKES

900 g/2 lb potatoes
2 tablespoons flour
1 dessertspoon powdered mustard
2 tablespoons finely-grated onion
2 eggs
Salt and pepper
Fat or dripping for frying

Peel the potatoes and soak in cold water for thirty minutes. Grate them and drain away any liquid. Add the flour, mustard powder, onion and beaten eggs. Mix thoroughly and season with salt and pepper. Melt a little fat or dripping in a pan and drop in the mixture in spoonfuls. When brown on one side, after about three minutes, turn over and brown the other side. Serve with bacon or sausages.

Makes 12

FLODDIES

1 large potato
1 tablespoon grated cheese
1 egg
Flour
Herbs and seasoning as in recipe
Fat for frying

Peel the potato and grate raw flesh. Mix this with the cheese and egg. Add enough flour to make a soft dropping consistency like a thick pancake mixture. Season to taste with salt and pepper and a pinch of mustard powder. Add some chopped fresh herbs such as chives, thyme, sage or parsley. Fry in spoonfuls in hot fat for about three minutes, and serve very hot.

Serves 4

KIPPER CAKES

225 g/8 oz cooked kippers
225 g/8 oz mashed potato
25 g/1 oz butter, softened
2 eggs
1 teaspoon chopped parsley
Salt and pepper
2 tablespoons browned breadcrumbs
Fat for frying

Remove bones from the kippers and flake the flesh. Mix with the mashed potato, softened butter and one of the eggs. Add the parsley and salt and pepper to taste and mix thoroughly. Divide the mixture into six pieces and form into cakes about 2.5 cm/1 in thick and two and a half inches across. Beat the other egg and dip the kipper cakes into it. Coat them in the breadcrumbs and fry in hot fat for about three minutes each side until golden-brown on both sides. Serve hot.

Serves 4

HERRINGS FRIED OR GRILLED IN OATMEAL

4 herrings
2 tablespoons oatmeal
½ teaspoon salt
Fat for frying

Scale and clean the herrings and wash and dry them well. Mix the oatmeal and salt and use this to coat the herrings. Fry in hot fat for five minutes each side. Grilled herrings can be coated likewise before cooking.

Serves 4

BUTTERED BLOATERS

4 bloaters
50 g/2 oz butter
2 tablespoons lemon juice
Salt and pepper

Cut off the heads, tails and fins of the bloaters and remove the backbones. Put into a greased ovenware dish and dot them with butter. Sprinkle on the lemon juice, salt and pepper. Cover and bake at 350°F, 180°C, gas mark 4 for ten minutes.

Serves 4

Bloaters are a speciality of East Anglia. They are whole fresh herrings which are dry-salted and lightly smoked. They were very popular in Victorian times and were often made into a strongly-flavoured paste.

BLOATERS GRILLED WITH MUSTARD

4 bloaters
25 g/1 oz butter, melted
2 teaspoons made mustard
2 tablespoons browned breadcrumbs

Clean and trim the bloaters and make three slashes along one side of each fish with a sharp knife. Brush with melted butter and grill the bloaters on both sides very lightly. Fill the slashes with mustard and sprinkle the breadcrumbs on bloaters. Pour on any remaining butter and brown the bloaters under a hot grill.

Serves 4

SMOKED HADDOCK IN MILK

1 large smoked haddock
600 ml/1 pint milk
Butter

Skin the haddock and remove the main bones. Put into a shallow heatproof buttered pan and cover with the milk. Cook gently for ten minutes until the fish is tender. Drain, and serve with knobs of butter.

Serves 2

SCRAMBLED EGGS WITH KIPPERS

2 kippers
6 eggs
Pepper
1 tablespoon butter
4 slices buttered toast

Grill the kippers and discard the bones and skin. Flake the flesh and keep warm. Beat the eggs lightly with a fork and season with a little pepper but no salt. Melt the butter in a pan and add the beaten eggs. Add the kipper flesh and cook over a low heat, moving the mixture constantly from the bottom of the pan but not stirring. While the eggs are still creamy, put them on the toast, and serve at once.

Serves 4

CREAMED EGGS

4 eggs
150 ml/¼ pint cream
Salt and pepper
Buttered toast

Break the eggs into a thick pan and stir with the cream, salt and pepper. Stir over a low heat until thick. Serve on buttered toast.

Serves 4

RUMBLED EGGS

4 eggs and 2 egg yolks
175 g/6 oz butter
1 tablespoon water
Toast or cooked bacon or kidneys
Salt and pepper

Put the eggs, egg yolks, butter and water into a thick saucepan. Season with salt and pepper. Stir over a low heat until thick. Serve on toast, or with bacon or kidneys.

Serves 4

CUMBERLAND SAUSAGES

675 g/1½ lb lean and fat pork
175 g/6 oz bread
Salt and pepper
Pinch of marjoram
Sausage skins (optional)

Mince the pork twice. Soak the bread in 300 ml (½ pint) cold water until very wet and mix this with the pork. Add the salt and pepper and the

marjoram. Put into skins, or form into sausage shapes for frying. The water in these sausages will form a good gravy when the sausages are fried.

Makes 900 g (2 lb)

GLAMORGAN SAUSAGES

150 g/5 oz soft breadcrumbs
75 g/3 oz grated cheese
Pinch of mixed herbs
A little chopped onion
Salt and dry mustard
1 egg, separated
Lard for frying

Combine the dry ingredients, season, bind with egg yolk and form into sausage shapes. Roll in flour, dip in egg white and crumbs, and fry in lard.

Serves 4

SUFFOLK SAUSAGES

2.75 kg/6 lb pork sausage meat
50 g/2 oz salt
Pinch of mace
Pinch of cloves
7 g/¼ oz pepper
Pinch of nutmeg
150 g/5 oz soft breadcrumbs
150 ml/¼ pint hot water
Sausage skins

Mix thoroughly and put into skins. Boil these sausages before frying them.

Makes 3 kg (7 lb)

OXFORD SAUSAGES

450 g/1 lb lean veal
450 g/1 lb pork
450 g/1 lb shredded suet
225 g/8 oz soft breadcrumbs
Rind of half lemon
7 g/¼ oz nutmeg
6 sage leaves
1 teaspoon pepper
2 teaspoons salt
Sprigs of thyme, marjoram and savory

Mince all the meats together. Add all the other ingredients and mix thoroughly. Fill skins.

Makes 1.5 kg (3½ lb)

SPICED PORK SAUSAGES

1.4 kg/3 lb bread
4 kg/9 lb lean pork
1.4 kg/3 lb firm fat from fat bacon
75 g/3 oz salt
25 g/1 oz white pepper
15 g/½ oz ginger
20 g/¾ oz mace
Sausage skins

Soak the bread in cold water and wring out. Put lean meat and fat through a coarse mincer. Mix in seasonings, then add the bread and run the whole lot through a fine mincer. Fill sausage skins.

Makes 7 kg (15 lb)

GRILLED KIDNEYS

8 lamb's kidneys
Salt and pepper
Butter, melted
Parsley, chopped

Skin the kidneys and split them in half without quite detaching them. Fasten them flat on skewers and season lightly with salt and pepper. Brush over with melted butter and grill on both sides for five minutes. Place on buttered toast and pour over a little melted butter and chopped parsley.

Serves 4

TOSSED KIDNEYS

8 lamb's kidneys
Butter
Salt and pepper
1 teaspoon flour
300 ml/½ pint stock
Juice of one lemon
1 teaspoon chopped parsley
Fried bread

Skin the kidneys and slice them. Heat a little butter in a pan and fry the kidney slices for one minute. Season, and stir in the flour. Add the stock, juice and parsley; heat, but do not boil. Serve with fried bread.

Serves 4

BACON FRAZE

8 eggs
50 ml/2 fl oz single cream
25 g/1 oz plain flour
225 g/8 oz thin rindless bacon rashers
Made mustard

Beat the eggs with the cream and flour to make a batter. Fry the bacon crisply, and remove from the pan. Lower the heat. Pour half the batter into the pan and cook for about five minutes until just set, lay the bacon rashers on top, and cover with the remaining batter. After a further five minutes, when this is set, turn and brown the other side. Serve very hot with mustard.

Serves 4

JOLLY BOYS

2 heaped tablespoons flour
Pinch of salt
1 egg
Milk
Bacon fat left from frying bacon

Mix the flour, salt, egg and enough milk to make a thick batter. When the bacon has been fried, bring the fat left in the pan almost to boiling point. Put in the batter in tablespoonfuls and cook for about three minutes. Spoon hot fat on top as they cook. The batter forms oval shapes and rises when fried. These can be served with the bacon when eggs are scarce, or can be eaten with marmalade afterwards in the old style.

Serves 4

WINTER OATMEAL CAKES

25 g/1 oz bacon fat, dripping or butter
150 ml/Scant ¼ pint water
100 g/4 oz coarse oatmeal
¼ teaspoon salt
¼ teaspoon bicarbonate of soda

Heat the fat with the water until the fat melts. Stir the oatmeal with the salt and bicarbonate of soda. Add the liquid and stir well to make a stiff paste. Form into eight balls and squash these flat, pressing more oatmeal into each side. They should be about 2.5 mm/⅛ in. thick. Cook on both sides on a lightly greased griddle, hotplate or frying pan, or bake at 350°F, 180°C, gas mark 4 for thirty minutes. Eat hot or cold with butter, cheese or marmalade. These may be kept in a tin, or more traditionally buried in oatmeal in a meal-chest. If not freshly-baked, they should be reheated before serving.

Makes 8

OATMEAL BREAKFAST CAKES

100 g/4 oz oatmeal
300 ml/½ pint milk
2 tablespoons flour
75 g/3 oz shredded suet
Salt and pepper
Bacon fat for frying

Soak the oatmeal in the milk. Add the flour, suet, salt and pepper, and mix well together. Shape into small round flat cakes on a floured board. Fry for about three minutes on each side in hot bacon fat and drain well. Serve very hot like scones.

Makes 12

BREAKFAST OATCAKES

100 g/4 oz medium oatmeal
25 g/1 oz plain flour
25 g/1 oz butter
25 g/1 oz lard
15 g/½ oz sugar
Pinch of salt
Pinch of bicarbonate of soda
2–3 tablespoons boiling water

Preheat oven to 450°F, 230°C, gas mark 8. Stir together the oatmeal and flour and lightly rub in the butter and lard. Stir in the sugar, salt and soda. Add boiling water until absorbed and knead the dough until smooth. Sprinkle a little oatmeal on a board and roll one-quarter of the mixture into a thin 18 cm/7 in round. Divide into four triangles and place on a well-greased baking sheet. Repeat with remaining mixture. Bake for 6 minutes. Turn the oatcakes over and continue baking for 3 minutes.

Put a cooling tray in a roasting tin and arrange the baked oatcakes on the tray. Leave in a plate warming oven or airing cupboard for about 6 hours until the oatcakes are crisp. The oatcakes may be eaten straight from the oven, but improve with keeping.

Makes 6

POTATO CAKES

225 g/8 oz cold mashed potato
25 g/1 oz butter
50 g/2 oz plain flour
5 tablespoons milk
Pinch of salt

Mash or sieve potatoes, work in butter and add flour and salt, working the mixture until the flour is well blended into the potatoes. Blend to a stiff dough with the milk. Roll out lightly on a floured board and cut into rounds or squares. Bake on a lightly greased hot griddle for about 3 minutes on each side, until golden-brown. Split and butter and serve while hot.

Makes 12

POTATO GRIDDLE CAKES

675 g/1½ lb potatoes
150 g/5 oz plain flour
1 egg
600 ml/1 pint milk
1 level teaspoon sugar
1 level teaspoon salt
Dash of pepper

Peel and grate the potatoes into a bowl. Mix in the flour, egg, milk and seasonings and leave the batter to stand for two hours or overnight. Grease a griddle or frying pan, and put on mixture in dessertspoonfuls. Cook for about 5 minutes on each side until deep golden in colour. Serve hot with curls of crisp bacon, or spread with cranberry sauce or marmalade.

Makes 20

COTTAGE CHEESE GRIDDLE CAKES

1 tablespoon melted butter
100 g/4 oz cottage cheese
2 eggs
50 g/2 oz self-raising flour
1 tablespoon milk

Add butter to cottage cheese and gradually whisk in eggs. Stir in flour and milk and mix to a smooth thick batter. Drop spoonfuls on to a hot greased griddle or frying-pan and turn several times. Serve freshly cooked with crisp hot bacon, honey, jam or jelly. These scones are very light and digestible, and particularly good for anyone who does not want much starch in his diet.

Makes 12

SAUTIE BANNOCKS

100 g/4 oz flour
100 g/4 oz fine oatmeal
1 tablespoon syrup
¼ teaspoon salt
½ teaspoon bicarbonate of soda
1 small teaspoon cream of tartar
1 egg
200 ml/7 fl oz milk

Mix dry ingredients, add syrup, beaten egg and enough milk to make a dropping consistency. Drop in spoonfuls on a hot, greased griddle. Cook for about three minutes on each side, until brown. Cool on a towel. Serve with syrup.

Makes 12

– AND MARMALADE TO END WITH

OLD-FASHIONED SCOTCH MARMALADE

900 g/2 lb Seville oranges
2.25 litres/4 pints water
1.75 kg/4 lb sugar

Remove the rind from the oranges as thinly as possible and cut it into small pieces (not shreds). Put the pips into some of the water allowed in the recipe and leave for twelve hours. Cover the fruit and the peel with the rest of the water brought to the boil. Leave to stand for twelve hours. Add the liquid from the pips and simmer for two hours. Stir in the sugar until dissolved. Bring to the boil and boil to setting point. Cool slightly and stir well. Pour into hot jars and cover.

Makes 3 kg (7 lb)

OXFORD MARMALADE

900 g/2 lb Seville oranges
1 lemon
2.25 litres/4 pints water
1.75 kg/4 lb sugar

Wash and wipe the fruit. Cut in half and squeeze out the juice and pips. Cut the peel into thick shreds and put into a pan with the pulp, juice and water. Tie the pips into a piece of muslin and put into the pan. Boil gently for about two hours, until the mixture is reduced by half. Take out the bag of pips and squeeze it well so that the liquid goes back into the pan. Add the sugar and stir until dissolved. Simmer for one and a half hours until the marmalade is dark and has reached setting point. Leave to stand for fifteen minutes, stir, and put into warm jars. Cover with lids.

Makes 3 kg (7 lb)

DARK ORANGE MARMALADE

1.4 kg/3 lb Seville oranges
1 lemon
3 litres/5 pints water
2.75 kg/6 lb sugar
1 tablespoon black treacle

Cut the oranges in half and squeeze out the juice. Put the pips into a muslin bag. Cut the fruit into thick shreds. Put into the pan with juice, the juice of the lemon, water and the bag of pips. Simmer for about two hours until the peel is tender. Take out the bag of pips, and squeeze out the liquid. Stir in the sugar and black treacle until dissolved and boil quickly to setting point. Cool slightly, stir well, pour into hot jars and cover. If liked, four tablespoons rum or whisky can be added just before pouring into pots.

Makes 4.5 kg (10 lb)

ORANGE SHRED MARMALADE

1.4 kg/2 lb Seville oranges
Juice of two lemons
2.5 litres/4½ pints water
1.4 kg/3 lb sugar

Peel enough thin rind from the oranges to weigh 100 g/4 oz, and cut into thin strips. Cut up all the fruit and put into a pan with 1.3 litres/2½ pints water and the lemon juice. Cover and simmer for two hours. Simmer the peel in one pint water with a lid on until the shreds are soft. Strain the liquid into the fruit pulp. Strain the pulp through a jelly bag and leave to drip for fifteen minutes. Simmer the pulp in the remaining water for twenty minutes, and then leave to strain through a jelly bag overnight. Put the two liquids together and stir in the sugar until dissolved. Add the peel and boil hard to setting point. Cool slightly and stir well. Pour into hot jars and cover.

Makes 1.8 kg (4 lb)

ORANGE MARMALADE WITH HONEY

Sweet oranges
Honey

Peel the oranges and shred the peel finely. Cook the peel in a little water until tender, and then drain. Remove the pith and pips from the oranges and measure the orange pulp. To each 600 ml/1 pint orange pulp, allow 450 g/1 lb honey and 225 g/8 oz prepared rinds. Simmer pulp, honey and rinds together gently for forty minutes, stirring often. Cool slightly, stir well, pour into hot jars and cover.

THREE FRUIT MARMALADE

2 grapefruit
2 sweet oranges
4 lemons
3.5 litres/6 pints water
2.75 kg/6 lb sugar

Cut all the fruit in half. Put the pips, and the pith and membranes from the grapefruit into a muslin bag. Shred all peel finely and cut up the flesh roughly. Put the peel, flesh, water and bag of pips into a pan and simmer for one-and-a-half hours. Take out the bag of pips and squeeze to extract the liquid. Stir in the sugar until dissolved, and boil rapidly to setting point. Cool slightly and stir well. Pour into hot jars and cover.

Makes 3 kg (7 lb)

GRAPEFRUIT MARMALADE

1 grapefruit
1 lemon
1 orange
1.75 kg/4 lb sugar

Cut all fruit up finely, removing seeds. Pour over four pints of cold water and let it stand for twenty hours or more. Tie pips in a piece of muslin and put in with the fruit. Boil until it is tender, then add the sugar (remove seed bag first). Stir until dissolved, then boil up again until it sets when tested.

Makes 2.7 kg (6 lb)

LEMON MARMALADE

8 large lemons
4.5 litres/8 pints cold water
Sugar

Peel lemons very thinly and cut peel into very fine shreds. Put pith and pips into muslin, and cut up the flesh of the lemons. Put fruit, peel and pips into a pan with water and boil until the contents of the pan are reduced by half. Remove pips. Weigh the contents of the pan and add an equal weight of sugar. Bring to the boil, boil for about twenty minutes until setting point is reached, and put into pots.

Makes 2.25 kg (5 lb)

GINGER MARMALADE

5 Seville oranges
3 litres/5 pints water
1.4 kg/3 lb cooking apples
3 kg/6½ lb sugar
225 g/8 oz crystallised ginger, diced
15 g/½ oz ground ginger

Cut the oranges in half and squeeze out the juice. Shred the peel finely and cut up the flesh. Put the pips and trimmings into a muslin bag in the pan with orange peel and flesh, juice and water. Simmer for one and a half hours, and remove the bag of pips, squeezing all the liquid out. Peel and core the apples and cut them into slices. Simmer in four tablespoons water until pulped. Add the apples to the oranges and stir in the sugar until dissolved. Add the ginger cut in pieces and the ground ginger. Boil rapidly to setting point. Cool slightly, stir well, pour into hot jars and cover.

Makes 4 kg (9 lb)

CHAPTER TWO

FARMER'S ORDINARY

In the past, the 'ordinary' was the meal traditionally served to farmers in the market town on market day. Each eating-house offered a meal at a fixed rate for all comers; sometimes the place itself was called an 'ordinary'. These meals were great favourites with the farmers. They usually started with a hearty soup, followed by a pie or savoury pudding, roast meat or poultry. The meal would finish with a sweet pie or pudding and plenty of cheese. With the main course, there would be an abundance of vegetables; creamed vegetables were particularly popular in the winter. In addition to potatoes, a variety of savoury, starchy puddings were prepared to eat with the meat and soak up the gravy. These were also made at other times, in the home, to quell appetites, and so eke out frugal portions of meat. Although cooked with the meat, they were often served first with the gravy so that the family would eat less meat.

SOUPS

PEA SOUP

450 g/1 lb dried green peas
2 medium-sized onions
2 carrots
1 small turnip
100 g/4 oz swede
1 ham-bone
Salt and pepper
2.25 litres/4 pints water

Soak the peas overnight. Put soaked peas and prepared vegetables into a large saucepan, add the ham bone, salt and pepper, and water. Bring to the boil, cover the pan and simmer until the peas are soft. Sieve the vegetables. Return the pulp to the liquid and reheat.

Serves 4

BARLEY SOUP

40 g/1½ oz pearl barley
300 ml/½ pint milk
1.1 litres/2 pints well-flavoured stock
25 g/1 oz butter
½ teaspoon yeast or meat extract (if needed)
Salt and pepper
Grated nutmeg

Blend the barley with the milk. Boil the stock with the fat and the yeast or meat extract, stir it into the barley and milk, return all to the pan and simmer until the barley thickens and becomes clear. Stir all the time, as the barley easily forms lumps. Season very carefully, adding the merest trace of nutmeg.

Serve with small cubes of fried bread, handed separately.

Serves 4

CARROT SOUP

450 g/1 lb carrots
600 ml/1 pint water
3 large tomatoes
25 g/1 oz butter
600 ml/1 pint milk
Salt and pepper
Chopped parsley
Toasted bread cubes

Scrape the carrots and chop them roughly. Put into a pan with the water and bring to the boil. Cover and simmer for 30 minutes. Drain well, reserving the liquid. Skin the tomatoes and discard the seeds. Melt the butter, add the tomatoes and simmer for 3 minutes. Add the carrots and stir together over low heat for 5 minutes. Add the reserved cooking liquid and simmer for 10 minutes, stirring often.

Sieve the mixture and return to a clean pan with the milk. Simmer for 15 minutes and season with salt and pepper to taste. Serve very hot, sprinkled with parsley and toast cubes.

Serves 4

COCK-A-LEEKIE

1 boiling chicken
900 g/2 lb veal knuckle
Salt
1 carrot
1 turnip
1 onion
2 cloves
4 leeks
50 g/2 oz rice

Put the chicken in a deep pan with the veal knuckle and cover with water, adding a pinch of salt. Bring to the boil, remove scum, then add the carrot, turnip and the onion which has been peeled and stuck with the cloves. Continue simmering till the chicken is tender, and remove the bird. Clean the leeks, removing outer leaves, and cut into short lengths. Strain the broth and add the leeks and the rice. Boil for a further thirty minutes and season to taste. Cut half the chicken meat into small pieces (use the remainder for another dish) and put into the soup. Just before serving add a teaspoonful of chopped parsley.

Serves 6

OATMEAL SOUP

1 leek
25 g/1 oz butter
50 g/2 oz fine oatmeal
600 ml/1 pint beef stock
300 ml/½ pint milk
50 ml/2 fl oz cream
Salt

Slice the leek finely and cook gently in the butter until the leek is soft but not coloured. Add the oatmeal and stock and stir until it comes to the boil. Simmer for one minute. Add milk and cream, and salt to taste, and reheat without boiling.

Serves 4

OXTAIL SOUP

1 oxtail
25 g/1 oz beef dripping
1 onion
1 carrot
1 piece of turnip
1 stick of celery
1.1 litres/2 pints water or bone stock
1 teaspoon salt
A bunch of herbs
6 peppercorns
25 g/1 oz flour

Cleanse the oxtail, remove outside fat and cut into joints. Make the dripping hot and in it fry half the meat till brown, then remove it. Slice the vegetables and fry them till golden-brown, then remove them. Put the fried and raw meat and the fried vegetables into a deep pan, cover with the liquid, and bring very slowly to boiling point. Add the salt, herbs and peppercorns and simmer very gently for 3–4 hours. Meanwhile fry the flour in the dripping until golden-brown. Strain the soup, return to the soup some of the thinner pieces of meat and small rounds of carrot. Whisk in the browned flour. Whisk till boiling, season and serve. The thicker pieces of meat may be served as stewed oxtail. A little sherry can be added to the soup just before serving.

Serves 6

BEEF BROTH AND PARSLEY DUMPLINGS

225 g/8 oz shin beef
1.1 litres/2 pints vegetable stock
Salt and pepper
1 carrot
1 onion
1 small turnip
1 stick celery
25 g/1 oz dripping

Parsley Dumplings
100 g/4 oz self-raising flour
50 g/2 oz shredded suet
Salt
1 dessertspoon parsley

Cut the meat in cubes and cook with the stock, pepper and salt for one hour. Dice the vegetables and fry in dripping for a few minutes. Add to the meat and simmer for one hour. To make the dumplings, mix the dry ingredients and form into a soft dough with water. Add the dumplings to the broth twenty minutes before the soup is ready. Sprinkle with a little extra chopped parsley before serving.

Serves 4

PHEASANT SOUP

1 pheasant
1 medium-sized onion
2 leeks
1 medium-sized carrot
1 stick celery
Bunch of fresh herbs
25 g/1 oz brown breadcrumbs
1 egg yolk
25 ml/1 fl oz cream

Using a sharp knife, remove the meat from the breast and wings of the pheasant and keep them to one side. Put the remaining carcass in a pan with sliced onion, leeks, carrot, celery and the herbs. Cover with water and simmer for 4–5 hours. Mince the breast meat and pound it finely. Mix with the breadcrumbs and egg yolk and shape the mixture into small balls. Strain the soup, and put the liquid into a clean saucepan. Add the meat balls and bring to the boil. Simmer for twenty minutes, stir in the cream and serve at once.

Serves 4

GAME SOUP

Carcass and trimmings of 2 partridges
    or equivalent amount of any game
25 g/1 oz lean bacon
25 g/1 oz butter
1 onion
1 carrot
½ parnsip
1 stick of celery
25 g/1 oz flour
1.1 litres/2 pints stock
A bunch of herbs
1 clove
Some neat pieces of breast of bird
Salt and pepper

Put the pieces of carcass, the trimmings, and the bacon, with the fat in a saucepan and fry them till brown. Remove the game and fry the sliced vegetables till brown. Add the flour and fry it till golden-brown. Stir in the stock, bring to the boil, add the herbs, return the game to the pan and simmer for 1½–2 hours. Meanwhile cut the pieces of breast meat into small inch dice. Strain the soup, and reheat the diced game in it. Season carefully and serve.

Serves 4

KIDNEY SOUP

1 ox kidney
Seasoned flour
25 g/1 oz dripping
2 small onions
2 carrots
A little beef extract
Salt and pepper

Remove fat from the kidney and cut the meat into slices. Roll them in the seasoned flour and fry them deep brown in the dripping. Slice the onions and carrots and put into 3.5 litres/6 pints boiling water. Simmer for three hours, skimming off the fat from time to time. Season to taste with beef extract, salt and pepper, and serve very hot.

Serves 10

POACHER'S SOUP

1–2 kg/2–4 lb venison
225 g/8 oz shin beef
450 g/1 lb mutton with bones
1 head celery
2 carrots and turnips
4 onions
Bunch of parsley
7 g/¼ oz peppercorns
1 woodcock
1 pheasant
½ hare or 1 rabbit
2 partridge or grouse
6 small onions
6 peeled potatoes
1 small white cabbage
3 litres/5 pints water

If liked
Red wine
Mushroom catsup
Forcemeat balls

Cut up the venison, beef, mutton, celery, carrots, turnips, onions, and put into the water with parsley and peppercorns. Simmer for three hours and strain the stock. Cut up the game, dust with flour and brown. Add to the stock with small onions, some more sliced celery, potatoes, and the cabbage cut in quarters. Season with some black pepper, allspice and salt, and simmer two hours. Remove bones. Add some red wine, mushroom catsup and forcemeat balls if liked.

Serves 10

IPSWICH PARTRIDGE (OR HARE) SOUP

2 partridges
1.75 litres/3 pints beef stock
6 medium-sized onions
12 cloves
1 carrot
100 g/4 oz lean ham
50 g/2 oz butter
50 g/2 oz plain flour
150 ml/¼ pint double cream
Cayenne pepper

Roast the partridges until they are just cooked. Crush the meat and bones very thoroughly and add to the stock. Stick two cloves in each onion, and add the onions and carrot to the stock, together with the ham. Cover and simmer very gently for four hours. Strain the liquid. Mix the softened butter and flour together and add a little of the hot soup. When the mixture is like thick cream, add it to the rest of the soup and bring it to the boil, stirring well. Simmer for ten minutes, then stir in the cream and a little Cayenne pepper and serve at once. This soup may also be made from cooked hare.

Serves 6

MAIN DISHES

ROAST BEEF WITH YORKSHIRE PUDDING AND HORSERADISH SAUCE

2.25 kg/5 lb sirloin of beef
Black pepper

Put the beef into a roasting tin without any fat. Sprinkle beef with pepper. Roast in a hot oven, 425°F, 220°C, gas mark 7 for fifteen minutes. Lower heat to 375°F, 190°C, gas mark 5 for the rest of cooking time, allowing fifteen minutes to 450 g/1 lb. Baste meat frequently with pan juices. Beef should be served underdone, and should be transferred to a heated dish and left to rest for fifteen minutes before carving.

For the Yorkshire Pudding

100 g/4 oz plain flour
½ teaspoon salt
2 eggs
300 ml/½ pint milk
1 tablespoon cold water

To make the Yorkshire Pudding, sieve flour and salt together into a mixing bowl. Add the eggs and stir into the flour. Add half the milk slowly, and stir until the mixture is smooth. Add the remaining milk slowly and beat batter well, and then beat in the cold water. Fifteen minutes before the beef is cooked, pour two tablespoons of its fat into a 25 cm/10 in square tin. Put tin into the oven, and when fat is sizzling hot, pour in the pudding batter. Bake at the top of oven for thirty minutes (the meat is removed fifteen minutes earlier to rest before carving). The pudding should be well-risen, puffy, crisp and brown on top and bottom, and should be served straight from the tin in which it is baked, cut in squares.

Serves 6–8

For the Horseradish Sauce

50 g/2 oz grated horseradish
150 ml/¼ pint double cream
1 teaspoon sugar
½ teaspoon dry mustard powder
½ teaspoon salt
½ teaspoon white pepper
2 teaspoons white wine vinegar

If fresh horseradish is to be used for the Horseradish Sauce, the root should remain in cold water for one hour, then be washed well, and scraped into very thin shreds with a sharp knife. If bottled horseradish is used, it must be drained and squeezed dry in a kitchen towel. To make the sauce, whip the cream to stiff peaks, and fold in the horseradish, sugar, mustard, salt, pepper and vinegar. Serve cold.

STUFFED SHOULDER OF LAMB

1 shoulder of lamb, boned
2 onions, skinned and chopped
50 g/2 oz butter
Rosemary or parsley to taste

Stuff meat with onions and rosemary or parsley. Skewer and tie well in round shape. Put in tin, brush melted butter over joint. Roast at 350°F, 180°C, gas mark 4 for twenty-five minutes per 450 g/1 lb and twenty-five minutes over. Remove the skewers and string, and serve in wedges. A shoulder of lamb is also excellent if lamb's kidneys are used in place of the onions. Three or four will be needed.

Serves 6

ROAST LAMB WITH MINT SAUCE

1 shoulder or leg of lamb
Salt and pepper
Juice of one lemon
Sprig of rosemary

The meat on a shoulder of lamb is succulent and sweeter than on a leg. It can be boned and rolled for easy carving. Remove any thick pieces of fat from the joint, chop small, and put them in the roasting tin to cook with the lamb. Rub the joint with salt and pepper and squeeze on the juice of a lemon. Put a sprig of rosemary under the joint. Put the meat into a hot oven for ten minutes, 425°F, 220°C, gas mark 7, then reduce heat to a moderate level, 350°F, 180°C, gas mark 4 and continue cooking for about one and a half hours according to the size of the joint. Lamb tastes best if it is still slightly pink near the bone. Place meat on a hot serving dish. Drain off excessive fat from the roasting tin, and add a little vegetable water to the pan drippings to make thin gravy. Serve with roast potatoes and vegetables in season, together with Mint Sauce.

1 dessertspoon chopped fresh mint
1 teaspoon sugar
1 dessertspoon hot water
Pinch of salt
2 tablespoons wine vinegar

To make the sauce, put the freshly-chopped mint into a bowl with sugar and hot water. Stir until sugar dissolves, and add salt and vinegar.

Serves 6

ROAST PORK WITH SAGE AND ONION STUFFING AND APPLE SAUCE

1 leg or loin of pork
Oil
Salt and pepper
2 large onions
50 g/2 oz fresh white breadcrumbs
75 g/3 oz butter
2 teaspoons chopped fresh sage
Salt and pepper

The skin of pork should be scored by the butcher with a sharp knife. A little oil rubbed into the skin, and a sprinkling of salt and pepper will give crisp crackling. Cook in a fairly hot oven, 375°F, 190°C, gas mark 5, allowing thirty minutes per 450 g/1 lb. Pork should be well cooked and not pink when served. Drain off excess fat, and use a little vegetable water with the pan juices to make a thin gravy.

The stuffing may be put into the pork if it has been boned, or cooked separately in the same oven. Peel the onions, chop them coarsely and simmer until soft in enough water to cover them. Add breadcrumbs, butter, sage, and plenty of salt and pepper. When stuffing is well mixed, pack it into the joint before roasting. To cook separately, put into a greased ovenware dish and dot with butter. Cook for one hour with the joint.

For the Apple Sauce

4 large cooking apples
40 g/1½ oz sugar
Juice of half lemon
4 cloves
25 g/1 oz butter

To make the sauce, use apples which become fluffy when peeled. Peel, core and slice them. Put into a saucepan with the sugar, lemon juice, cloves and a little water. Simmer until soft, and then beat apples to a pulp. Remove cloves, and stir in butter. Serve hot.

Serves 8

Right: A selection of savoury flans can be made with fish, meat, poultry, egg and cheese fillings to serve hot or cold.
Over: Scrambled egg with a hint of smoked salmon and garnished with freshly ground black pepper and herbs for a special breakfast.

COLLARED BREAST OF VEAL

1.25–1.5 kg/2½–3 lb breast of veal
Grated nutmeg
Ground mace
Salt and pepper
Fresh or dried mixed herbs, finely-
  chopped
Chopped parsley
Grated lemon peel
½ slice bread, crumbled
2 tablespoons clean dripping
Flour to dredge
25–50 g/1–2 oz unsalted butter

Bone the meat carefully, without cutting the breast right through. Put the bones in the stew-pan, ready to make the sauce. Lay the veal flat, and sprinkle the inside with the nutmeg, mace, salt and pepper, herbs, parsley, lemon peel and breadcrumbs. Roll up tightly, secure with skewers, and wrap in foil greased with the dripping.

Roast or pot-roast at 170°C, 325°F, gas mark 3 for about 1–1½ hours until done. Twenty minutes before the end of the cooking time, remove the foil, dredge with the flour, baste with the butter and allow to brown.

For the Sauce

225 ml/8 fl oz stock
Flour
1 onion
Bundle of fresh herbs
½ slice bread, toasted
2–3 blades mace
2–3 whole cloves
2–3 whole black peppercorns
The veal bones

To make the sauce: put the stock in a saucepan. Use a little to make 1–2 tablespoons flour (depending on the amount of bouillon) into a paste. Add this to the liquid in small bits while heating the stock, and stir until the sauce thickens. Add water to thin it enough to cook the shredded onion without burning if required.

Peel and shred the onion and add it to the sauce with the bundle of herbs, toasted bread, mace, cloves and peppercorns. Add the veal bones too, and simmer until thick and well blended. You can add a few mushrooms for the last five minutes, if you wish; and you should test for seasoning before serving.

For Garnish
Forcemeat balls
Lemon wedges

Serve in a gravy boat and surround the meat with forcemeat balls and lemon wedges.

Serves 6

ROAST MICHAELMAS GOOSE

1 goose
100 g/4 oz pork
100 g/4 oz veal
1 large onion
15 g/½ oz butter
2 slices bread soaked in milk
1 egg yolk
Parsley, thyme, sage
75 ml/3 fl oz red wine

Chop the pork, veal, onion, and the goose liver very finely and brown them in the butter. Squeeze the milk out of the bread and mix together all the ingredients, chopping the herbs finely, and using only a little of the wine to moisten. Season with salt and pepper to taste. Stuff the goose and put into a very hot oven, say 450°F, 230°C, gas mark 8, for fifteen minutes. Reduce heat to 350°F, 180°C, gas mark 4 and cook for fifteen minutes per 450 g/1 lb, basting with the remaining wine.

Serves 6

Left: Braised beef makes a deliciously warming winter meal.
Page 35: Cider and fresh herbs enhance succulent mackerel.

ROAST CHICKEN STUFFED WITH HERBS

1 chicken
40 g/1½ oz butter
1 tablespoon chopped onion
2 tablespoons chopped carrot
25 g/1 oz flour
450 ml/¾ pint stock
Salt and pepper
100 ml/4 fl oz white wine or cider
  (optional)
1 teaspoon parsley
1 teaspoon chervil
1 teaspoon tarragon

For Herb Stuffing
2 tablespoons breadcrumbs
1 teaspoon chopped shallot
1 teaspoon chopped tarragon
1 teasponn chopped parsley
1 teaspoon chopped chervil
Salt and pepper
Liver from chicken
25 g/1 oz melted butter
  (approximately)

Remove gall bladder, wash and chop the liver finely. Mix the chopped liver with breadcrumbs, herbs, seasoning and sufficient oiled butter to moisten. Stuff the bird with stuffing, truss for roasting. Roast in moderately hot oven (350–375°F, 180–190°C, gas mark 4–5) until tender, 1–1½ hours, basting frequently.

Melt butter in saucepan, fry onion and carrot lightly, stir in flour, cook gently until lightly browned. Stir in stock, boil until cooked, add seasoning and wine (if used) together with one teaspoon each of parsley, chervil, tarragon or other herbs, as liked. Simmer sauce gently for quarter of an hour. Remove trussing string from bird.

Serve with a little sauce poured round, and remainder of sauce in a sauceboat.

Serves 6

CHICKEN CASSEROLE

1.75 kg/4 lb chicken
Seasoned flour
100 g/4 oz bacon
450 g/1 lb potatoes
225 g/8 oz onions
225 g/8 oz sausage meat
Salt and pepper
450 ml/¾ pint stock
Dripping

Cut the chicken into large pieces, and coat lightly with seasoned flour. Cut the bacon into small pieces and put them into a thick frying pan. Heat them until the fat runs out, and then remove the bacon. Fry the chicken pieces in this fat until golden. In a casserole, put a layer of sliced potatoes and the bacon pieces. Place on top of a layer of onion slices and then chicken, potato, onion, and sausage meat. Continue in layers until all the ingredients are used, seasoning lightly with salt and pepper. Finish with a layer of potato slices and dot lightly with pieces of dripping.

Pour in the stock and cover with a lid. Bake at 325°F, 170°C, gas mark 3 for two hours. Take off the lid and leave in the oven for twenty-five minutes to brown the potatoes.

Serves 6

COUNTRY CHICKEN BAKE

225 g/8 oz mashed potato
175 g/6 oz plain flour
50 g/2 oz butter
50 g/2 oz lard
225 g/8 oz leeks
225/8 oz cooked chicken
3 eggs
150 ml/¼ pint milk

Sieve the flour, rub in the fats, add the mashed potato and mix to a fairly stiff dough. Roll out half this pastry and line an 18 cm/7 in shallow dish. Roll out the remaining pastry, cut out rounds about 4 cm/1¾ in diameter, and place them overlapping round the top edge of the dish. Prick the base and leave in a cool place for about thirty minutes. Wash the leeks and cut into thin slices, and cook in boiling salted water for ten minutes, then drain. Slice the chicken and place in the pie shell. Add the leeks, reserving some to decorate.

Whisk together the eggs and milk, season and pour into the pastry shell. Arrange leek slices on top. Brush the pastry with a little egg and milk. Bake at 350°F, 180°C, gas mark 4 for 35–40 minutes until set. Serve with vegetables or a salad.

Serves 4

BOILED HAND OR SHOULDER OF PORK AND PEASE PUDDING

1.4 kg/3 lb shoulder (or hand) pork
3 sage leaves
6 peppercorns
3 carrots
1 large onion
½ turnip
2 or 3 stalks celery

450 g/1 lb split peas, soaked overnight
Sprig mint
25 g/1 oz butter
1 egg
Salt and pepper

Prepare the vegetables and tie the sage and peppercorns in a muslin bag. Put the pork in a large pan, cover with warm water and bring to the boil. Skim, boil for fifteen minutes, then add the quartered carrots, sliced onion, turnip, chopped celery, peppercorns and sage. Boil steadily for one and a half hours with the pease pudding.

To make the pudding: tie the peas in a pudding cloth with the mint, allowing room for the peas to swell. Suspend the bag in a pan with boiling pork and boil for one hour. Then take out, rub peas through a sieve, mix in the butter, egg and seasoning. Replace in a clean cloth and boil with pork again for a further thirty minutes. Lift out pudding and unroll from the cloth on to a hot dish. Serve with the pork and vegetables.

Serves 6

COLLARED BEEF

1.4–1.75 kg/3–4 lb fresh silverside or
    brisket
Salt and pepper
A sprinkling each of ground cloves,
    ground mace and ground ginger
A few drops of red colouring
¼ teaspoon each of whole allspice,
    peppercorns, sage and thyme
1 bay leaf

Lay out the meat in a flat strip; if thick, cut it through horizontally, and lay the two pieces end to end. Season it with salt and pepper and sprinkling spices, and rub with red colouring. Roll it up tightly, and tie it with string at each end and in the middle. Wrap it in one thickness of butter muslin, to keep it moist. Place it in a stewpot and water to cover, and bring gently to the boil. Remove the scum, add the remaining spices and herbs, and simmer very gently for 3–4 hours, or until tender. Serve hot with a savoury suet pudding such as Herb Pudding, and pickles, or press and serve cold with a salad which includes herbs and pickled mushrooms or gherkins.

Serves 6–8

BOILED BEEF AND CARROTS WITH DUMPLINGS

1.75 kg/4 lb salt beef brisket or
  silverside
1 bay leaf
Parsley and thyme
10 peppercorns
4 onions
12 carrots

Dumplings
100 g/4 oz self-raising flour
Water to mix
2 oz suet

Tie the meat into a neat shape and put in a large pan with enough water to cover. Add the bay leaf, thyme, parsley and peppercorns, and bring to the boil. Skim, then simmer for one and a half hours. Add the whole onions, and the carrots cut in pieces, and cook for fifteen minutes. Make the dumplings by mixing the flour, finely-chopped suet and water into a firm paste, and rolling with the hands into eight round balls. Drop the dumplings into the liquid with the meat and vegetables and continue cooking for thirty minutes. Remove the meat to a serving dish, surround with the vegetables and dumplings, and serve some of the cooking liquid.

Serves 6–8

OVEN BEEF AND BAKED HERB DUMPLINGS

1.4 kg/3 lb salt brisket
225 g/8 oz carrots
225 g/8 oz onions
4 celery sticks
2 bay leaves
6 peppercorns

Soak the meat in cold water overnight, and drain. Line the inside of a roasting tin with foil and put the joint in the centre. Cut onions, carrots and celery in large pieces, put round the joint, add bay leaves and peppercorns, and pour 150 ml/¼ pint water over the meat. Cover the tin with a second piece of foil, tucking the edges well under the tin. Cook in the centre of the oven, 400°F, 200°C, gas mark 6 for one hour and fifty minutes.

FOR THE DUMPLINGS

175 g/6 oz plain flour
1½ teaspoons baking powder
1 level teaspoon salt
1 level teaspoon mixed herbs
75 g/3 oz shredded suet

Make the dumplings by sifting flour, baking powder and salt into a bowl with herbs and suet, mixing to a fairly stiff dough with cold water and dividing into eight pieces. Form each piece into a ball. At the end of cooking time, take foil off the meat, put the dumplings on vegetables round the joint and re-cover with foil. Continue baking for forty minutes until dumplings are well risen and cooked.

Serves 6–8

BOILED BACON WITH PARSLEY SAUCE

1.75 kg/4 lb bacon joint
1 bay leaf
6 peppercorns
1 tablespoon brown sugar

Soak the bacon joint for four hours. Put into a saucepan with fresh cold water, bay leaf, peppercorns and sugar. Bring to the boil, then reduce heat and simmer for two hours. Drain bacon and strip off skin. Sprinkle fat surface of bacon with a little oatmeal or browned breadcrumbs.

FOR THE PARSLEY SAUCE

50 g/2 oz butter
50 g/2 oz plain flour
300 ml/½ pint milk
300 ml/½ pint bacon stock
Salt and pepper
1 tablespoon chopped parsley

To make the sauce, melt the butter and stir in the flour gradually, away from the heat, until the mixture is smooth. Add milk and stock gradually, beating well, and stir over low heat until boiling. Simmer gently, stirring often, and add parsley, salt and pepper to taste.

Serves 6–8

STUFFED LAMB ROSETTES

2 breasts of boned lamb

Stuffing
100 g/4 oz lamb's liver, chopped
1 small onion, skinned and chopped
25 g/1 oz butter
4 tablespoons soft, white breadcrumbs
1 teaspoon finely-grated lemon peel
1 dessertspoon chopped parsley
Salt and pepper to taste
Milk to bind stuffing

Vegetables
900 g/2 lb thinly-sliced potatoes
225 g/8 oz tomatoes, skinned and
  thinly sliced
1 onion, skinned and thinly sliced
2 level teaspoons flour
300 ml/½ pint stock

Put the lamb breasts on a board, skin side down. Mix the stuffing and spread it on the lamb. Roll and tie each breast in four places; cut to make eight rosettes. Arrange vegetables in layers in an ovenproof dish, sprinkling each layer with flour. Add rosettes and stock. Cover with foil. Cook on the centre shelf of the oven for thirty minutes at 375°F, 190°C, gas mark 5. Take off the foil and cook for further forty-five minutes. Remove the string before serving.

Serves 6

IRISH STEW

1.4 kg/3 lb lean neck of lamb chops
900 g/2 lb potatoes
450 g/1 lb onions
Sprig of thyme
Sprig of parsley
450 ml/¾ pint water
Salt and pepper

Make sure the meat is trimmed of fat and gristle. Keep the bones in the chops as this adds flavour. Peel the potatoes and slice one-third thinly, leaving the rest whole. Slice the onions, and chop the thyme and parsley. Put the sliced potatoes into a pan, then a layer of onions and the meat. Add the herbs and remaining onion, and top with the whole potatoes. Add water and salt and pepper. Cover tightly. Cook in a warm oven, 325°F, 170°C, gas mark 3 for two and a half hours. The stew may be cooked on the top of the stove, very gently, for the same time.

Serves 6

WILTSHIRE MARKET DAY DINNER

6 pork chops
2 pigs' kidneys
450 g/1 lb onions
1 apple
1 teaspoon sage
Salt and pepper
450 g/1 lb potatoes

Put the chops into a casserole. Cover with sliced kidneys and onions. Peel, core and slice the apple and put this on top. Sprinkle on the sage and season well with salt and pepper. Peel and slice the potatoes and cover the top of the dish with them. Pour on 150 ml/¼ pint water. Cover and cook at 325°F, 170°C, gas mark 3 for three hours.

Serves 6

JOHN FARLEY'S LEG OF MUTTON WITH CAULIFLOWER AND SPINACH

3.5–4 kg/8–9 lb leg well-aged mutton
Salt
8 medium-sized carrots
4 onions
Bay leaf, thyme and parsley
2 small cauliflowers
675 g/1½ lb leaf spinach
Sea salt and freshly-ground black
*   pepper*
100 g/4 oz butter
150 ml/¼ pint milk
450 ml/¾ pint thick brown gravy or
*   leftover sauce or 2–3 tablespoons*
*   double cream and 2 hard-boiled eggs*

Trim unwanted fat off the meat, but take care not to skin it or spoil its shape. Wrap it tightly in foil after salting it lightly. Clean the vegetables and cut into presentable pieces. Bring to the boil enough water almost (but not quite) to cover the joint. Lay the meat in it when boiling. Boil briskly for 3–5 minutes. Then reduce the heat, so that the liquid barely simmers. Leave for twenty-five minutes for each 450 g/lb of meat, with a firm lid on the pan. Add the vegetables and herbs for the last one and a half hours.

Towards the end of the cooking time, cut the cauliflowers into sprigs and prepare the spinach for cooking. Steam both, well salted and peppered, over boiling water or stock for 7–12 minutes.

Melt 50 g/2 oz butter in a stewpan, add the milk, and when very hot simmer the cauliflower in the mixture for four or five minutes. Dish the steamed spinach either with the heated brown gravy poured over it, or with a garnish of the cream and chopped hard-boiled eggs.

Unwrap the meat (which will have made a good gravy in the foil package), place it on a serving dish and pour the butter and milk over. Serve vegetables (including carrots and onions) separately.

This size of joint takes four hours to boil, and should rest at least three-quarters of an hour before serving.

Serves 10

BEEF IN BEER

1.75 kg/4 lb brisket of beef
6 rashers lean bacon
450 g/1 lb onions
300 ml/½ pint brown ale
300 ml/½ pint beef stock
150 ml/¼ pint wine vinegar
Salt and pepper
Bay leaf

Have the beef rolled and tied. Cut bacon into thin strips and put into casserole. Put in the meat. Slice the onions thinly and put round the beef. Add salt and pepper, depending on possible saltiness of bacon; add bay leaf. Heat together ale, stock and vinegar and pour over the meat. Cover tightly and cook at 300°F, 150°C, gas mark 2 for three and a half hours. The gravy is rich and delicious, and the meat has a good flavour when eaten cold or in sandwiches.

Serves 6–8

BACON AND BEER CASSEROLE

1.25 kg/2½ lb bacon collar
1 carrot
1 onion
Pepper
1 tablespoon black treacle
1 bay leaf
600 ml/1 pint ale
25 g/1 oz butter
25 g/1 oz flour

Soak the bacon for six hours (two hours if unsmoked). Put in a casserole, and add sliced carrot and onion, a shake of freshly ground black pepper, treacle, bay leaf and beer. Bring to the boil, skim, and simmer for one hour (or cook in the oven at 350°F, 180°C, gas mark 4). Remove the bacon, take off the skin, and keep the joint hot. Blend the butter with flour and thicken the strained liquid. This is very good with baked parsnips.

Serves 6

SCOTCH COLLOPS

450 g/1 lb fresh minced beef
1 large onion
25 g/1 oz butter or dripping
Salt and pepper
1 tablespoon oatmeal
250 ml/8 fl oz water
Mashed potato
Poached eggs (if liked)

Form the beef into patties if desired. Brown the beef and finely-chopped onion in the fat. Season with salt and pepper, and add the oatmeal and water. Cover with a lid and simmer for thirty minutes. Put into a serving dish and surround with mashed potato. Poached eggs may be served on top.

Serves 4

TRIPE AND BACON

450 g/1 lb pre-cooked tripe
225 g/8 oz bacon rashers
15 g/½ oz plain flour
150 ml/¼ pint water
1 dessertspoon tomato sauce
Salt and pepper

Fry the bacon slowly so that the fat runs. Put the bacon on a warm dish. Slice the tripe and fry it until golden in the bacon fat. Put the tripe with the bacon on the dish. Sprinkle the flour into the fat and cook for one minute, stirring well. Add the water, sauce, salt and pepper, stirring all the time. When hot and thick, pour over the tripe and bacon.

Serves 4

LANCASHIRE HOT-POT

10 large potatoes
6 onions
3 lamb's kidneys
900 g/2 lb neck of mutton chops
Salt and pepper
Water
Pickled red cabbage

Peel and slice the potatoes and onions, skin and slice the kidneys. Place the chops in the bottom of a casserole, cover with alternate layers of potatoes, onions and kidneys, seasoning well. Cover with a layer of potatoes, and brush well with melted butter. Add a little water, and cook with lid on in a hot oven, 425°F, 220°C, gas mark 7 for thirty minutes, then in a cool oven, 300°F, 150°C, gas mark 2 for two hours. Remove the lid for thirty minutes before serving to brown the top. Serve with pickled red cabbage.

Serves 4

LAMB AND MUSHROOM HOT-POT

675 g/1½ lb best-end lamb cutlets
25 g/1 oz plain flour
50 g/2 oz butter
1 onion
175 g/6 oz button mushrooms
450 ml/¾ pint stock
Salt and pepper
Pinch of rosemary
450 g/1 lb potatoes

Trim fat from the cutlets and coat them with flour. Melt the butter and fry the cutlets and sliced onion until golden. Put into a casserole with the mushrooms, stocks, salt and pepper and rosemary. Peel the potatoes and cut in 5 mm/¼ in slices. Arrange the potatoes on top of the meat, cover and bake at 300°F, 150°C, gas mark 2 for one and a half hours. Take off the lid and continue baking for thirty minutes.

Serves 4

STOVED CHICKEN

1.4 kg/3 lb chicken joints
2 large onions
1.25 kg/2½ lb potatoes
50 g/2 oz butter
600 ml/1 pint giblet stock
Salt and pepper
Chopped parsley

Wipe the chicken joints. Cut the onions in slices, and the potatoes in medium-thick slices. Brown the chicken pieces in half the butter. In a casserole, put a thick layer of potatoes, then onions and chicken pieces. Season well with salt and pepper and add small pieces of butter. Put on another layer of potatoes, then onions, chicken and finally potatoes.

Season again and pour on the stock. Put on a piece of buttered paper and a lid. Cook at 300°F, 150°C, gas mark 2 for two and a half hours, adding a little more stock or water if needed. If an iron casserole is used, this dish may be simmered gently on a low heat on top of the stove. Sprinkle with parsley before serving.

Serves 6

BACON WITH CIDER SAUCE

600 ml/1 pint cider
1.25–1.4 kg/2½–3 lb bacon joint
8 small onions
4 eating apples
25 g/1 oz plain flour
1 tablespoon redcurrant jelly

Put the cider into a large casserole with the bacon joint, which should have been soaked overnight in cold water if necessary. Add the peeled onions and cover with a lid. Cook for one and a half hours at 325°F, 170°C, gas mark 3. Remove from the oven and turn the bacon over. Core the apples but do not peel them. Arrange

round the bacon, baste and return to the oven for a further thirty minutes.

Transfer the bacon to a heated serving dish and arrange the onions and apples round it. Pour the cider into a pan, add the flour mixed to a smooth paste with cold water and the redcurrant jelly. Bring to the boil, stirring continuously and boil for three minutes. Serve in a sauceboat.

Serves 6

BRAISED PORK WITH APPLE RINGS

900 g/2 lb loin of pork
450 g/1 lb breadcrumbs
50 g/2 oz chopped suet
1 tablespoon thyme
2 tablespoons parsley
1 cooking apple
1 egg
Squeeze of lemon juice
4 tablespoons olive oil
6 tablespoons cider
3 eating apples
2 tablespoons butter
Salt and pepper

Combine the breadcrumbs with the suet, herbs and chopped cooking apple, and add salt and pepper to taste. Add the egg and lemon juice and mix well, adding a little milk if necessary. Slice the pork down to the bone and place stuffing between the cuts. Use long skewers to keep the joint together. Heat two tablespoons oil in casserole, and toss pork in this until golden. Pour cider over, cover and cook at 375°F, 190°C, gas mark 5 for forty-five minutes. Core the eating apples but do not peel them. Slice and fry them in butter and the remaining oil until golden. Put pork on to a very hot dish and garnish with the apples.

Serves 4

FAGGOTS

675 g/1½ lb pig's liver
175 g/6 oz bacon
2 onions
200 g/7 oz white breadcrumbs
75 g/3 oz shredded suet
2 teaspoons sage
1 teaspoon basil
Salt and pepper

Mince the liver, bacon and onions. Place all the ingredients together in a bowl and mix well. Form the mixture into eight balls and roll in flour. Pack closely together in a baking tin. Bake in the centre of the oven at 350°F, 180°C, gas mark 4 for thirty minutes. When cooked, divide with a knife and serve with a rich brown gravy and pease pudding.

Serves 4

LIVER AND POTATO CASSEROLE

350 g/12 oz liver
675 g/1½ lb potatoes
6 rashers bacon
300 ml/½ pint stock or water
15 g/½ oz flour
4 medium-sized onions
Salt and pepper
Dripping

Cut the liver into small pieces. Dip into flour seasoned with salt and pepper, and brown on each side in hot dripping. Remove from the pan, and fry the sliced potatoes. Put layers of potatoes, onions, and liver in a casserole, seasoning well, and put the rashers of bacon on top. Pour in stock to come half way up the dish. Bake in a moderate oven 375°F, 190°C, gas mark 5 for one hour.

Serves 4

LIVER AND BACON CASSEROLE

450 g/1 lb pig's liver
4 rashers lean bacon
2 cooking apples
2 large onions
100 g/4 oz breadcrumbs
1 tablespoon chopped parsley
1 teaspoon salt
¼ teaspoon pepper
300 ml/½ pint stock or water

Slice the liver, and cut the bacon into small pieces. Peel and chop apples and onions. Grease a casserole, put in a layer of liver, then bacon. Top with a layer of breadcrumbs, onions, parsley, salt and pepper, then apple. Repeat the layers, finishing with breadcrumbs, and pour in the stock or water. Bake at 375°F, 190°C, gas mark 5 for two hours, removing the cover for the last thirty minutes.

Serves 4

KIDNEY CASSEROLE

450 g/1 lb lamb's or veal kidneys
2 medium-sized onions
2 tablespoons dripping
4 bacon rashers
Flour
Salt and pepper
150 ml/¼ pint stock

Clean the kidneys, skin and remove cores, and cut in slices. Chop the onions finely and fry until golden in melted dripping. Put the onions in a casserole, arrange the kidneys on top, then pieces of chopped bacon. Season with salt and pepper and dust lightly with flour. Pour over stock and cook at 350°F, 180°C, gas mark 4 for forty minutes.

Serves 4

BROWN OXTAIL

1 jointed oxtail
4 carrots
2 onions
1 turnip
25 g/1 oz dripping
25 g/1 oz flour
4 rashers bacon
450 ml/¾ pint stock
4 tablespoons red wine
Salt and pepper
1 bay leaf
Sprig of parsley
Sprig of thyme

Slice the carrots, onions and turnip and brown in the melted dripping. Remove from the pan and put into a casserole. In the same fat, brown the oxtail pieces, and stir in the flour. Blend well, then put into the casserole. Add the chopped bacon, stock and wine, herbs, salt and pepper. Cook at 325°F, 170°C, gas mark 3 for four hours. Remove the herbs before serving, and skim off excess fat.

Serves 4

POTTED BEEF

450 g/1 lb chuck steak
175 g/6 oz bacon rashers
150 ml/¼ pint stock
1 bay leaf
1 sprig of parsley
1 sprig of thyme
Salt and pepper
Nutmeg

Slice steak and bacon in very small pieces, and arrange in a small casserole in alternate layers, sprinkling each layer with a dash of salt, pepper and nutmeg. Put the herbs halfway up the dish, and pour on the stock. On top of the casserole, put the rinds cut from the bacon. Cover tightly and cook in slow oven, 300°F, 150°C, gas mark 2 for three hours. Remove the bacon rinds and herbs before serving. Serve hot, or leave until cold, when the gravy will form a clear pink jelly.

Serves 4

BRAISED LAMB

1.35 kg/3 lb shoulder of lamb
Salt and pepper
2 carrots
4 onions
1 garlic clove
1 clove
Bunch of mixed herbs
Stock

Have the lamb boned, and season it with salt and pepper. Roll and tie the meat, and brown it in its own fat on all sides. Put into a casserole with the sliced carrots and onions, crushed garlic, clove and herbs. Add stock to come halfway up the meat. Cover and cook at 325°F, 170°C, gas mark 3 for four hours.

Serves 6

JUST PUDDING AND PIE

STEAK, KIDNEY (AND OYSTER) PUDDING

225 g/8 oz suet
450 g/1 lb self-raising flour
Water to mix
900 g/2 lb rump steak
2 veal kidneys
Oysters or mushrooms if liked
Salt and pepper
1 bay leaf

Chop the suet finely and rub into the flour, then add enough water to make a stiff paste which can be rolled out on a floured board. Roll out 5 mm/$\frac{1}{4}$ in thick, giving enough paste to line and cover a 1.1 litres/2 pint pudding basin. Line the basin with the paste, and fill with alternative layers of steak and kidney cut in small pieces. If oysters are added, they should be raw; mushrooms should be sliced and tossed for two minutes in a little butter. Season the layers with salt and pepper, and insert the bay leaf halfway up. When the basin is full, put in enough water to reach within an inch of the top, moisten the edges of the lining paste and put on the top, cutting off the surplus and pinching the two edges together. Wring out a cloth in hot water, flour it, and tie over the top of the basin with string. Bring up the ends of the cloth and knot on top of the pudding, and then put the basin in a pan of boiling water and boil for four hours. The water in the pan must be topped up with boiling water from time to time. When ready for serving, untie the cloth and make a small cut in the top paste to let the steam escape. Serve in the pudding basin with a table napkin wrapped round it.

Serves 6

CHICKEN PUDDING

350 g/12 oz self-raising flour
175 g/6 oz suet
1 old chicken
1 chopped onion
Bay leaf
Salt and pepper
1 dessertspoon chopped parsley

Make up suet pastry with enough water to give a firm paste. Cut the flesh from legs, wings and breast of bird. Line a 1.1 litres/2 pint basin with suet pastry. Fill with alternate layers of meat and onion, with some seasoning and parsley. Put bay leaf in the centre. Just cover meat with stock or water, and top with pastry. Steam for four hours. Serve with gravy made from chicken stock, using carcass of bird, or with parsley sauce.

Serves 6

KENTISH PORK AND APPLE PUDDING

225 g/8 oz self-raising flour
100 g/4 oz shredded suet
225 g/8 oz lean pork
1 cooking apple
Salt and pepper
Sage
Stock or water

Prepare pastry with flour, suet and enough water to make a firm paste. Line a 600 ml/1 pint basin with pastry, and put in pork, cut in squares, the chopped apple, salt and pepper, a good pinch of chopped sage and stock to cover. Put on pastry lid, cover and boil for four hours.

Serves 4

NORFOLK PLOUGH PUDDING

225 g/8 oz self-raising flour
100 g/4 oz shredded suet
450 g/1 lb pork sausage meat
100 g/4 oz bacon
1 large onion
2 teaspoons chopped sage
15 g/½ oz Demerara sugar
Fresh tomato sauce

Mix together the flour and suet with a pinch of salt and enough cold water to make a firm dough. Roll out the dough, and use two-thirds to line a 1.1 litre/2 pint pudding basin. Press the sausage meat into the pastry all around the basin. Chop the bacon and onion and mix together with the sage and sugar. Put this mixture into the centre of the pudding and cover with the remaining pastry. Cover with grease-proof paper and a piece of foil or a pudding cloth. Steam for four hours, and serve with a hot tomato sauce.

Serves 6

BACON LAYER PUDDING

175 g/6 oz self-raising flour
75 g/3 oz shredded suet
225 g/8 oz chopped bacon
2 onions
2 carrots

Make a suet pastry by adding the suet to the flour with a pinch of salt, and enough water to make a firm dough. Roll out the pastry thinly and cut out a round to fit the bottom of a greased 1.1 litre/2 pint basin. Put in a layer of bacon pieces. Grate the onions and carrots, and put a little of the mixture on top of the bacon and vegetables. Continue until the basin is full, and cover with a layer of pastry. Cover and steam for two hours. Serve with gravy.

Serves 4

DUCK PUDDINGS

75 g/3 oz bread without crust
225 ml/7½ fl oz milk
1 egg
50 g/2 oz shredded suet
1 teaspoon salt
1 teaspoon flour
1 onion
½ teaspoon chopped sage
Salt and pepper

Pour the milk over the bread and leave for ten minutes, then beat well with a spoon. Stir in the egg, suet, flour, finely-chopped onion, sage and seasoning. Grease and warm some small patty tins, and put in the mixture. Bake for fifteen minutes at 425°F, 220°C, gas mark 7. Take out of the tins and put round a roasting duck or pork for the last fifteen minutes' cooking time.

Makes 12

SALT BEEF PIE

350 g/12 oz cooked salt beef
1 onion
1 carrot
1 potato
Pepper
175 g/6 oz shortcrust pastry

Mince the meat and vegetables. Put meat and vegetables on a 18 cm/7 in pie plate, moisten with a little water and season with pepper. Cover with the pastry. Brush with beaten egg or milk. Bake for twenty minutes at 400°F, 200°C, gas mark 6 then reduce to 350°F, 180°C, gas mark 4 for a further twenty minutes.

Serves 4

FARMHOUSE PLATE PIE

1 onion
1 carrot
50 g/2 oz mushrooms
2 tablespoons oil
350 g/12 oz cooked meat
1 dessertspoon flour
150 ml/¼ pint beef stock
450 g/1 lb mashed potato
50 g/2 oz grated cheese

Dice the onion and carrot, and slice the mushrooms. Gently fry the vegetables in the oil until just cooked. Add chopped or minced meat with seasoning to taste. Stir in the flour then the stock, bring to the boil and cook for a few minutes. Press just under half the potato on to a 20 cm/8 in greased ovenproof plate, rather like pastry. Pile the meat mixture into the centre. Press the remaining potato flat over the top or roll out on a floured surface and lift on. Press the edges well together, brush the top with a little melted butter and spinkle the cheese on top. Bake at 400°F, 200°C, gas mark 6 for thirty minutes.

Serves 4

DEVONSHIRE LAMB PIES

350 g/12 oz puff pastry
225 g/8 oz cold cooked lamb
100 g/4 oz cooked ham
1 teaspoon plain flour
1 teaspoon chopped parsley
½ teaspoon mixed fresh herbs
Salt and pepper
150 ml/¼ pint thick brown gravy

Roll out the pastry and cut into six rounds to line individual tins, and six rounds for lids. Chop the lamb and ham finely and mix together. Sprinkle with flour, parsley, herbs, salt and pepper, and mix well. Divide the mixture between the lined tins. Sprinkle gravy over the filling and put on the pastry lids, sealing the edges with water. Make a small slit in the centre of each lid. Bake at 400°F, 200°C, gas mark 6 for 30 minutes. Serve hot with additional gravy if liked.

Serves 6

PORK AND KIDNEY PIE

450 g/1 lb pork shoulder or hand of pork
3 pig's kidneys
2 teaspoons basil
300 ml/½ pint stock
Pinch of nutmeg
1 medium-sized onion
2 medium-sized carrots
175 g/6 oz shortcrust pastry

Cut the pork and the kidneys in pieces and put them into a 1.1 litre/2 pint pie dish with basil, stock, nutmeg, chopped onion and carrots. Cover with a lid or piece of foil and cook at 325°F, 170°C, gas mark 3 for one hour. Cover with pastry lid and bake at 400°F, 200°C, gas mark 6 for thirty minutes.

Serves 4

STEAK AND KIDNEY PIE

675 g/1½ lb beef skirt
175 g/6 oz ox kidney
25 g/1 oz seasoned flour
50 g/2 oz dripping
2 large onions
150 ml/¼ pint dry red wine if liked
150 ml/¼ pint stock
½ teaspoon dried thyme
1 bay leaf
225 g/8 oz puff pastry

Trim the meat and cut it into 2.5 cm/1 in pieces. Cut the kidney into pieces of about the same size. Discard the core. Dust the meat and kidney with well-seasoned flour. Heat the fan and brown the meat very slowly. Remove from the heat, pour over the red wine and the stock (or omit the wine and make up the total amount of liquid in stock). Add the thyme and the crushed bay leaf and additional salt and pepper if necessary. Allow to cool, and if possible stand for two or three hours (covered). Transfer to a 1.1 litre/2 pint pie dish with a centre cone. Cover with the pastry supported in the centre; seal the edges of the dish. Cut slits in the pastry cover. Decorate if wished and brush with a little milk or beaten egg to glaze. Place on a low shelf in the oven at 400°F, 200°C, gas mark 6 and cook for about twenty minutes or until the pastry is golden-brown. Cover the pie completely with grease-proof paper, then reduce the oven heat to 300°F, 150°C, gas mark 2 and continue cooking for a further three hours or until the meat is tender. If necessary, additional stock may be added through the slits in the pastry during or after cooking.

Serves 4–6

BEEF AND BACON PIE

1 onion
225 g/8 oz bacon
225 g/8 oz minced raw beef
1 tablespoon plain flour
150 ml/¼ pint water
Pinch of fresh mixed herbs
Salt and pepper
225 g/8 oz shortcrust pastry

Chop the onion and bacon in small pieces, put in a heavy pan, and cook gently until the fat runs from the bacon, and the onion and bacon are soft and golden. Add the mince and cook until mince browns. Stir in flour mixed with a little water, and the rest of the water, herbs and seasonings, and cook until mixture is thick and well blended. Roll pastry into two rounds and line a 20 cm/8 in pie plate with one. Put in filling, and cover with second round of pastry. Bake at 400°F, 200°C, gas mark 6 for thirty minutes.

Serves 4

CHICKEN PARSLEY PIE

1 chicken
600 ml/1 pint basin full of washed parsley
600 ml/1 pint milk
Stock made from chicken giblets
225 g/8 oz shortcrust or puff pastry
150 ml/¼ pint double cream
Salt and pepper

Joint the chicken and place the pieces in a 1.1 litre/2 pint pie dish. Scald the parsley in milk. Season and add to the chicken with the stock. Cover with pastry, leaving an air hole in the middle and bake for one and a half hours, starting at 425°F, 220°C, gas mark 7 but reducing to 350°F, 180°C, gas mark 4 when the pastry has risen. Cover the pastry with foil if it begins to get too brown. When baked, pour the cream through the air hole and shake gently to mix with the other liquid inside the pie.

Serves 6

SAVOURY HERBED PUDDING

175 g/6 oz stale bread
300 ml/½ pint milk
50 g/2 oz shredded suet
50 g/2 oz fine oatmeal
3 eggs
Salt and pepper
Cayenne pepper
Thyme, sage and marjoram

Soak the bread in hot milk and leave it to get cold. Mix the dry ingredients with the bread. Beat the eggs and mix it well. Over heat, melt some dripping in an 18 cm/7 in flameproof ovenware dish to boiling point. Spread in the mixture with a fork. Bake from 30–40 minutes in the oven with a joint. Serve in squares with the meat and gravy.

Serves 6

YORKSHIRE SAVOURY PUDDING

225 g/8 oz bread without crust
4 large onions
2 teaspoons chopped sage
25 g/1 oz oatmeal
75 g/3 oz shredded suet
Salt and pepper

Pour some boiling water over the bread and leave it to stand for thirty minutes. Drain well but do not squeeze out moisture. Chop the onions finely and mix with the bread and other ingredients. Put into a greased baking dish and bake at 375°F, 190°C, gas mark 5 for one hour until well browned. Cut into slices to serve with thick gravy and vegetables.

Serves 4

SEASONING PUDDING

2 large onions
225 g/8 oz fresh breadcrumbs
2 teaspoons chopped sage
1 egg
1 tablespoon melted butter
Salt and pepper
Gravy

Boil the onions and chop them finely. Mix with the breadcrumbs, sage, egg, melted butter, salt and pepper. Put into a greased oven tin, and spread about 1.25 cm/½ in thick. Bake at 425°F, 220°C, gas mark 7 for thirty minutes until crisp and brown. Serve with gravy.

Serves 4–6

NORTH COUNTRY TASTY BATTER PUDDING

25 g/1 oz shredded suet
100 g/4 oz flour
2 eggs
600 ml/1 pint milk
Pinch of salt

Mix the suet and the flour with salt. Beat the eggs, and add to the mixture, and make into a batter with the milk. Put into a greased 1.1 litre/2 pint pie dish and bake at 350°F, 180°C, gas mark 4 for one and a half hours. Serve with meat, or make it into a sweet pudding by adding two tablespoons sugar and a few currants.

Serves 4–6

POTATO DUMPLINGS

7 medium-sized potatoes, peeled
2 medium-sized onions
12 slices white bread
¾ teaspoon salt
½ teaspoon black pepper
¾ teaspoon dried dill seeds
3 eggs
175 g/6 oz plain flour
Boiling water or light stock

Grate the potatoes coarsely, squeeze out as much water as possible, then press between paper towels to squeeze out any further liquid. Grate or mince the onions, put in a fine sieve, and press out all juices with the back of a spoon. Mix the onion juice and three tablespoons onion pulp with the grated potatoes; keep the rest of the onion pulp for another dish.

Soak the bread in water until soft. Squeeze out as much water as possible and place the bread in a bowl. Add the salt, pepper and dill, stir in the grated potato and onion mixture, and mix in the eggs. Blend all ingredients thoroughly. Form the mixture into dumplings. Bring 4 litres/7 pints salted water or stock to a full boil. Spread a good quantity of flour on a pastry board, and roll the dumplings in it until thickly coated. Drop into the water or stock, and lower the heat. Cook gently for 15–17 minutes. Remove with a perforated spoon and serve very hot.

Makes 12

VEGETABLES

CREAMED CABBAGE

1 large white cabbage
25 g/1 oz butter
25 g/1 oz plain flour
300 ml/½ pint creamy milk
Salt and pepper

Shred the cabbage and put into boiling water. Boil for ten minutes and drain very well, pressing out moisture. Melt the butter in a saucepan and work in the flour. Cook for two minutes and then gradually add the milk and seasoning. Heat and stir for five minutes, and then stir in the drained cabbage. Cook gently for ten minutes.

Serves 4–6

BASHED 'NEEPS'

6 large turnips
25 g/1 oz butter
150 ml/¼ pint single or thin cream
1 teaspoon plain flour

Peel the turnips and cut them into slices. Boil them in salted water until tender. Mash the turnips and sieve them. Return the sieved turnips to the saucepan with the butter and cream. Scatter in the flour and stir over the heat until the mixture is thick and creamy.

Serves 6

SAVOURY LENTILS

450 g/1 lb lentils
3 rashers streaky bacon
1 small carrot
1 small onion
1 bay leaf
1 sprig of thyme

Rinse the lentils and leave them soaking overnight in cold water. Drain them and put them in a saucepan with chopped bacon, carrot and onion, and the bay leaf and thyme. Just cover with cold water, and bring slowly to the boil. Reduce the heat and continue simmering until the lentils are soft, adding more liquid if necessary during the cooking. (The lentils can be left to simmer in a low oven if preferred.) Serve them with bacon, pork or ham.

Serves 4–6

CREAMED HARICOT BEANS

450 g/1 lb haricot beans
1 medium-sized onion
25 g/1 oz butter
25 g/1 oz flour
300 ml/½ pint stock

Soak the beans overnight in cold water and drain them. Chop the onion finely and cook it in the butter until lightly browned. Work in the flour and stock and simmer until the liquid thickens. Add to the beans and simmer until they are soft.

Serves 4–6

ONIONS IN THE JACKETS

6 large onions
Butter
Salt and pepper

Remove any loose outer skin from the onions, but leave as much skin as possible. Put on to a baking tin in the bottom of the oven in which the joint is cooking. Cook until the onions are tender, testing them with a skewer, which will easily go into the centre when they are done. Serve with plenty of butter, salt and pepper.

Serves 6

BRAISED ONIONS

6 large onions
100 g/4 oz dripping
300 ml/½ pint stock
Flour
Salt and pepper
Juice of half lemon

Peel the onions and put into a pan with the dripping. Cover with a tight lid and cook the onions gently until golden. Drain off the excess fat and cover the onions with stock. Simmer until the onions are soft but unbroken. Thicken the liquid with a little flour, and season with salt, pepper and lemon juice before serving.

Serves 6

BAKED PUMPKIN

1 small, very ripe pumpkin (with a
   hard shell)
Milk as required

Slice the stem end from pumpkin, to form a cover with a handle. Scoop out the seeds and stringy fibres so that only the solid meat remains. Fill the shell with milk, cover with foil, and bake very slowly in the bottom of the oven for 6–7 hours when doing other baking.

To serve, add more milk to the brim and eat straight from the shell.

CHAPTER THREE

SPORTING LIFE

Until about thirty years ago, many country families never saw 'butcher's meat' except when they could barter it for the chickens they had reared. All kinds of game were eaten however, particularly rabbits, hares and pigeons which were considered to be vermin. Occasionally, young game in season was roasted, but the older or badly-shot birds were mainly used for soup, casseroles, pies and puddings, with plenty of onions, herbs and root vegetables.

Pigeons have no close season. They need not be hung, but if they are hung head downwards for an hour immediately after killing, they will bleed, and the flesh will be paler.

Rabbits have no close season. A plump rabbit feeds six people.

Hares are in season from the early autumn to the end of February. A young hare is best roasted, and a hare should feed 8–10 people easily. Often a hare can be served roast or jugged for a smaller number and the remains used for a casserole, soup or cold dish.

Partridges are in season from September 1st to February 1st. The grey partridge needs only 3–4 days hanging, but the red-legged birds need 6–7 days hanging. One bird will usually serve two people, and if plainly roasted is good with watercress, wafer potatoes, and an apple and celery salad.

Pheasants are in season from October 1st to February 1st. Hen birds are smaller but less dry and more tender with good flavour. A good bird should serve four people. A pheasant is best hung for about seven days before cooking. Only young birds should be roasted; the others are fine for casseroles. When roasted, the bird needs additional fat such as butter or bacon for basting, and should be served with bread sauce, fried crumbs and wafer potatoes. Mushrooms, chestnuts and braised celery are all good accompaniments.

Grouse are in season from August 12th to December 10th. A good bird should serve three people, and is usually preferred roasted, but older birds are best in a casserole or pudding. The roast birds are best served on a piece of toast spread with the cooked liver mashed in a little stock, with bread sauce, buttered crumbs, wafer potatoes and watercress, and with rowanberry jelly.

Venison is in season from late June to January. It is best hung for 8–10 days, and needs larding and marinading before roasting. Large joints are best roasted, but venison is excellent in casseroles, soups, cottage pies and pasties. A sharp jelly, made with rowanberries, cranberries, or redcurrants is the most usual traditional accompaniment.

GAME DISHES

ROAST PHEASANT WITH GAME CHIPS AND BREAD SAUCE

1 pheasant
4 rashers bacon
50 g/2 oz butter

Spread a plump young pheasant with butter and put some butter inside the bird. Cover with bacon rashers and roast in a moderate oven, 350°F, 180°C, gas mark 4 for forty-five minutes. Remove to a warm dish and keep hot. Use the pan drippings with a little stock or vegetable water to make clear gravy, and serve the bird with Brussels sprouts or braised celery.

For the Game Chips

4 medium-sized potatoes
Deep fat for frying

To make the *Game Chips*, cut peeled potatoes in wafer-thin slices across. Soak in ice-cold water and dry very thoroughly. Fry in a wire basket in deep fat heated to 395°F, 200°C. Shake the pan as they cook so that they do not stick together. They will float to the surface when ready. Drain on absorbent paper, sprinkle with salt and serve hot.

For the Bread Sauce

1 medium onion
4 cloves
300 ml/½ pint milk
Pinch of mace
6 peppercorns
100 g/4 oz soft white breadcrumbs
15 g/½ oz butter
2 tablespoons cream

To make the *Bread Sauce*, stick the onion with cloves and put into a saucepan with the milk, mace and peppercorns. Bring to the boil, and then remove from heat and leave to stand for thirty minutes. Strain the milk into another pan and add the breadcrumbs. Heat until boiling, stirring gently. Stir in butter and cream, and season to taste with salt and pepper.

Serves 3–4

ROAST VENISON

1 joint of venison
300 ml/½ pint red wine
300 ml/½ pint vinegar
1 sliced onion
Parsley, thyme and bay leaf

Mix together the wine, vinegar, onion and herbs and put the venison in it to soak for two days, turning the meat from time to time. When ready to cook the meat, put the joint on a rack in a baking tin, with the marinade in the tin. Cook at 375°F, 190°C, gas mark 5 until meat is tender (for 15–20 minutes per 450 g/lb if young or well marinated); baste frequently. Strain the pan juices through a sieve, thicken with a little flour, and 150 ml/¼ pint of sour cream or yogurt.

ROAST GROUSE WITH CRANBERRIES

2 grouse
100 g/4 oz butter
225 g/8 oz fresh cranberries

Hang the grouse to taste, until the feathers loosen easily. Pluck and truss them, and fill the cavities with the butter and cranberries. Roast at 450°F, 230°C, gas mark 8 for twenty-five minutes.

Serves 4

RABBIT PUDDING

1 jointed rabbit
225 g/8 oz self-raising flour
100 g/4 oz shredded suet
1 large onion
2 teaspoons sage
100 g/4 oz mushrooms
2 rindless rashers streaky bacon
Salt and pepper

Soak the rabbit joints in salted water for two hours and dry well. Mix together the flour and suet with a pinch of salt and enough cold water to make a firm dough. Roll out the dough and use two-thirds to line a 1.1 litre/2 pint pudding basin. Slice the onion and chop the sage, mushrooms and bacon. Arrange alternate layers of rabbit, onions, sage, mushrooms and bacon in the basin, adding a sprinkle of flour, salt and pepper to the layers. Cover with water and put on the remaining suet dough as a lid. Put on a piece of greaseproof paper and foil or a pudding cloth, and steam for three hours.

Serves 6

GROUSE PUDDING

225 g/8 oz plain flour
1 teaspoon baking powder
½ teaspoon salt
100 g/4 oz shredded suet
1 old grouse
450 g/1 lb stewing steak
1 onion
25 g/1 oz butter
Salt, pepper, nutmeg

Sift together flour, baking powder and salt, and add the grated or chopped suet. Stir in enough cold water to make a pliable dough, and line a 1.1 litre/2 pint pudding basin with two-thirds of the pastry. Cut the flesh of the grouse into neat chunks, stewing the bones and trimmings in water to make a good stock. Brown the grouse and cubes of steak in the butter and put into the basin with salt, pepper and a pinch of nutmeg, chopped onion, and enough stock or water to half fill the basin. Cover with the top crust, put on paper and a cloth, and steam for three hours, adding boiling water to the saucepan to keep it almost to the top of the basin. Make a hole in the top crust before serving and pour in hot stock.

Serves 6

PARTRIDGE PUDDING

675 g/1½ lb flour
225 g/8 oz suet
100 g/4 oz rump steak
Brace of old partridges
½ teaspoon pepper
1 teaspoon salt
100 g/4 oz mushrooms
1 teaspoon each freshly-chopped
  parsley, thyme and tarragon
450 ml/¾ pint brown stock
150 ml/¼ pint sweet stout

Line a 1.1 litre/2 pint pudding basin with a suet crust made with the flour, suet and enough cold water to make a stiff dough, leaving enough crust for a cover. Cut the rump steak in thin slices and put on the bottom, cut the partridges into neat joints and season with pepper and salt, and put in the basin mixed with sliced mushrooms and herbs. Pour in stock mixed with stout, cover with suet crust and pinch the edges together. Tie a pudding cloth or foil over the basin, place in boiling water, and keep boiling for three hours.

Serves 6

GAME PUDDING

225 g/8 oz suet pastry
4 pigeons or 2 partridges or 2 grouse
225 g/8 oz stewing steak
3 hard-boiled egg yolks
Salt, pepper and nutmeg
Stock made from game trimmings

If pigeons are used, the breasts only can go into the pudding, and the rest can be simmered for stock. If partridges are used, they can be split in half. A little bacon and chopped onion, and sometimes a few mushrooms, can be added to this pudding, but they are optional. If appetites are very hearty, the quantity of suet pastry may be increased so that the bowl can be lined.

Line a 1.1 litre/2 pint pudding basin with 1.25 cm/½ in thick pastry, if liked. Put in pigeon breasts or halved partridges or halved grouse, chopped steak, egg yolks, seasoning and gravy to come half way up the bowl. Put on pastry lid and cover with cloth. Steam for three hours.

Serves 4

HARE PIE (COLD)

3 joints hare
1 teaspoon fresh herbs
Salt and pepper
3 tablespoons cider
225 g/8 oz plain flour
Pinch of salt
50 g/2 oz lard
65 ml/2½ fl oz milk and water
Stock
1 egg, beaten

Chop or mince the hare finely, season with herbs, salt and pepper, and leave to stand overnight in cider. Sieve flour and salt in a warm bowl. Bring lard, milk and water to boil together and pour into the middle of the flour; stir until cool enough to handle. Knead until smooth, adding more hot milk and water if necessary. Cover with a tea towel damped in hot water and wrung out, and stand bowl in warm water for fifteen minutes, keeping dough only just warm. Roll out three-quarters of the pastry and line an 18 cm/7 in pie mould or cake tin with a removable bottom. Mix hare meat well and stir in a spoonful of stock; put filling into pastry case to within 2.5 cm/1 in of the top. Brush top edge with egg, cover with pastry lid, and glaze with beaten egg. Make a hole in the centre of the lid. Bake at 400°F, 200°C, gas mark 6 for twenty minutes, then reduce heat to 350°F, 180°C, gas mark 4 for another hour, covering the pastry with thick paper to prevent burning. When pie is cool, pour in a little cold jellied stock almost at setting point, using a funnel in the hole. Leave in tin until completely cold.

Serves 6

PARTRIDGE, VEAL AND BACON PIE (HOT OR COLD)

2 partridges
25 g/1 oz butter
225 g/8 oz lean veal
225 g/8 oz boiled bacon or ham
150 ml/¼ pint onion sauce
2 hard-boiled eggs
1 tablespoon chopped parsley
100 g/4 oz mushrooms
Salt and pepper
Pinch of nutmeg
225 g/8 oz puff pastry
Rich stock or gravy
1 egg, beaten

Cut the birds in halves and cook them lightly in butter until just coloured. In a 1.1 litre/2 pint pie dish put a layer of mixed chopped veal and bacon. Put in partridges. Add parsley, mushrooms and seasoning, and put on a second layer of veal and bacon. Pour on the onion sauce and cover with slices of egg. Cover with pastry, glaze with beaten egg and bake at 400°F, 200°C, gas mark 6 for one hour. When the pie is removed from the oven, pour in a little rich hot stock or gravy. Serve hot or cold.

Serves 6

RABBIT PIE (HOT OR COLD)

1 jointed rabbit
100 g/4 oz pork sausage meat
225 g/8 oz stewing steak
Salt and pepper
1 tablespoon chopped parsley
Ground nutmeg
225 g/8 oz shortcrust pastry

Soak the rabbit joints in salted water for two hours and dry well. Make the sausage meat into small balls and cut the stewing steak into cubes. Arrange layers of the steak, rabbit and sausage meat balls in a 1.1 litre/2 pint pie dish, sprinkling well with salt and pepper, parsley and nutmeg.

Cover with stock or water. Put on a pastry lid, and bake at 450°F, 230°C, gas mark 8 for twenty minutes. Reduce heat to 350°F, 180°C, gas mark 4 and cook for one hour.

Serves 6

VENISON PASTY

225 g/8 oz shortcrust pastry
350 g/12 oz cold cooked venison
300 ml/½ pint beef stock
1 bayleaf
6 peppercorns
¼ teaspoon ground mace
2 teaspoons redcurrant jelly
Beaten egg for glazing

Line an 18 cm/7 in pie plate with half the pastry. Mince the venison coarsely. Put the remaining ingredients into a pan and simmer together for 20 minutes. Strain over the meat and leave to stand for a few minutes so that the meat absorbs the liquid. Spread over the pastry case and cover with the remaining pastry. Cut two or three slits in the lid. Brush over the surface with beaten egg. Bake at 400°F, 200°C, gas mark 6 for 20 minutes. Serve hot with gravy and root vegetables.

Serves 4

GROUSE PIE

2 grouse
225 g/8 oz puff pastry
225 g/8 oz pork sausage meat
Salt, pepper and herbs
4 hard-boiled egg yolks
1 egg, beaten
100 g/4 oz raw ham

Cut up the grouse, each of them in five parts, and season with pepper and salt. Cover the bottom of a 1.1 litre/2 pint dish with a layer of sausage meat on which place the pieces of grouse. Sprinkle over a few herbs. Fill the cavities between the pieces with the hard-boiled yolks, and place pieces of ham on top of the grouse; pour in good gravy to half the height, cover the pie with pastry and brush with egg. Bake at 350°F, 180°C, gas mark 4 for one and a half hours.

Serves 6

PIGEON PIE

3 pigeons
225 g/8 oz rump steak
100 g/4 oz ham or rindless lean bacon
100 g/4 oz mushrooms
2 hard-boiled eggs
Salt and pepper
450 ml/¾ pint beef stock
225 g/8 oz puff pastry
1 egg yolk

Cut each pigeon into four pieces. Cut steak into squares, and ham or bacon into strips. Chop the mushrooms roughly, and cut eggs into quarters. Put steak into the bottom of a 1.1 litre/2 pint pie dish, and then add the pigeon pieces, ham or bacon, mushrooms and eggs. Season well with salt and pepper and pour in the stock. Roll out pastry and cover pie, using pastry trimmings to make decorative 'leaves' to finish the crust. Brush pastry with the egg yolk beaten with a pinch of salt. Bake in a hot oven, 425°F, 220°C, gas mark 7 for fifteen minutes, then lower heat to 350°F, 180°C, gas mark 4 for one and a quarter hours.

Serves 6

PUPTON OF PIGEONS

For the forcemeat
175 g/6 oz cooked lamb or veal
175 g/6 oz lamb fat or beef dripping
2 egg yolks
225 g/8 oz soft white breadcrumbs
White pepper and salt
½ teaspoon each grated nutmeg, ground
  mace and grated lemon peel
¼ teaspoon each chopped parsley and
  thyme
2 egg yolks

For the filling
4 thin rindless slices bacon, diced
150–175 g/5–6 oz cooked braised or
  roast beef, thinly sliced
2 cooked pigeons
50 g/2 oz cooked lamb's sweetbreads
50–75 g/2–3 oz green asparagus tips
  (optional)
75 g/3 oz mushrooms
2 hard-boiled egg yolks
1 egg

This is a very old dish, very like a plate pie but made in a forcemeat crust instead of pastry. It is a good way to use up leftovers.

Make the forcemeat first. Mince and pound the lamb or veal (or process with the fat in an electric blender). Make it a smooth paste. Add the fat, seasonings, herbs, egg yolks and enough breadcrumbs to make a firm dough-like paste. Grease a 20 cm/8 in round baking dish or pie plate. Halve the forcemeat. Roll out one half, if possible, and lay it in the dish to line it; if too crumbly, press it on the bottom and sides of the dish as when making a crumb shell. Scatter a little flour over the bottom. Spread the diced bacon over the flour, and the beef. Halve the pigeons lengthways, and remove the spines and wings. Place in one layer in the dish. Chop the sweetbreads and press them into the spaces between the birds, do the same with the asparagus tips if used, and with the mushrooms, chopped if large. Top with the sliced hard-boiled egg yolks and a little more flour. Season with pepper and salt. Cover with the second half of the forcemeat, rolled out or pressed on as before. Glaze with the egg. Bake at 350°F, 180°C, gas mark 4 for 30–35 minutes until the forcemeat crust is cooked and golden. Serve with rich gravy and green vegetable.

NOTE: The quantity of forcemeat given above can also be used to stuff 5–6 pigeons.

Serves 6

CAMBRIDGE HARE IN BEER

1 hare
2 large onions
225 g/8 oz carrots
40 g/1½ oz plain flour
300 ml/½ pint brown ale or stout
300 ml/½ pint stock

Joint the hare. Slice the onions thinly and the carrots rather thickly. Fry the onions in a little dripping until soft but not coloured and put them into a casserole. Coat the hare joints in a little of the flour seasoned with salt and pepper, and cook them in the dripping until golden. Put on top of the onions and add the carrots. Work the remaining flour into the fat in the pan and cook for two minutes. Gradually add the beer and stock and cook until smooth. Pour over the hare, cover the casserole, and cook at 350°F, 180°C, gas mark 4 for two and a half hours. Very good with jacket potatoes.

Serves 6

OCTOBER PARTRIDGE

2 partridges
Salt and pepper
Juice of half lemon
50 g/2 oz butter
2 rindless rashers bacon
1 small onion
1 small red cabbage
150 ml/¼ pint cider
1 teaspoon vinegar
6 chestnuts
25 g/1 oz butter

Wipe the partridges inside and out, dust with salt and pepper and sprinkle with lemon juice. Melt the butter in a pan and brown the birds slowly all over. Cool slightly, then wrap each bird in a slice of bacon. Slice the onion and red cabbage very finely, season with salt and pepper and put into a saucepan with the cider and vinegar. Bring to the boil and simmer for twenty minutes. Put birds on top and put on lid, then simmer for one and a half hours. Peel the chestnuts, toss in butter and add to the dish ten minutes before cooking is finished.

Serves 4

PARTRIDGE CASSEROLE WITH CABBAGE

2 old partridges
2 onions
2 carrots
100 g/4 oz streaky bacon
225 g/8 oz chipolata sausages
1 savoy cabbage
300 ml/½ pint stock
Thyme and parsley
Salt, pepper

Cut the vegetables into neat pieces and brown them in a little butter, together with the partridges. Cut the cabbage into quarters and cook in boiling water with the bacon for five minutes. Drain well. Cut bacon and cabbage into small pieces. Put half the cabbage into a casserole, season with salt and pepper, and lay it on the partridges. Cover with bacon and vegetables, chopped herbs, and the rest of the cabbage. Pour in stock, cover with a lid and cook at 300°F, 150°C, gas mark 2 for three hours. Grill the sausages lightly and add half an hour before serving time. The addition of a glass of dry perry (using a little less stock) makes a good dish.

Serves 4

PHEASANT AND HERB CASEROLE

1 pheasant
225 g/8 oz onions
Salt and white pepper
¼ teaspoon thyme
¼ teaspoon parsley
450 ml/¾ pint chicken stock
25 g/1 oz butter

Cut the pheasant into eight pieces. Slice the onions and mingle with the pheasant, salt and pepper. Leave to stand for three hours or overnight in a cool place. Chop the giblets finely. Remove the onions from the pheasant and cook them in the butter until golden. Add the giblets, thyme and parsley, and stock, and simmer on a low heat. Carefully fry the pheasant pieces in a little cooking oil for about five minutes, turning occasionally. Put the pheasant and onion gravy together in a casserole and cook at 350°F, 180°C, gas mark 4 for one hour twenty minutes

Serves 3–4

PHEASANT WITH MUSHROOMS AND SHERRY

75 g/3 oz butter
225 g/8 oz mushrooms
1 pheasant
3 tablespoons flour
450 ml/¾ pint stock
75 ml/3 fl oz sherry
Salt and pepper
Watercress

Melt half the butter and cook the sliced mushrooms gently for ten minutes. Season lightly and cool. Stuff the pheasant with three-quarters of the mushrooms. Brown the bird in the rest of the butter, and put in a casserole. Blend the flour into the pan juices, and gradually work in the stock and sherry. Season well and pour over pheasant. Cover tightly and cook in the oven at 325°F, 170°C, gas mark 3 for one and a half hours, but allow an extra thirty minutes for an old bird. Just before serving, add remaining mushrooms, and garnish with watercress. The sauce is rich and delicious.

Serves 3–4

PHEASANT WITH CELERY SAUCE

1 large old pheasant
650 ml/1 pint stock

The stock for cooking the pheasant should include a carrot and onion, a couple of cloves, salt and pepper with a good sprig of parsley. Poach the pheasant in this until tender (this will depend on the age of the bird). Cut the bird into neat pieces for serving with the celery sauce.

For the Celery Sauce

1 head celery
50 g/2 oz butter
1 onion
Parsley, theyme and bay leaf
1 clove
Salt and pepper
25 g/1 oz butter mixed with 25 g/1 oz
  flour
150 ml/¼ pint cream

Make sauce by cooking the chopped celery in butter with the onion, herbs, clove, salt and pepper until tender, then simmering in 300 ml/½ pint of the pheasant stock until really soft. Put the celery through a sieve and thicken with the butter and flour worked together. Finally, stir in the cream and pour over the pheasant. The sauce should be rather thick. If time is short and the celery young and without strings, the pieces may be left whole without sieving. If money is short, use a little top of the milk instead of cream for the sauce. The same recipe may be used for partridges and this quantity of sauce will be enough for two birds.

Serves 3–4

HAMPSHIRE RABBIT

1 rabbit
Seasoned flour
225 g/8 oz onions
2 leeks
100 g/4 oz rindless streaky bacon
*   rashers*
Dripping
Stock
Salt and pepper

Dumplings
75 g/3 oz self-raising flour
45 g/1½ oz shredded beef suet
1 tablespoon chopped chives

Joint the rabbit and soak in salt and water until blanched. Dry joints and toss in seasoned flour. Put joints in a fireproof dish and surround with sliced onions, celery and leeks and top with diced bacon rashers. Dot with dripping, and brown in a hot oven for twenty minutes. Add stock to come half way up the dish, season well with salt and pepper, and cover with a lid. Cook at 325°F, 170°C, gas mark 3 for one and a half hours.

Make twelve dumplings, add to the rabbit, cover and cook for twenty to twenty five minutes.

Serves 4

IRISH ROAST RABBIT

1 rabbit
4 rindless rashers bacon
2 medium-sized onions
1 tablespoon flour
50 g/2 oz butter
300 ml/½ pint scalded milk
Pepper
1 dessertspoon chopped parsley

Cut up rabbit and soak in vinegar and water. Dry pieces well and coat in flour seasoned with pepper. Brown in the butter and put into a casserole. Add chopped bacon, onions and parsley and pour over milk. Cover and bake at 375°F, 190°C, gas mark 5 for one hour. Serve with plenty of floury potatoes. Parsley sauce is also good with this.

Serves 4

MUMBLED RABBIT

575 g/1¼ lb rabbit joints
Bay leaf, thyme and parsley
1–2 teaspoons anchovy essence
3 eggs, hard-boiled
50 g/2 oz butter
Salt and pepper

Bring a saucepan of salted water to the boil. Cut the rabbit into serving pieces if necessary. Simmer with the herbs and anchovy essence for about forty minutes, until tender. Add the hard-boiled eggs for the last 2–3 minutes of the cooking time, just for long enough to heat them through.

Take out the eggs first, and chop them finely. Drain the rabbit, discard the herbs, and mix the meat and seasoning lightly with the eggs and butter. Toss briefly over gentle heat if the butter does not melt at once.

Add 150 ml/¼ pint of the cooking liquid as a sauce if you wish. But if the accompanying vegetables are sauced, keep all the cooking liquid for stock.

This dish is not only easy, cheap and labour-saving, it is very good. It goes particularly well with cooked celery.

Serves 4

RABBIT WITH LENTILS

100 g/4 oz lentils
1 rindless rasher bacon
1 onion
1 rabbit
150 ml/¼ pint cider
Bunch of mixed herbs
Salt and pepper

Soak the lentils in water to cover overnight. Next morning, chop the bacon and fry till the fat runs, then add chopped onion, and soften without browning. Stir in the lentils and any water if necessary to prevent burning. When lentils are soft, put through a sieve. Put the jointed rabbit in a casserole with cider, herbs, salt and pepper. Cover and cook in a slow oven at 325°F, 170°C, gas mark 3 till rabbit is tender. Drain off the rabbit liquid and mix with the lentil purée. Pour over the rabbit and continue cooking for fifteen minutes.

Serves 4

RABBIT IN CIDER

1 jointed rabbit
4 large onions
1 bay leaf
Sprig of thyme
50 g/2 oz chopped bacon
225 g/8 oz peeled sliced tomatoes
300 ml/½ pint dry cider
Salt and pepper

Soak the rabbit joints in salted water for two hours and dry well. Fry them until golden in a little fat (bacon fat if possible). Slice the onions and add them to the rabbit. Cook until soft. Add the bayleaf and the thyme, bacon and tomatoes, and simmer for ten minutes. Pour on the cider and cover the pan. Simmer for one hour. Season with salt and pepper just before serving, and garnish with plenty of chopped parsley if liked.

Serves 4

JUGGED RABBIT

1 rabbit
1 onion
1 bay leaf
Salt and pepper
Pinch of nutmeg
1 teaspoon sugar
300 ml/½ pint dry cider

Soak rabbit joints overnight in one pint water with two tablespoons vinegar, together with chopped onion, bay leaf, salt and pepper and nutmeg. Drain joints, keeping the liquid, and dry joints well. Fry rabbit in dripping or bacon fat until golden, then cover with liquid and simmer very gently until tender (about one hour). Add sugar and cider to pan and continue cooking for fifteen minutes. Thicken gravy with a little flour or cornflour, and serve with forcemeat balls and redcurrant jelly.

Serves 4

STEAMED AND BROWNED PIGEONS

2 pigeons
4 rindless rashers streaky bacon
1 large onion
Salt and pepper

This method can be used to make dry birds succulent. When they have been steamed, the birds can be browned under a grill or in the oven. Rub the pigeons with salt and pepper and tie two rashers of bacon over each bird. Steam them until tender together with the onion. When the birds are tender, brown them lightly under the grill or in the oven. Use the juices and pieces of onion in the steamer to make a rich gravy.

Serves 4

PIGEON AND MUSHROOM CASSEROLE

2 pigeons
25 g/1 oz butter
225 g/8 oz stewing steak
1 rindless rasher bacon
300 ml/½ pint stock
50 g/2 oz mushrooms
Salt and pepper
1 tablespoon redcurrant jelly
1 tablespoon lemon juice
1 tablespoon plain flour

Cut the pigeons in half and brown them lightly in the butter. Put into a casserole with the steak cut in cubes and the bacon cut in pieces. Cover with stock and sliced mushrooms, and season with salt and pepper to taste. Cover and simmer for two hours. Mix together the redcurrant jelly, lemon juice and flour with a little water and stir this into the casserole. Simmer for fifteen minutes. Serve with plainly boiled or mashed potatoes.

Serves 4

SLOW-COOKED PIGEONS

4 pigeons
12 small onions
3 rindless rashers lean bacon
225 g/8 oz mushrooms
600 ml/1 pint stock
225 ml/7½ fl oz rosé wine
25 g/1 oz butter
20 g/¾ oz flour
1 teaspoon sugar
Parsley, thyme and bay leaf

Use an oven-to-table fireproof dish which will allow the pigeons to fit side by side. Peel the onions, cut the bacon into thin strips and wipe the mushrooms. Heat the butter and lightly fry the bacon. Put on a warmed dish, and reserve; cook onions until lightly golden, sprinkling with sugar. Remove to dish. Cook the mushrooms in the same fat, and remove to the dish. Brown the pigeons in the fat, very slowly and

carefully, and lift out. Work the flour into the fat, cooking until brown. Gradually add stock and wine, bring to the boil and strain. Rinse out the pan, put back the sauce and bring to the boil. Add all the ingredients, cover with greased paper and well-fitting lid. Cook at 300°F, 150°C, gas mark 2 for 2½–3 hours. Remove bunch of herbs before serving.

Serves 4

JUGGED PIGEONS

2 pigeons
2 hard-boiled egg yolks
Pinch of nutmeg
Salt and pepper
Bunch of fresh herbs
225 ml/8 fl oz beer
75 g/3 oz soft white breadcrumbs
25 g/1 oz melted butter
A little grated lemon peel
600 ml/1 pint water
1 onion
25 g/1 oz butter
25 g/1 oz flour

Pluck and draw the birds. Boil the livers and chop them finely. Make a stuffing with the chopped livers, the yolks of hard-boiled eggs, nutmeg, pepper, salt, breadcrumbs, and finely-chopped suet or melted butter. Mix well together. Stuff the birds, and place them in the top of a double saucepan with the water, peeled and sliced onion, the sweet herbs, and the beer. Cover with a close fitting lid and place on the bottom pan, which should be kept three-quarters full with boiling water (and when refilling, fill from kettle of boiling water), and allow the pigeons to stew until tender. This will take 1½–2 hours.

Strain off the gravy. Melt the butter in a saucepan, add the flour, stir well and dilute with one pint of the pigeon broth, and bring to the boil. Stir, and, when thickened, pour over pigeons.

Serves 4

PIGEON AND APPLE CASSEROLE

2 pigeons
25 g/1 oz butter
1 small apple
1 small onion
15 g/½ oz flour
300 ml/½ pint cider
300 ml/½ pint stock
Salt and pepper
Bay leaf, thyme and parsley

Brown the pigeons in the butter and then cut them in half. Peel and slice the apple and onion, and brown them in the fat drained from the pigeons. Sprinkle in the flour, and cook and stir well for two minutes. Add the cider and stock and bring to the boil. Season well with salt and pepper and add the herbs. Put the pigeons into a casserole and pour over the liquid from the pan. Cover and simmer for two hours. Put the pigeons on a serving dish. Strain the liquid and boil quickly to reduce by half. Pour this sauce over the pigeons and garnish with fried apple rings and crisp bacon.

Serves 4

PIGEON LOAF

2–3 pigeons
225 g/8 oz pork sausagemeat
1 medium onion
1 slice bread, toast thickness
150 ml/¼ pint red wine
1 teaspoon mixed fresh herbs
Salt and pepper
225 g/8 oz bacon rashers

Using a sharp knife, strip the flesh from the pigeons and mince finely. Mix with the sausagemeat and finely chopped onion. Remove the crusts from the bread and soak the bread in the wine. Mash with a fork and add to the meat mixture with the herbs and plenty of salt and pepper.

Remove the rinds from the bacon and put half the rashers into a 450 g/1 lb loaf tin. Cover with the pigeon mixture and the remaining bacon rashers. Cover with foil and bake at 325°F, 160°C, gas mark 3 for 2 hours. Cool slightly before turning out to serve hot with gravy. If liked, cool under weights and cut into thick slices to serve with salad.

Serves 4–6

DEVONSHIRE VENISON

2 kg/4 lb roasting joint of venison
Seasoned flour
Butter or dripping
Stock
Fresh herbs
Stuffing using thyme and parsley

Soak the venison in cold salted water for thirty minutes, and then drain and dry it well. Cut the meat in thick slices and dust them with seasoned flour. Fry in butter or dripping until brown on both sides. Put the slices into a casserole and cover with stock which has been lightly thickened with flour. Add a good pinch of fresh herbs, cover and cook at 325°F, 170°C, gas mark 3 for two hours. Add small balls of any favourite stuffing flavoured with thyme and parsley and continue cooking for thirty minutes.

Serves 6

New Forest Venison Roll

900 g/2 lb venison
225 g/8 oz fat bacon
1 medium-sized onion
Salt and pepper
175 g/6 oz soft white breadcrumbs
1 tablespoon chopped parsley
2 eggs
Stock

Mince the venison, bacon and onion and add salt and pepper, breadcrumbs and chopped parsley. Beat the eggs and add to the other ingredients. Add sufficient stock to bind. Flour a pudding cloth or foil and place the mixture on it in a long roll, wrap up, tie the end with string or twist to secure, and boil for two and a half hours. Serve with brown gravy and cranberry or quince jelly. Rowanberry jelly is also good with this dish.

Serves 6

Venison in Ale

1.4 kg/3 lb stewing venison
225 g/8 oz Demerara sugar
2 tablespoons black treacle
600 ml/1 pint beer

Dissolve the sugar and treacle in the beer. Put the well-hung meat into a stewpan or casserole, cover with the liquid, put on the lid and bring to the boil. Simmer gently for two hours.

Serves 6

CHAPTER FOUR

FRESH FROM THE
SEA AND RIVER

Until about a hundred years ago, fresh fish from the sea was rarely seen inland, and farmers' wives used smoked or salted sea fish. They did, however, get fresh fish from rivers, streams and ponds. It was abundant, from perch and bream to salmon, carp and pike. So were eels and fresh-water shellfish.

Many housewives used estuary and coastal fish too. The coastal areas of the West Country and East Anglia in particular were rich in herring, mackerel and pilchard, as well as cockles, mussels and oysters. There are many traditional ways of preparing all these in cider or vinegar which make delicious dishes, and which also serve to preserve the fish for a while.

COD WITH BACON

675 g/1½ lb cod cutlets
25 g/1 oz bacon fat
4 rindless rashers streaky bacon
Salt and pepper

Dry the fish well. Put the bacon fat into a fairly deep ovenware dish which will hold half the fish. Put in half the cutlets and season well. Cut each bacon rasher in two pieces and put half the slices over the fish. Lay the remaining fish on top and then the remaining bacon rashers. Cover and bake at 350°F, 180°C, gas mark 4 for thirty minutes. Remove the lid and continue cooking for ten minutes so that the top layer of bacon becomes crisp.

Serves 4

HAMPSHIRE HADDOCK OR COD

900 g/2 lb whole haddock or cod
75 g/3 oz soft white breadcrumbs
40 g/1½ oz shredded suet
1 teaspoon chopped parsley
1 teaspoon chopped thyme
Grated rind of half lemon
Salt and pepper
Pinch of nutmeg
1 egg
25 g/1 oz butter or dripping

Use a middle cut for this dish. Clean the fish, removing the head, fins and tail. Mix together the breadcrumbs, suet, herbs, lemon rind, seasoning and egg and stuff the fish with this mixture. If preferred, the stuffing mixture may be spread over the surface of the fish instead. Dot the fish with pieces of butter or dripping and bake at 350°F, 180°C, gas mark 4 for forty-five minutes. This is very good served with plenty of melted butter or with parsley sauce.

Serves 4

WEST COUNTRY MACKEREL (A COLD DISH)

8 mackerel
8 bay leaves
20 black peppercorns
1 tablespoon brown sugar
300 ml/½ pint mixed cold tea and white vinegar

Clean the mackerel and put a bay leaf inside each one. Put the fish side by side in an ovenware dish. Sprinkle on the peppercorns and sugar, and add the mixed tea and vinegar. Cover and bake at 350°F, 180°C, gas mark 4 for one hour. Serve cold.

Serves 8

CORNISH MACKEREL

4 mackerel
1 teaspoon fresh horseradish
75 g/3 oz sour clotted cream, or cream cheese
1 teaspoon chopped onion
150 ml/¼ pint cider

If cream or cream cheese are not obtainable, nor fresh horseradish, the fish can be prepared with butter creamed with some bottled horseradish sauce, but the flavour is less good. Split and clean the fish. Work the horseradish into the cream cheese together with the onion and just enough cider to make a soft spreadable cream. Spread this inside the fish and fold them back into shape. Place side by side in an ovenware dish and sprinkle with the remaining cider. Bake at 350°F, 180°C, gas mark 4 for forty-five minutes. Serve very hot.

Serves 4

YORKSHIRE HERRING PIE

4 herrings
6 potatoes
2 cooking apples, peeled, chopped and dipped in mild vinegar
Butter or bacon fat
Salt and pepper

Clean the herrings and cut them into fillets. Peel the potatoes and cut them into thin slices like crisps. Arrange these potato slices round the sides and bottom of a greased ovenware dish. Put a layer of herring in the dish, and then a layer of peeled and finely-chopped apple. Put on another layer of herrings and apples, then herrings, and finish with pieces of potato as a top layer. Put one or two knobs of butter or bacon fat on top and cover with greased paper. Bake at 350°F, 180°C, gas mark 4 for thirty minutes. Remove the paper and continue cooking for twenty minutes.

Serves 4

Right: Cooked on a griddle, Drop Scones are delicious when eaten as soon as they are ready.
Over: Freshly-baked scones, together with home-made strawberry jam, are firm favourites for a traditional farmhouse tea.

SCOTCH SALMON PUDDING

225 g/8 oz cooked salmon
3 tablespoons cooked rice
1 egg
2 tablespoons milk
Salt and pepper
½ teaspoon mixed chopped chervil and
  tarragon
½ teaspoon chopped celery leaves

Flake the salmon and mix it with the rice, egg, milk, seasoning and herbs. Put into an 18 cm/7 in buttered ovenware dish and cover with a buttered paper. Steam for thirty minutes. Turn out and serve with briefly-steamed cucumber marbles and with melted butter, which can be flavoured with a little anchovy essence or grated horseradish.

NOTE: Make cucumber marbles by cutting out with a potato baller.

Serves 3

SCOTTISH SALT FISH PIE

900 g/2 lb salt fish
900 g/2 lb potatoes
Salt and pepper
50 g/2 oz butter

This pie can be made with any salt fish, but cod is the most easily obtainable. Soak the fish for twenty-four hours, and then simmer until tender in enough fresh cold water to cover. Remove the bones, and flake the flesh into small pieces. Boil and mash half the potatoes with the butter, seasoning to taste. Parboil the remaining potatoes and cut them into slices. Put one layer of potatoes in an ovenware dish and season lightly. Put on a thick layer of fish, then the remaining sliced potatoes. Top with the remaining fish and cover with the mashed potatoes. Bake at 375°F, 190°C, gas mark 5 for forty-five minutes. Mustard sauce is very good with it.

Serves 6

WELSH COCKLE PIE, HOT OR COLD

225 g/8 oz cooked cockles
225 g/8 oz shortcrust pastry
6 spring onions
75 g/3 oz streaky bacon, diced
Salt and pepper

Line a 20 cm/8 in pie dish with pastry, reserving some for a lattice decoration. Put a layer of the cockles in the dish. Sprinkle with chopped onions (chives can be used instead), and a layer of diced bacon, seasoning well. Repeat the layers until the dish is full and pour in the cockle liquid. Make a pastry lattice over the pie and bake at 400°F, 200°C, gas mark 6 for thirty minutes. Serve hot with new potatoes, or cold with salad.

Serves 4

FISH STAND-BY

175 g/6 oz shortcrust pastry
175 g/6 oz kipper fillets
1 hard-boiled egg
25 g/1 oz butter
25 g/1 oz plain flour
150 ml/¼ pint milk
225 g/8 oz mashed potato
2 eggs, separated
1 tablespoon chopped parsley

Use the pastry to line a 20 cm/8 in flan ring. To make the filling, cook the kipper fillets, skin and flake them. Chop and mix in the hard-boiled egg. Melt the butter in a small saucepan, stir in the flour, then remove from the heat and stir in the milk. Return to the heat, bring to the boil and simmer for a few minutes, stirring continuously. Mix in the kipper mixture, season to taste and pour into the pastry case. To make the topping, beat the egg yolks and parsley into the mashed potato. Stiffly whisk the egg whites and fold in. Pile this mixture on top of the filling and bake at 375°F, 190°C, gas mark 5 for forty-five minutes until golden-brown.

Serves 4

Left: Tea has always been a very important meal in a farmhouse.
Page 71: Moist, dark and spicy, gingerbread keeps well.

TRELLIS PIE

225 g/8 oz mashed potato
175 g/6 oz plain flour
100 g/4 oz butter
50 g/2 oz lard
100 g/4 oz sliced mushrooms
1 chopped onion
225 g/8 oz canned fish or cooked
  smoked haddock
Milk
1 heaped tablespoon flour
1 egg yolk

Sieve the flour with a pinch of salt, and rub in half the butter and all the lard. Add the potato and mix to a fairly stiff dough. Line a 20 cm/8 in pie plate with this potato pastry, reserving the scraps. Fry the vegetables in the remaining butter, and when cooked, take out a few mushroom slices. Drain off the liquid from canned fish if used and make it up to 300 ml/½ pint with milk, otherwise Use 300 ml/½ pint milk. Add the flour, stirring continuously to make a smooth sauce. Add the flaked fish and egg yolk, and adjust seasoning. Spoon the mixture into the flan case. Decorate with a lattice of potato pastry and brush with a little milk. Bake the flan at 400°F, 200°C, gas mark 6 for 25–30 minutes until cooked through. Decorate with the reserved mushrooms before serving.

Serves 4

HADDOCK OR BREAM PUDDING

450 g/1 lb haddock or bream
1 chopped onion
2 eggs
300 ml/½ pint milk
75 g/3 oz soft white breadcrumbs
Juice of half lemon
Salt and pepper
Grated Lancashire cheese

Poach the fish and cool it. Flake the flesh and mix with the finely-chopped onion, beaten eggs,

milk, softened butter, breadcrumbs and lemon juice. Season well and put into a greased 1.1 litre/2 pint pie dish. Sprinkle with grated cheese. Bake at 375°F, 190°C, gas mark 5 for forty minutes.

Serves 4

WEST COUNTRY BAKED PILCHARDS, HOT OR COLD

8 pilchards
Salt and black pepper
1 teaspoon ground cloves
1 teaspoon ground allspice
1 medium-sized onion
300 ml/½ pint pale ale
300 ml/½ pint vinegar
4 bay leaves

Clean and fillet the fish. Sprinkle salt, pepper and spices on the inside of the fish, roll them up and put them into an ovenware dish. Slice the onion finely and scatter the onion rings on the fish, together with the bay leaves. Pour over the ale and the vinegar. Cover and bake at 350°F, 180°C, gas mark 4 for one hour. Serve hot or cold.

Serves 4

WELSH TROUT WITH BACON

175 g/6 oz rindless streaky bacon
  rashers
4 river trout
Salt and pepper
1 teaspoon chopped parsley

Line an ovenware dish with the slices of bacon. Split and clean the trout and put them on the bacon. Sprinkle with salt, pepper and parsley. Cover and bake at 350°F, 180°C, gas mark 4 for twenty minutes.

Serves 4

SUFFOLK TROUT

4 river trout
4 bay leaves
50 g/2 oz butter
Juice of one lemon

Clean the trout and remove their heads. Put a bay leaf inside each trout. Melt the butter in a thick frying pan, and put in the trout. Add the lemon juice and cover with a lid. Cook on a very low heat for twenty minutes, turning the trout once during cooking. Serve very hot with lemon slices, peas and new potatoes.

Serves 4

STUFFED HERRINGS WITH GOOSEBERRY SAUCE

4 herrings
1 tablespoon chopped parsley
1 tablespoon chopped thyme
1 teaspoon grated lemon rind
1 tablespoon lemon juice
25 g/1 oz white breadcrumbs
Seasoned flour
25 g/1 oz browned breadcrumbs
225 g/8 oz gooseberries
Sugar to taste

Wash and dry the herrings, and clean them. Mix the parsley, thyme, lemon rind, lemon juice and soft breadcrumbs and stuff the herrings with this mixture. Roll the fish lightly in seasoned flour. Melt a little dripping in a baking pan and when it is very hot, put in the herrings.

Put into the oven and bake at 350°F, 180°C, gas mark 4 for twenty minutes. Sprinkle lightly with browned crumbs and return to the oven for five minutes. Meanwhile, for the *Gooseberry Sauce* simmer the gooseberries in very little water until they are soft. Rub them through a sieve and sweeten lightly. Add a little green vegetable colouring if the colour is pale. Serve the gooseberry sauce with the herrings.

Serves 4

Mackerel can also be cooked in this way. Omit the crumbs.

So can *Sprats*; the stuffing is put between pairs of the little fish so they remain flat.

CIDER-SOUSED MACKEREL

2 large mackerel
1 onion
thinly pared rind of ½ lemon
2 fresh bay leaves
6 peppercorns
300 ml/½ pint dry cider
150 ml/¼ pint water
1 teaspoon arrowroot

Clean the herrings and remove their heads, tails and side fins. Put them side by side in an oven dish, close together and head-to-tail. Cover with finely sliced onion, lemon rind, bay leaves and peppercorns. Pour on the mixed cider and water and bake at 350°F, 180°C, gas mark 4 for thirty to forty minutes. Transfer fish to a serving dish and keep warm. Blend the arrowroot with a little of the cooking liquor. Strain in 300 ml/½ pint more, stirring. Boil in a saucepan, stirring, until clear. Pour over fish and garnish with fresh herbs.

Serves 4

SEFTON BLOATERS

2 bloaters
25 g/1 oz grated Lancashire cheese
75 g/3 oz breadcrumbs
1 egg, beaten
Lard
Chopped parsley

Put the lard in a pan. Fillet the fish and cut into pieces. Dip them in flour, then in egg, and then roll in the breadcrumbs and cheese mixed together. When the lard smokes, put them in and fry until golden. Drain them well and serve with chopped parsley.

Serves 2

FISHERMAN'S PIE

350 g/12 oz puff pastry
40 g/1½ oz butter
40 g/1½ oz plain flour
300 ml/½ pint dry cider
150 ml/¼ pint milk
450 g/1 lb smoked haddock fillet,
  cooked
3 hard-boiled eggs
100 g/4 oz cooked peas
Salt and pepper

Roll the pastry into a rectangle 28 × 20 cm/11 × 8 in. Mark out a rectangle with a sharp knife 2.5 cm/1 in from the edge to form a lid. Brush with a little milk or beaten egg and bake at 425°F, 220°C, gas mark 7 for 20 minutes. Carefully remove the lid from the pastry case.

Melt the butter and work in the flour. Cook for 1 minute and gradually stir in the cider and milk. Bring to the boil, stirring well. Boil for 1 minute and remove from the heat. Flake the haddock and chop the eggs roughly. Stir into the sauce with the peas and plenty of salt and pepper. Pour into the pastry case and cover lightly with the lid. Reheat at 375°F, 190°C, gas mark 5 for 15 minutes.

CHUTNEY-STUFFED MACKEREL

4 mackerel fillets
4 tablespoons apple chutney (see page
  00).
4 teaspoons soured cream or natural
  yoghurt (optional)

Spread the chutney equally over the flesh side of the fillets. Fold in half and arrange in a shallow heatproof dish. Cover and bake for 12–15 minutes at 200°C/400°F/gas 6 for 15–20 minutes.

Spoon over soured cream or yoghurt if using, and serve hot or cold with potatoes, rice and steam pieces of young marrow.

Serves 4

JAMAICA HERRINGS

12 herrings, or more
100 g/4 oz salt
20–35 whole allspice
600 ml/1 pint white wine vinegar as
  required

Clean the herrings, take off the heads and (only if necessary) run briefly under the cold tap. Wipe dry with soft kitchen paper. Scrape each fish on both sides with a blunt knife held almost parallel to the fish. Work from the tail downward, holding the tail in your left hand. Sprinkle your fingers with salt for a firm grip.

Lay a row of herrings side by side in a deep square or loaf tin. Sprinkle well with salt. Repeat the layers until you have used all the herrings. Cover the container, and leave in a cool place for twenty-four hours.

Remove the herrings, wipe off the surface salt with soft kitchen paper, and lay them on paper to dry slightly. Drain and dry the container. Replace the fish, sprinkling each layer with whole allspice berries. Fill the container with white wine vinegar. Cover tightly with aluminium foil, and leave in the oven overnight at a very low heat (not more than 300°F, 150°C, gas mark 1–2).

Next day, skim off any fat floating on the surface of the vinegar, replace the foil cover, and leave in a cool place until required for use.

It is not worth pickling fewer than twelve herrings, nor is it effective. They should be used within 4–6 weeks.

CHAPTER FIVE

THE DAIRY

Eggs, milk, cream, butter and cheese have always been important to the countryman. Milk fresh from the cow has been used for a variety of puddings, notably, in the past, for junkets, 'creams' and syllabubs. The milk from a newly-calved cow, called beestings, was once used in many areas to make curds and cheesecakes (although, today, we usually make the latter with cottage cheese). Buttermilk was used likewise, and whey had many uses.

Soured milk was often made into the local cheese, either soft or semi-firm. In poorer households, a piece of cheese and slab of bread was often the complete meal; since butchered meat was too costly to obtain, eggs and cheese might well be the only protein food available. These farmhouse cheeses were matured for a long time, and developed rich, strong flavours; so they were also used to make many nourishing, tasty dishes.

There used to be many different regional British cheeses, and each had its own characteristics and flavour. The ones which are still made have kept these.

CHEESES

Cheddar cheese is close-textured, golden or orange-red, with a clean, mellow and nutty flavour. It is excellent for cooking, or for eating with fruit, and cider or beer.

Cheshire is more crumbly, and may be orange-red or white. It is particularly good with fruit, or with a piece of cake or semi-sweet biscuits. A blue Cheshire is sometimes available.

Derby is a buttery open cheese, with a clean and tangy flavour and the colour of honey. It, too, is very good with fruit. Derby flavoured with sage leaves is sometimes available and is criss-crossed, if genuine, with thin green lines; a thick green line through the centre of the cheese indicates a synthetic Sage Derby.

Double Gloucester is also buttery and open, with a delicate, creamy flavour and an orange-red colour. It is good with beer, and is one of the most useful cooking cheeses.

Leicester has a mild flavour and buttery texture, and is reddish in colour. It is good for both eating and cooking.

Caerphilly is a white, close-textured cheese with a clean, mild and slightly salt flavour. It is nice with celery.

Lancashire is white, soft and crumbly with a mild flavour. It is particularly good for toasting and for crumbling on soups and hotpots.

Wensleydale is generally white, and is moderately close with a mild, slightly salt flavour. A blue Wensleydale is also obtainable. It is good with apples or apple pie.

Stilton is the prince of British cheeses. It is a rich, creamy blue cheese with a soft, close texture. It is traditionally eaten after a meal with port and nuts, but it is superb with, or after, cold meats and game, apples and many other foods. It is also excellent cooked, and when potted.

Much more could be written about our cheeses; about the Scottish cheeses for instance, or the difference between present-day farmhouse cheeses, which still take long to mature, and our excellent but different creamery-made cheeses of the same types. For anyone who is interested in cheese, both well repay study by offering satisfying, flavoursome foods.

COTTAGE CHEESE

There are several different ways to make even the basic, simple soft cheese we call Farmer's Cheese, Pot Cheese, Clabber Cheese, Cottage Cheese, Crowdie and so on. This is just one of them.

Put sour, whole or skimmed milk in a warm place until thick. Add half teaspoon salt to each 550 ml/1 pint of milk. Put into a muslin bag and leave to drain overnight. Press between two plates for an hour, then mix with a little fresh cream to serve. Keep refrigerated.

SOUR MILK SOFT CHEESE WITH HERBS

1.1 litre/2 pints thick sour milk
25 g/1 oz butter
1 tablespoon salt
Salt and pepper
Chopped fresh herbs

Scald the sour milk until the curd separates from the whey, but do not boil. Discard whey. Add all other ingredients to the curd except the herbs and beat well. Add herbs to taste.

Makes 225 g (8 oz)

HOME-MADE YOGHURT

Yogurt can be made at home without elaborate equipment. For a family of four, a week's supply of yogurt can be made from 2.2 litre/4 pints milk. Besides the milk, a little *genuine live* yogurt is needed, as a 'starter'.

Use a large casserole with a well-fitting lid, and be sure the dish retains heat well. Put the milk into a saucepan, and bring it just to the boil. Pour it immediately into the casserole and cover with the lid. Leave the milk until it is just cool enough to leave your finger in for a little while. Add a teaspoon of the live yogurt and stir gently. Put on the lid, wrap the casserole in a blanket, and put it in a place which remains gently warm, such as an airing cupboard. Leave overnight, and the yogurt should be set, in which case it will 'cut' like a junket. If it is not successful, it is probably because the milk was either too hot or too cold when the 'starter' was added. (A spoonful of this yogurt when successful can be used to 'start' a new batch.)

Junket or renneted curd is very like yogurt although it lends itself more to sweet flavours.

DEVONSHIRE JUNKET

1.1 litre/2 pints milk
3 tablespoons brandy
40 g/1½ oz Demerara sugar
Grated nutmeg
1½ tablespoons rennet

Heat the milk to lukewarm (about 104°F, 50°C). Put the brandy and sugar into a china serving dish with nutmeg to taste. Pour in the milk and stir well to blend the flavours. Stir in the rennet, and leave the milk in a cool place to set. This junket should be served with a sprinkling of nutmeg or a covering of thick cream, topped with a sprinkling of Demerara sugar and a little more brandy.

Serves 4

CHEESECAKES

The following cheesecakes are made with cottage cheese but by no means all cheesecakes contain cheese. Many traditional cheesecakes were (and are) made with milk 'set' with rennet, eggs, herbs or other mildly acid products instead of using a cheese curd.

YORKSHIRE CHEESECAKE

100 g/4 oz plain flour
Pinch of salt
65 g/2½ oz butter
Juice of one-and-a-half lemons
225 g/8 oz curd or cottage cheese
2 tablespoons caster sugar
2 eggs
Grated rind of one lemon
2 teaspoons cornflour
2 tablespoons double cream
1 tablespoon melted butter
25 g/1 oz raisins

Sift the flour and salt, rub in the butter, and add the juice of half lemon and enough water to bind. Roll out thinly and use to line a 25 cm/10 in plate. Bake blind at 425°F, 220°C, gas mark 7 for ten minutes. Sieve the cheese and mix with the sugar, eggs, lemon rind and the remainder of the lemon juice. Beat until smooth and add the cornflour mixed with cream to a smooth paste. Fold in the melted butter and blend well. Pour into the pastry case and sprinkle with raisins. Bake at 350°F, 180°C, gas mark 4 for thirty minutes. Serve cold.

Serves 6

LITTLE COUNTRY CHEESECAKES

225 g/8 oz puff pastry
225 g/8 oz cottage cheese
175 g/6 oz sugar
6 egg yolks
50 g/2 oz butter
Pinch of nutmeg and salt
Grated rind of two lemons

Line small tart tins with the pastry. Sieve the cheese and mix with all the other ingredients, and put into the tart cases. Sprinkle the top of each with a mixture of chopped candied peel, currants and sultanas. Bake at 375°F, 190°C, gas mark 5 until pastry is golden, about twenty minutes.

Makes 15

LEICESTER CHEESECAKES

350 g/12 oz puff pastry
100 g/4 oz smooth curd (not cottage)
  cheese
50 g/2 oz butter, softened
1 whole egg, beaten
1 egg yolk, beaten
50 g/2 oz fine dry white breadcrumbs
50 g/2 oz granulated sugar
175 g/6 oz mixed currants and
  sultanas
1 tablespoon single cream
Grated nutmeg and lemon rind to
  taste
1 dessertspoon brandy

Roll out the pastry to 2.5 mm/⅛ in thick and line deep patty pans or small bun tins with it. Prick the bottoms to prevent rising, and chill. Mix the cheese with the butter, then fork in the beaten eggs, breadcrumbs, sugar, fruit, cream and flavourings. The mixture will be fairly wet. Fill the pastry shells three-quarters full only. Bake for fifteen minutes at 425°F, 220°C, gas mark 7, then lower the heat and bake at 325°F. 170°C, gas mark 3 for a further fifteen minutes, or until the cheesecakes are firm in the centre. Eat warm or cold.

Makes 12

FARMHOUSE CURD CAKES

225 g/8 oz shortcrust pastry,
*   homemade or frozen*
225 g/8 oz unsalted curd cheese from
*   skimmed milk*
50 g/2 oz caster sugar
2 eggs
100 g/4 oz mixed currants and candied
*   chopped peel*
1 teaspoon ground cinnamon

Roll out the pastry and use it to line 6.25 cm/2½ in patty pans or bun tins, well greased. Leave to 'rest' in a cool place. Put the curd in a basin. Sift the sugar. Beat the eggs until frothy, then gradually beat in the sugar. When the mixture is pale and light, mix thoroughly with the curd, adding the dried fruit and spice dusted over it. Fill the pastry shells about two-thirds full. Bake for 30–35 minutes at 350°F, 180°C, gas mark 4.

Makes 12

HONEY CHEESECAKE

100 g/4 oz cottage cheese
50 g/2 oz honey
50 g/2 oz caster sugar
½ level teaspoon cinnamon
2 beaten eggs
175 g/6 oz shortcrust pastry
Cinnamon
Caster sugar

Blend together the sieved cottage cheese, honey, sugar, cinnamon and eggs. Line an 18 cm/7 in pie plate with shortcrust pastry and fill with the cheese mixture. Sprinkle thickly with a mixture of cinnamon and caster sugar and bake at 375°F, 190°C, gas mark 5 for thirty-five minutes.

Serves 4

OTHER CHEESE DISHES

CHEESE AND ONIONS

4 medium-sized onions
150 ml/¼ pint milk
Salt and pepper
100 g/4 oz grated cheese

Peel and slice the onions. Cook until tender in very little water. Add milk and seasoning. Bring to the boil and turn into an ovenproof dish. Cover with cheese and brown under the grill. Serve with bread and butter.

Serves 4

CHEDDAR CHEESE PUFFS

50 g/2 oz butter
100 g/4 oz grated Cheddar cheese
2 eggs
225 g/8 oz soft white breadcrumbs
Salt and Cayenne pepper
Deep fat for frying

Melt the butter and add the cheese. Mix well and add the beaten eggs, salt and pepper. Mix in the breadcrumbs to make a stiff consistency. Divide and form into balls. Fry in deep hot fat for three minutes. These are good served with baked tomatoes.

Makes 12

CHEDDAR FRITTERS

50 g/2 oz butter
150 ml/¼ pint water
100 g/4 oz plain flour
3 eggs
75 g/3 oz grated Cheddar cheese
Salt and pepper

Boil the butter and water together. Add the sieved flour to the boiled liquid, beating well until smooth. Add the eggs and beat well. Beat in the grated cheese, salt and pepper. Fry spoonfuls in hot fat, turning to brown on both sides.

Makes 12

LANCASHIRE CHEESE AND EGGS

25 g/1 oz butter
1 teaspoon olive oil
225 g/8 oz Lancashire cheese
4 eggs
Pepper

Melt the butter and oil in a shallow dish on top of the stove. Cut the cheese into slices, reserving about 25 g/1 oz for grating. Put the cheese into the dish and melt cheese gently. Break the eggs on top. Cook at 350°F, 180°C, gas mark 4 for eight minutes. Sprinkle with pepper and grated cheese, and brown under the grill.

Serves 4

GLOUCESTERSHIRE POTATO CAKES

225 g/8 oz cooked potatoes
50 g/2 oz flour
50 g/2 oz Double Gloucester cheese
1 egg
A little butter

Mash the potatoes thoroughly with a little butter. Work in the flour and cheese. Beat the egg and add it to the mixture. Roll out the cut

into small round cakes. Cook in the butter on a girdle or heavy frying pan until golden on both sides.

Makes 10

COTTAGE CHEESE AND HAM TART

175 g/6 oz shortcrust pastry
25 g/1 oz butter
1 large onion
450 g/1 lb cottage cheese
2 eggs
50 g/2 oz chopped ham
Salt and pepper

Line a 20 cm/8 in flan ring or pie plate with the pastry. Melt the butter and fry the finely-chopped onion until golden. Sieve the cottage cheese finely, and mix it with the beaten eggs, ham, salt and pepper. Pour into the pastry and bake at 375°F, 190°C, gas mark 5 for fifteen minutes, and then reduce the heat to 325°F, 170°C, gas mark 3 for forty-five minutes. Serve hot. Finely-chopped mushrooms, or some chopped parsley may be used instead of the ham, or can be added to the recipe if liked.

Serves 4

CHEESE AND POTATO PIE

675 g/1½ lb potatoes
4 tablespoons milk
1 egg
1 teaspoon dry mustard
175 g/6 oz grated cheese
3 tablespoons chopped parsley
Salt and pepper

Cook the potatoes until they are tender, and then drain them. Mash them with the milk, egg, mustard, half the cheese, the parsley, salt and pepper. Put into a greased ovenware dish and sprinkle with the remaining cheese. Bake at 425°F, 220°C, gas mark 7 for fifteen minutes until golden-brown.

Serves 4

CHEESE BREAD AND BUTTER PUDDING

6 slices bread and butter
175 g/6 oz grated cheese
300 ml/½ pint milk
2 eggs

Butter a shallow ovenware dish. Line with bread and butter, and cover the bread thickly with cheese. Put on the remaining bread with the buttered side upwards. Beat the milk and eggs together and pour over the bread. Leave for one hour. Bake at 425°F, 220°C, gas mark 7 for thirty minutes; eat at once while very hot.

Serves 4

BAKED CHEDDAR PUDDING

175 g/6 oz grated Cheddar cheese
220 g/8 oz white breadcrumbs
1.1 litre/2 pints milk
2 onions, peeled and grated
50 g/2 oz butter
4 eggs
Salt and pepper
Butter

Boil the milk with the grated onions. Pour on to the cheese, breadcrumbs, butter, salt and pepper. Mix well with the beaten eggs. Pour into a buttered pie dish and bake at 375°F, 190°C, gas mark 5 for thirty minutes.

Serves 6

BAKED CHEESE AND CREAM

100 g/4 oz cheese
Salt and pepper
150 ml/¼ pint single cream

Butter an ovenware dish. Cut the cheese into matchstick slices and arrange them so that they are not packed together in the dish. Season well and pour the cream over them. Bake at 350°C, 180°C, gas mark 4 for fifteen minutes.

Serves 2

CHEESE AND PARSLEY CUSTARD PUDDING

2 eggs
300 ml/½ pint milk
75 g/3 oz grated cheese
50 g/2 oz soft white breadcrumbs
½ teaspoon dry mustard
½ teaspoon salt
2 tablespoons chopped parsley

Separate the eggs. Beat the yolks with lukewarm milk and cheese. Mix the crumbs with mustard, salt and parsley and gradually stir in the milk mixture. Leave to stand for thirty minutes. Beat the egg whites stiffly and fold them into the mixture. Put into a greased ovenware dish and bake at 400°F, 200°C, gas mark 6 for thirty minutes. (Instead of the parsley, 50 g/2 oz chopped ham can be used.)

Serves 4

LEICESTERSHIRE RAREBIT

15 g/½ oz butter
100 g/4 oz Leicestershire cheese
2 tablespoons milk
Salt and pepper
1 teaspoon made mustard
Hot buttered toast

Melt the butter and add the crumbled cheese. Heat gently, stirring until melted, and gradually add the milk. This must be done carefully or the cheese becomes hard and lumpy. Season with salt, pepper and mustard and pour over hot buttered toast.

Serves 2

The rabbit, rare-bit or rarebit was first made by soaking a toasted slice of bread in front of the open fire in red wine or beer. The thinly-cut cheese was then laid on top and left before the fire until the cheese was toasted and browned. If a fried or poached egg were added on top, the dish became Buckinghamshire Rare-bite, or Buck Rabbit.

'BOILED' CHEESE

100 g/4 oz mild cheese
50 g/2 oz butter
2 tablespoons double cream
1 egg

Cut the cheese in very thin slices and put it into a thick pan with the butter and cream. Stir the mixture over very gentle heat until it is smooth. Beat the egg lightly and stir into the mixture. Pour into a fireproof dish and brown under the grill. Serve with dry toast.

Serves 2

STEWED CHEESE AND ALE

100 g/4 oz Cheshire cheese
100 ml/4 fl oz ale

Cut the cheese into very thin slices and put into a thick-bottomed saucepan. Cover with the ale and heat very gently until the mixture is like custard. Serve very hot on toast.

The cheese and ale can, if you wish, be heated in a bowl over hot water or in an ovenware dish in a very low oven.

Serves 2

CHESHIRE SAVOURY

50 g/2 oz Cheshire cheese
25 g/1 oz butter
1 hard-boiled egg yolk
1 slice buttered toast

Crumble the cheese finely and mix with the butter and egg yolk until a smooth paste is formed. Spread on the buttered toast and put under a grill to brown.

Seves 1

POTTED CHEDDAR (NOT FOR KEEPING)

100 g/4 oz butter
Salt and pepper
½ teaspoon made English mustard
225 g/8 oz Cheddar cheese
3 tablespoons milk
5 drops Worcestershire sauce

Cream the butter and season with salt, pepper and mustard. Grate the cheese finely and mix it with the butter, gradually adding the milk and sauce. Chill before use.

Serves 4

MOCK CRAB

15 g/½ oz butter
1 large tomato, skinned and de-pipped
1 egg
25 g/1 oz grated cheese
Salt and pepper

Melt the butter and add the tomato, skinned and de-pipped. Simmer for five minutes. Beat the egg with the cheese and season well. Add to the tomato mixture and cook gently until thick. Use hot on toast, or cool for use as a sandwich filling.

Serves 1

EGGS

SLIPPERY JACK OR POTTED EGGS

6 eggs
100 g/4 oz butter, softened
1 teaspoon anchovy paste

Boil the eggs hard and cool them. Put the yolks through a sieve and chop the whites very finely. Mix with the softened butter and paste. Chill before use. This is very good on toast or in sandwiches.

Serves 6

YORKSHIRE BAKED EGGS

2 eggs
3 tablespoons creamy milk
1 teaspoon chopped parsley
Salt and pepper
15 g/½ oz butter

Beat the eggs and milk with the parsley, salt and pepper. Put the butter into an ovenproof dish and heat it in the oven until just melted. Pour into the egg mixture and bake at 375°F, 190°C, gas mark 5 for ten minutes. Serve hot with toast.

Variations A little crisp bacon or chopped ham, or a few shrimps, can be put at the bottom of the dish before the egg mixture is poured in.

Serves 2

EGG AND MINT PASTY

175 g/6 oz plain flour
Pinch of salt
75 g/3 oz clarified dripping
Cold water
1 tablespoon scratchings (see recipe)
9 eggs
1 tablespoon chopped fresh mint
Salt and freshly-ground black pepper

Preheat the oven to 425°F, 220°C, gas mark 7. Grease a shallow 18 cm/7 in pie plate and line with two-thirds of the pastry. Scatter on the scratchings which are crisp scraps of pork fat left after rendering lard. (Scraps of crisp fat from a roast joint serve quite well.) Break eight eggs very carefully into the shell, taking care not to break the yolks. Sprinkle with the mint, salt and pepper. Separate the last egg, beat the yolk lightly in a bowl and glaze the edge of the pastry lining. Make sure the remaining one-third rolled-out pastry will cover the lining, and lay it gently on top of the eggs. Press down the edges of the pie to seal. Glaze the whole lid very gently with beaten egg yolk; the pie is very fragile. Bake for 20–30 minutes until the pastry is golden-brown and set; the eggs should then be half set but still moist. Serve hot with steamed spring greens or spinach and parsley sauce.

Serves 4–6

This old farm dish is clearly of peasant origin, using as it does the dripping and crisp fat which, being precious meat products, the farmer's wife dared not waste, and whose flavour she 'stretched' as far as possible. It was usually made in spring when the first fresh wild herbs appeared and the farm hens started laying. So although its many eggs make it seem quite a luxurious dish, it was a cheap one.

MARIGOLD EGG PIE

Butter
Shortcrust pastry, using 4 oz flour
2–4 tart eating apples
2 eggs
300 ml/½ pint milk
Salt and pepper
Thyme
Sage
Marigold petals

Grease an 18 cm/7 in flan ring or pie plate with butter, and line it with pastry. Peel, core and slice the apples, and lay them in the dish; flake a little more butter over them, and bake the dish at 400°F, 200°C, gas mark 6 until the apple slices are tender and the pastry rim is set. This will take 15–20 minutes.

While the dish is baking, make a custard mixture with the eggs beaten in the milk, and season it strongly with salt, pepper, thyme and sage. Add about half a teacup of marigold petals, or to your taste.

When the apple slices are done, pour this savoury custard over them, cover the pastry with buttered pepper or aluminium foil, and return the pie to the oven at a reduced heat of 325°F, 170°C, gas mark 3–4, until the custard is set. It will take 20–30 minutes. Serve with roast pork just as you would serve Yorkshire pudding with beef. The pungent marigold flavour is first-class with it.

Serves 4

BUTTERMILK AND WHEY

After making butter, a good deal of buttermilk and whey were left. These were never thrown away, for they were nourishing and flavoursome. They were used for various purposes, such as making curds for cheesecakes, for moistening bread and cakes, and for refreshing drinks.

CURDS AND WHEY

1.1 litre/2 pints milk
Setting agent as described in recipe
 (rennet, eggs or buttermilk)
Vanilla essence or rose-water to taste
Caster sugar to taste
½–1 teaspoon ground cinnamon or
 grated nutmeg

There are several ways to make curds. Bottled rennet has been widely used since the late nineteenth century when it replaced the prepared calf's stomach lining. A more extravagant method in eighteenth century use was to add three beaten eggs with one teaspoon salt to each 550 ml/1 pint of milk; the mixture was heated very gently until at simmering point, and the curds were then tipped into a cloth laid on a sieve over a basin, to drain. A more practical method for use now is to make 1.1 litre/2 pints milk scalding (not boiling) hot and tip them into 2.2 litres/4 pints commercial buttermilk. Let the mixture stand until cold and firm before tipping into a cloth to drain as above.

Sweeten and flavour both curd and whey with sugar and spice to suit your taste. Serve the curd chilled, as a dessert, either alone or with fresh stewed fruit, and pour some of the whey over it as a sauce, just before serving.

Variation

An older way to serve curds and whey is to add only a little salt to the curd and then to mix it lightly with one stiffly-beaten egg white. Place in a small mould or dish and chill. Unmould to serve, and offer the whey sweetened as above and single cream to pour over it.

Serves 4

BUTTERMILK CURD CREAM

600 ml/1 pint milk
1.1 litre/2 pints buttermilk
Caster sugar
Single cream
Icing sugar
Salt
Vanilla essence or ground cinnamon

Make the milk scalding (not boiling) hot, and stir it quickly into the buttermilk. Let the mixture stand until cold and firm, then tip it gently on to a cloth laid over a sieve. Allow to drain until set and crumbly.

Turn gently out of the cloth on to a board, and pat squares with the side of a knife. Cut into square individual helpings, and lift them with a spatula into serving bowls.

Sprinkle each lightly with sifted caster sugar. Then pour over a small amount of single cream flavoured with sifted icing sugar, a pinch of salt and vanilla essence or cinnamon to suit your taste. Flavour some of the whey like the cream, and serve it in a jug as a sauce.

Serves 6

GUERNSEY BUTTERMILK CAKE

225 g/8 oz currants
150 ml/¼ pint cider
450 g/1 lb plain flour
100 g/4 oz unsalted butter
1 teaspoon grated nutmeg
2 teaspoons cream of tartar
1 teaspoon bicarbonate of soda
225 g/8 oz caster sugar
2 eggs, beaten
150 ml/¼ pint buttermilk
2 teaspoons lemon juice

Steep the currants in the cider until plumped. Rub the butter into the flour until the mixture resembles fine crumbs. Sift together the nutmeg, cream of tartar, soda and sugar, and add to the mixture. Mix the eggs into the buttermilk with the lemon juice. Make a well in the dry ingredients. Mix in the cider and the buttermilk alternately, adding about one-third each time. Mix thoroughly to blend. Place the mixture in a 20 cm/8 in cake tin, lined and greased, and bake at 325°F, 170°C, gas mark 3 for two hours or until the cake is springy and brown. Cool well before cutting.

Makes one 20 cm/8 in cake

CHAPTER SIX

HARVEST HOME

The harvest was always important in corn-growing Britain, and was widely celebrated by a 'horkey' or party; it is still commemorated by autumn thanksgiving services in churches throughout the land. Even the poorest labouring families would glean enough corn from the fields to supply their flour for the winter months.

Wheat, barley and oats were the three grains used for home baking. Wheat predominated in East Anglia, barley in the North, and oats in Scotland and Wales. Bread was made in most farm and cottage kitchens, and so were a wide variety of scones, pancakes or bannocks. All these plain baked goods were first made on a hot hearthstone since ovens were not built in most small homes until the nineteenth century. (Meat,

cakes and pies were taken to the local baker's oven.) From the eighteenth century on, however, most farmhouses of any size had a brick bread oven in which the bread was baked on the hot floor after raking out the hot ashes of a fire. Later still, the bread came to be baked in tins, to make the shapes of loaves we know now; but many traditional small baked goods are still griddle baked.

Baking Day was busy, but the men and children could usually look forward to a special treat for tea. This was often a piece of bread dough left from the loaf-making, made richer and sweeter with fat and sugar. For extra special days, fruit and peel were added to make (among others) the still-popular Lardy Cakes.

SUCCESSFUL BREADMAKING

Flour and Yeast Ordinary plain flour, both white and wholemeal, is satisfactory for bread-making, but the best kind is 'hard' or 'strong' flour. If a large quantity of flour can be bought direct from a mill for regular breadmaking, it can be stored for about three months in a small dust-bin. Fresh baker's yeast is cheap and will keep for about ten days in a covered bowl or refrigerator. It can also be frozen in 25 g/1 oz cubes which are convenient to use; the yeast should be thawed at room temperature before using. Dried yeast is convenient to store and use, but it sometimes has a stronger flavour. The maker's specific instructions for using dried yeast should be followed carefully; note that only half as much dried as fresh yeast is needed in a recipe. Dried yeast needs about twenty minutes to start working well, before being added to flour.

Other ingredients Fat and sugar are sometimes added to a basic bread mixture to give richer, longer-keeping bread. When yeast is creamed with sugar, the 'working' time is speeded up. Salt is an essential in bread, and is best dissolved first in a little liquid, as dry salt affects the growth of the yeast cells.

Procedure In breadmaking, the yeast is set working by the addition of sugar and warm liquid, and is mixed and kneaded with flour and left to prove, or rise. The dough then has to be knocked back or lightly rekneaded, and shaped to fit the tins when these are used. Dough should be kneaded on a floured board, which means folding it over on itself and pushing with a firm rocking motion until the dough becomes smooth and shiny. A dough hook on an electric mixer is an inexpensive attachment which speeds up the work, and ensures that the yeast is worked right through the dough. If bread is to be baked as rolls or freehand shapes, a slightly firmer dough is needed than for baked bread in tins.

After a second rising, bread is baked in a really hot oven or on a piping hot griddle; the heat kills the yeast and prevents further rising. A container of water in the oven during baking gives a crisp crust. Bread is properly baked when it sounds hollow if tapped underneath with the knuckles. If it is not quite cooked, it should be returned to the oven without the tins and cooked for a further 5–10 minutes.

If plain loaves are painted with rich milk or cream before baking, they will have a gleaming brown crust; beaten eggs give a dark crust, while melted butter or margarine gives a crisp, crunchy crust. A thick milk and sugar syrup painted on *after* baking gives loaves and buns a sweet sticky finish.

If a batch of bread is not successful, it may only be because one or two details have been over-looked. For instance, during breadmaking, the implements and the ingredients should be *warm* to speed up the working of the yeast; but if the dough is made too hot during rising, the result is a very coarse, breakable crumb of irregular texture. The dough must be *worked thoroughly* to give an even distribution of the yeast, which enables the dough to rise properly. It should be on the *soft* side to achieve a light loaf; if it is too stiff, it cannot expand properly under the influence of the yeast. Again if the dough is not proved long enough, a heavy, soggy loaf will result, with a crust which breaks away from the top. If dough is left to rise for too long, however, there will be a loss of strength, colour, scent and flavour. It is also important to bake bread at a high temperature, or the result will be pale, moist and flavourless.

Using a griddle As I have said, bread and scones used to be cooked on a griddle or heavy bake-stone because few rural houses had ovens. Today, heavy iron griddles are still obtainable, but the hotplate of an electric or solid fuel cooker can be used equally well, or a heavy frying pan with a flat base.

The griddle should be put on to heat before the dough is mixed. To test the heat, a little flour should be sprinkled on. If it browns at once, the griddle is too hot. If the flour takes a few seconds to brown, the heat is right. For scones and bannocks, the griddle was traditionally floured; for crumpets and drop scones it was lightly greased to prevent sticking, using a piece of suet wrapped in a clean rag. The general rule was 'floured for dough, greased for batter'. A griddle should never be washed, but should be rubbed when hot with coarse salt and a piece of clean paper, and then dusted with a cloth.

WHITE BREAD

1.4 kg/3 lb of plain white flour
25 g/1 oz fresh yeast
50 g/2 oz fat (butter or lard)
15 g/½ oz salt
900 ml/1½ pints warm water

Put flour in a large bowl, make a well in the centre, and sprinkle salt around the edge. Cream yeast with a little warm water and pour into the well. Add the rest of the water and the warmed fat and mix well to a soft putty-like consistency. Leave to prove until double in size. Put into four 450 g/1 lb tins and leave to prove again until bread reaches top of the tins. Bake at 450°F, 230°C, gas mark 8 for forty-five minutes, turning bread once in the oven. Cool on a wire rack.

Makes four medium loaves

WHOLEMEAL BREAD

1.4 kg/3 lb wholemeal flour
25 g/1 oz salt
25 g/1 oz sugar
40 g/1½ oz fresh yeast
900 ml/1½ pints warm water

Take half the flour and make into a batter with all the water. Cream the yeast with two table-spoons of warm water and mix well into the batter. Cover the basin with a damp cloth and let the batter stand for fifteen minutes. Add the rest of the flour, salt and sugar, and make the dough. Mix well and knead for ten minutes. Warm and lightly grease four 450 g/1 lb-loaf tins, and divide dough between them. Flatten each piece and roll up to fit lengthwise in the tin, pressing down to avoid cracks and folds. Leave for one hour in a warm place until the dough doubles in volume. Bake at 450°F, 230°C, gas mark 8 for forty-five minutes, turning the loaves (move them through a right angle in the oven) half-way through cooking time. Turn out the loaves on to a wire tray and cool thoroughly before cutting.

Makes four medium loaves

MILK BREAD

1 teaspoon sugar
15 g/½ oz fresh yeast
675 g/1½ lb plain white flour
½ teaspoon salt
50 g/2 oz butter
450 ml/¾ pint warm milk

Cream yeast and sugar together in a warm basin and cover with a little warm milk. Leave in a warm place for fifteen minutes. Sift together the flour and salt and rub in the butter. Make a well in the centre and pour in the yeast mixture. Add the warm milk and knead the soft dough lightly. Cover and leave in a warm place until double in size. Grease two 450 g/1 lb-loaf tins and divide the dough between them. Leave to rise for fifteen minutes. Brush over with a little warm milk and bake at 400°F, 200°C, gas mark 6 for thirty minutes.

Makes two medium loaves

This light dough is also excellent for forming into plaits, twists or buns or fruit loaves. For a fruit loaf, add 50 g/2 oz currants, 50 g/2 oz raisins and 25 g/1 oz chopped candied peel to the basic recipe.

IRISH GRIDDLE BREAD

225 g/8 oz wholemeal flour
225 g/8 oz plain flour
1 dessertspoon sugar
1 teaspoon bicarbonate of soda
1 teaspoon salt
1 dessertspoon dripping
Milk

Mix together flours, and add sugar, soda and salt. Rub in dripping and mix to a batter with milk, to make a dough which is stiff but will roll easily. Roll out in a round 2.5 cm/1 in thick, and cut into four sections. Cook on a hot griddle for ten minutes on each side.

Makes four pieces

IRISH SODA BREAD

450 g/1 lb plain flour
1 level teaspoon salt
1 level teaspoon bicarbonate of soda
25 g/1 oz lard
300 ml/½ pint buttermilk or milk

Sift the dry ingredients into a basin and rub in the fat. Make a well in the centre and stir in enough buttermilk or milk to give a soft spongy dough. Knead lightly on a floured surface. Shape quickly into a round cake about 5 cm/2 in thick. Put on a floured baking sheet and score the top lightly three times with a sharp knife. Bake at 400°F, 200°C, gas mark 6 for thirty-five minutes, or until well risen.

Makes one medium loaf

THRESHING DAY BARLEY BREAD (NORTHUMBERLAND)

450 g/1 lb barley flour
100 g/4 oz plain white flour
1 teaspoon salt
1 teaspoon bicarbonate of soda
2 teaspoons cream of tartar
450 ml/1 pint buttermilk

Mix together the barley flour, white flour, salt, bicarbonate of soda and cream of tartar. Stir in the buttermilk to make a firm dough. Shape into a round cake 2.5 cm/1 in thick, and cook on a very hot griddle, hotplate or heavy frying pan. When cooked on the underside, turn over and cook the second side. This may also be baked at 475°F, 240°C, gas mark 9 for twenty minutes without turning.

Makes one medium loaf

PLAITED HARVEST BREAD

450 g/1 lb plain flour
½ teaspoon salt
150 ml/¼ pint milk
50 g/2 oz butter
1 egg, beaten
25 g/1 oz fresh yeast
25 g/1 oz caster sugar
1 tablespoon currants
Pinch of grated nutmeg
2 teaspoons grated lemon rind

Put the flour and salt in a warm bowl. Warm the milk to blood heat, stir in the butter and continue stirring until it melts. Cool, then mix in the egg. Mix the yeast with a little of the sugar, and mix well. Add the remaining sugar, currants, spices and lemon to the flour and salt. When the yeast mixture froths, add it to the milk, mix in and stir both into the flour. Leave in a warm place to rise. When double the original size, cut into three pieces. Form each piece into three strips, and plait them. Damp the ends with milk to secure them. Place on a lightly-greased baking sheet, and allow to prove for 10–15 minutes. Bake at 425°F, 220°C, gas mark 7 for fifteen minutes or until golden-brown.

Makes one medium loaf

CURRANT BREAD

675 g/1½ lb white flour
100 g/4 oz sugar
Pinch of salt
25 g/1 oz fresh yeast
100 g/4 oz warm butter
150 ml/¼ pint warm milk
225 g/8 oz mixed dried fruit
50 g/2 oz chopped mixed peel

Mix flour, sugar and salt, and add yeast creamed with a little sugar. Work in warm butter and milk. Knead and leave to prove for one and a half hours. Knead in fruit and peel, and shape into loaves or buns to prove for forty-five minutes. Bake at 375°F, 190°C, gas mark 5 for forty-five minutes, turning after twenty minutes. Small buns will need about twenty minutes cooking time. Remove to a wire tray and glaze with a mixture of milk and sugar.

Makes one large loaf or 20 buns

MALT BREAD

675 g/1½ lb white flour (or a mixture of
plain white and wholemeal flour)
15 g/1 oz fresh yeast
½ teaspoon salt
450 ml/¾ pint lukewarm water
2 tablespoons black treacle
2 tablespoons extract of malt
50 g/2 oz butter
50 g/2 oz sultanas

Sieve flour into a bowl. Cream yeast with a little water, and dissolve salt in rest of water. Add the yeast and water to the flour, then add treacle, malt, butter and sultanas. Knead to an even texture, prove till double in size, knead again and shape into three 450 g/1 lb tins. Prove until the mixture reaches the top of the tins, then bake at 425°F, 220°C, gas mark 7 for forty-five minutes, turning the loaves halfway through cooking time. Remove to a wire tray and glaze with milk and sugar syrup.

Makes three small loaves

BANNOCK WITH FRUIT

Batter ingredients
50 g/2 oz plain flour
25 g/1 oz melted butter or lard
5 tablespoons warm milk
7 g/¼ oz fresh yeast

Additional ingredients
175 g/6 oz plain flour
25 g/1 oz caster sugar
5 tablespoons warm milk
25 g/1 oz sultanas
25 g/1 oz currants
15 g/½ oz candied peel

Blend batter ingredients together in a mixing bowl and leave for 20–30 minutes until the batter is frothy. Add the additional ingredients and mix well. Knead the dough thoroughly for about ten minutes on a lightly-floured board. Put the dough to rise in a warm place under a damp cloth and leave for one hour, until the dough springs back when pressed gently with a floured finger. Knead the dough again and shape into a ball. Flatten with the hands to approximately 20 cm/8 in across and 1.25 cm/½ in thick. Put on a greased and floured tray and slash half through with a sharp knife into eight equal sections. Brush top with milk, cover with a greased paper and leave to rise until the dough feels springy (about forty-five minutes). Brush top again with milk, and bake towards the top of the oven set at 400°F, 200°C, gas mark 6 for twenty minutes. Cool on a wire tray.

Makes one 20 cm/8 in loaf

MUFFINS

1 egg
300 ml/½ pint milk
25 g/1 oz butter
450 g/1 lb flour
1 teaspoon salt
15 g/½ oz fresh yeast

Beat together egg, milk and warm butter. Put flour and salt into a bowl, and pour in yeast creamed with a little warm water. Add butter, milk and egg mixture, and knead thoroughly to a soft but not sticky dough. Cover and prove for one and a half hours. Roll out dough to 1.25 cm/½ in thickness on a floured board, and cut out muffins with a large tumbler. Bake on a griddle, turning as soon as bottoms are browned, or on a baking sheet in a hot oven at 450°F, 230°C, gas mark 8 for fifteen minutes, turning halfway through cooking.

Makes 10

KENTISH HUFFKINS

675 g/1½ lb plain flour
1½ teaspoons salt
15 g/½ oz yeast
1 teaspoon caster sugar
450 ml/¾ pint warm milk and water
50 g/2 oz lard

Sift the flour and salt into a warm bowl. Cream the yeast and sugar and add the warm liquid. Make a well in the centre of the flour and work in the yeast mixture. Knead to a soft dough. Cover and leave in a warm place until double in size. Rub in the lard and leave to rise again. Divide into pieces weighing 50 g/2 oz and roll into balls with the hands. Roll out flat about 2.5 cm/1 in thick and leave on a baking tin for twenty minutes to prove. Bake at 425°F, 220°C, gas mark 7 for fifteen minutes. Turn over and continue baking for ten minutes.

Makes 15

ABERDEEN BUTTERY ROWIES

450 g/1 lb flour
1 teaspoon salt
25 g/1 oz fresh yeast
1 tablespoon caster sugar
450 ml/¾ pint tepid water
175 g/6 oz lard
175 g/6 oz butter

Sieve the flour and the salt into a warm basin. Cream the yeast and the sugar in a smaller bowl, then add the flour along with the water. Set in a warm place to rise to twice its bulk. Beat the lard and butter together until thoroughly blended. Divide into three portions and divide each into small pieces. Roll out the dough on a floured board and dot the first portion of fat over it in small pats. Fold into three and roll out as for flaky pastry. Repeat the operation twice, so as to use up all the fat. Divide into pieces of equal size and form into oval shapes. Put on a greased and floured baking tray and prove in a warm place for thirty minutes. Bake at 400°F, 200°C, gas mark 6 for twenty–twenty-five minutes.

Makes 20

SALLY LUNNS

350 g/1 oz plain flour
½ teaspoon salt
15 g/½ oz fresh yeast
1 teaspoon sugar
450 ml/¼ pint milk
50 g/2 oz melted butter
1 egg

Warm the flour and salt. Cream the yeast with the sugar, add warm milk, and stir into the flour with melted butter and egg. Knead well and divide in half. Shape the pieces to fit two greased 15 cm/6 in round cake tins or soufflé dishes. Leave in a warm place until risen to the top of the tins. Brush with egg and bake at 450°F, 230°C, gas mark 8 for thirty minutes. If the Sally Lunns are to be eaten hot, they should be split in four and spread thickly with butter, then the slices replaced and cut into wedges. They should be covered with a damp cloth and reheated in the oven until the butter has melted.

Makes 8 slices

BAPS

450 g/1 lb plain flour
50 g/2 oz lard
2 level teaspoons salt
1 level teaspoon sugar
25 g/1 oz fresh yeast
300 ml/½ pint lukewarm milk and
  water

Sieve the flour, rub in the lard and sugar. Cream the yeast in half the liquid and dissolve the salt in the rest. Mix into the flour, knead and prove until double in size. Divide into pieces and make into small loaves about 10 cm/4 in across. Brush with milk, put on to a greased baking sheet, prove again, and bake at 450°F, 230°C, gas mark 8 for twenty minutes.

Makes 12

DEVONSHIRE SPLITS

450 g/1 lb plain flour
½ teaspoon salt
15 g/½ oz fresh yeast
1 teaspoon caster sugar
25 g/1 oz butter
300 ml pint/½ pint skim milk (or
  150 ml/¼ milk and 150 ml/¼ pint
  water)

Sieve the flour and salt into a basin. Cream the yeast with a little lukewarm milk. Melt the butter in the remaining milk. Pour all the liquid into a well in the centre of the flour and mix to a dough. Leave to prove in a warm place for one hour. Divide mixture into twelve pieces and knead each into a ball. Flatten into a round 1.25 cm/½ in thick with the hands. Leave to prove for twenty minutes on a greased and floured baking tin in a warm place. Brush with milk and bake at 450°F, 230°C, gas mark 8 for fifteen minutes. Cut through and serve hot with butter or Devonshire cream. (If serving the splits cold, sandwich them with jam and Devonshire cream.)

Makes 12

CORNISH SPLITS

450 g/1 lb plain flour
¼ teaspoon salt
15 g/½ oz fresh yeast
15 g/½ oz caster sugar
300 ml/½ pint milk
25 g/1 oz butter

Sieve the flour and salt into a warm basin. Cream the yeast and sugar together and gradually add the milk. Add the milk mixture and the melted butter to the flour and mix to a smooth dough. Cover and leave in a warm place for forty-five minutes. Shape into small round cakes and put on to a floured baking sheet. Bake at 475°F, 240°C, gas mark 9 for fifteen minutes. Split and butter and serve very hot. Otherwise, leave them until cold, then split and butter; or split and eat with cream, jam or treacle. Splits eaten with cream and treacle are known as 'Thunder and Lightning'.

Makes 12

TEA CAKES

225 g/8 oz plain flour
Pinch of salt
15 g/½ oz butter
15 g/½ oz fresh yeast
1 teaspoon sugar
1 egg
150 ml/¼ pint milk
50 g/2 oz sultanas

Warm the flour and salt and rub in the butter. Cream the yeast and sugar and add to the flour together with the egg, milk and sultanas. Knead well and leave in a warm place until double its size. Knead well again and divide into three, shaping into rather flat, round cakes. Put on greased tins, and prove for ten minutes. Bake at 450°F, 230°C, gas mark 8 for twelve minutes. Brush over with milk and glaze with sugar immediately after removing from oven.

Makes 3

OVEN BOTTOM CAKE (YORKSHIRE)

100 g/4 oz bread dough
25 g/1 oz lard

Take the lump of dough and put on to a pastry board. Cut the lard into six pieces and push the pieces roughly into the dough. Fold over the dough and with the knuckles of one hand press the fat into the dough, giving it a lumpy appearance. Put on to a greased baking sheet and bake at 450°F, 230°C, gas mark 8 for about fifteen minutes until golden-brown. Take out of the oven, wrap in a tea towel and place on a cushion. To serve, cut the cake in irregular pieces, split open and spread thickly with butter and jam. This cake was traditionally made at the end of baking day, having been put into the bottom of the oven when the loaves were taken out.

Makes 6 pieces

DERBYSHIRE PYCLETS

225 g/8 oz plain flour
1 teaspoon salt
7 g/¼ oz fresh yeast
1 teaspoon sugar
1 egg
300 ml/½ pint milk

Put the flour and salt into a warm bowl. Cream the yeast and sugar, and add the beaten egg and warm milk. Add the liquid to the warm dry ingredients to make a thin batter, adding a little more warm milk if necessary. Cover the bowl and leave in a warm place for thirty minutes until double in size. Heat a griddle, hotplate or heavy frying pan and grease it lightly. Pour 7 small cupfuls of the yeast mixture on to the griddle. Cook one side, turn and cook the other side.

Makes 7

SAVOURY WILTSHIRE TEABREAD

100 g/4 oz rindless streaky bacon,
  finely chopped
4 sticks celery, chopped
1 small onion, skinned and grated
450 g/1 lb self-raising flour
¼ level teaspoon salt
Pepper
50 g/2 oz dripping
2 level tablespoons chopped parsley
300 ml/½ pint less 2 tablespoons milk
1 egg

Place finely-chopped bacon in a pan and fry gently for two minutes. Add chopped celery and grated onion and fry gently for five minutes. Cool. Sift together the flour, salt and pepper and rub in the dripping until the mixture resembles fine breadcrumbs. Stir bacon mixture into flour with the parsley. Beat together the milk and the egg and stir into the flour. Knead very lightly on a floured surface, shape into a rectangle and place in a greased 900 g/2-lb loaf tin. Bake at 375°F, 190°C, gas mark 5 for one hour. Remove from the tin and serve sliced, warm or cold, with butter.

Makes one loaf

POTATO WHOLEMEAL BREAD

225 g/8 oz potatoes
675 g/1½ lb 100% wholemeal flour
300 ml/½ pint hot potato water
½ level tablespoon sugar
25 g/1 oz butter
15 g/½ oz fresh yeast
3 level teaspoons salt

Use freshly boiled and sieved potatoes. Mix the potatoes, hot water, sugar and butter in a bowl, stirring until the mixture is well blended. Allow to cool to lukewarm. Crumble in the yeast, mix and leave in a warm place for ten minutes. Add the flour and salt gradually to make a soft dough that does not stick to the bowl or hands. Knead until smooth and elastic. Put in a large bowl, cover with a clean cloth, and put in a warm place to rise until the dough is double in size. Knead again and shape into three loaves. Put into three 450 g/1-lb loaf tins, cover and leave to rise until double in bulk. Bake at 450°F, 230°C, gas mark 8 for fifteen minutes. Reduce heat to 375°F, 190°C, gas mark 5 and continue baking for 35–40 minutes until the bread gives a hollow sound when tapped on the bottom. Thorough cooking is essential. Turn out on a wire rack and cool. Potatoes give a pleasingly different flavour and texture to bread and cakes, and help keep them fresh and moist. Choose 'floury' potatoes and make sure they are well drained after cooking.

Makes three loaves

CHEESE AND WALNUT LOAF

225 g/8 oz self-raising flour
1 level teaspoon dry mustard powder
1 level teaspoon salt
Pepper
75 g/3 oz butter
100 g/4 oz Cheddar cheese, grated
25 g/1 oz walnuts, chopped
2 eggs
150 ml/¼ pint milk

Sieve the flour, mustard and seasoning into a bowl and rub in the fat until the mixture resembles fine breadcrumbs. Stir in the grated cheese and chopped walnuts. Beat the eggs and milk together and add to the dry ingredients to give a soft dropping consistency. Place the mixture in a greased 450 g/1 lb loaf tin, smooth the top and bake in the centre of oven at 350°F, 180°C, gas mark 4 for ¾–1 hour until golden-brown and cooked through. Cool on a wire tray.

Makes one loaf

SCOTTISH BARLEY BANNOCKS

450 g/1 lb barley meal
100 g/4 oz plain white flour
2 teaspoons cream of tartar
½ teaspoon salt
350 ml/12 fl oz buttermilk
2 teaspoons bicarbonate of soda

Mix together barley meal, flour, cream of tartar and salt. Stir the bicarbonate of soda into the milk and stir quickly. When it fizzes up, pour into the flour mixture. Make into a soft dough and roll out very lightly to 1.25 cm/½ in thick. Cut into rounds the size of a meat plate and put on a hot griddle, hotplate or thick frying pan. Bake gently until the underside is brown. Turn and brown the other side.

Makes 10

SCONES AND SUCH

BASIC DRY SCONE MIX

450 g/1 lb self-raising flour
2 rounded teaspoons baking powder
75 g/3 oz butter

Sift together flour and baking powder, and rub in butter until the mixture looks like fine bread-crumbs. Store in a plastic container in a cold place, keeping tightly covered. Half this mixture with the addition of 150 ml/¼ pint milk or water.

Makes 12

For sweet scones, use milk, or an egg for three tablespoons of milk.

For cheese scones, add 75 g/3 oz finely-grated dry cheese, and use water for a fluffy texture.

With plain flour, use one teaspoon bicarbonate of soda and two teaspoons cream of tartar as raising agents. If sour milk is used, for better texture, use only one teaspoon cream of tartar.

When the scones are mixed, roll out and cut in rounds. Place close together on greased baking sheet, and bake at 450°F, 230°C, gas mark 8 for twelve minutes.

SKYE SCONES

225 g/8 oz plain flour
Pinch of salt
2 rounded teaspoons baking powder
1 heaped tablespoon caster sugar
50 g/2 oz butter
1 egg
Milk

Sift the flour with the salt and baking powder. Stir in the caster sugar and rub in the butter. Break the egg into a measuring cup and make up to 150 ml/¼ pint with milk. Whisk the egg and milk together. Make a well in the centre of the flour mixture and pour in the liquid (saving a little for brushing the scones). Using a knife, cut and fold to moisten all the mixture until a spongy, non-sticky ball of dough is formed. Turn the dough on to a floured board, and knead for thirty seconds to smooth the underside. Turn the dough over and roll out gently to 1.25 cm/½ in thickness. Form into one large round cake (for breakfast) or cut into 5 cm/2 in (for tea). Place on a buttered baking sheet, and brush with the reserved egg and milk. Sprinkle thickly with granulated sugar. Put into an oven set at 500°F, 250°C, gas mark 10, and then immediately turn the oven down to 425°F, 220°C, gas mark 7 for 10–12 minutes for small scones, 15–18 for a large one, until puffy and a rich brown. Serve slighly warm, spread with cool butter.

Makes 10

WHEATMEAL SPOON SCONES

275 g/10 oz wholemeal flour
175 g/6 oz plain flour
1 level teaspoon salt
50 g/2 oz granulated sugar
1 level teaspoon bicarbonate of soda
2 level teaspoons cream of tartar
50 g/2 oz butter
1 tablespoon black treacle
285 ml/scant ½ pint milk

Sieve together dry ingredients and stir in sugar. Rub in butter, then mix with the treacle and milk to give a heavy dropping consistency. Drop spoonsful of the mixture on to a baking sheet dusted with wholemeal flour. Brush lightly with milk and dredge with flour or rolled oats. Bake at 450°F, 230°C, gas mark 8 for fifteen minutes.

Makes 15

SCOTCH PANCAKES OR DROP SCONES

225 g/8 oz plain flour
1 level teaspoon salt
2 level teaspoons cream of tartar
1 level teaspoon bicarbonate of soda
1 dessertspoon caster sugar
2 eggs
1 dessertspoon golden syrup
250 ml/8 fl oz milk

These are best cooked on a heavy iron griddle; but they can be cooked on the solid hotplate of an electric cooker, or in a frying pan with a cast iron base. Sieve together the flour, salt, cream of tartar and bicarbonate of soda. Add the sugar and mix to a very thick batter with the beaten eggs, syrup and milk, so that the mixture will only just fall from the spoon yet will flow into a pancake on the hot griddle. Leave the batter to stand just long enough for bubbles of gas to rise to the surface. Lightly, grease the pan or griddle and heat until you can feel the heat 2.5 cm/1 in above the surface. Drop the mixture into small rounds from a dessertspoon, held point downwards. When bubbles start to burst, and the underside is a pale brown, turn each pancake over. Allow approximately three minutes for the first side and two minutes for the second. As the pancakes come off the pan, slip them into a folded tea towel to keep the steam in. Serve fresh and buttered. Any left over can later be toasted, or fried and served topped with eggs.

Makes 20

CREMPOG OR WELSH PANCAKES

175 g/6 oz plain flour
½ teaspoon bicarbonate of soda
½ teaspoon cream of tartar
50 g/2 oz sugar
25 g/1 oz butter
½ teaspoon vinegar
1 egg
Milk to mix

Sieve together the flour, bicarbonate of soda and cream of tartar. Stir in the sugar, and rub in the butter. Make a well in the centre and stir in the beaten egg and enough milk to make a thin batter. Add the vinegar last. Heat a griddle, hotplate or heavy frying pan, and grease it well. Put two tablespoons of the batter on to the hot surface and cook until brown on the underside – about three minutes. Turn and finish cooking the other side – about two minutes. Butter well and eat hot. These were traditionally made as large pancakes and spread with butter, then piled on a plate and cut into quarters.

Makes 15

WELSH OATMEAL PANCAKES (CREMPOG GEIRCH)

175 g/6 oz fine oatmeal
450 g/1 lb plain white flour
15 g/½ oz fresh yeast
1 teaspoon sugar
A little warm milk

Mix the oatmeal and flour. Cream the yeast with the sugar and add a little warm milk. Add to the flour mixture, adding more warm milk as necessary to make a thin batter. Cook like pancakes in a thick frying pan, and eat hot with butter.

Makes 20

TYNESIDE SINGIN' HINNY

225 g/8 oz plain flour
½ level teaspoon baking powder
½ level teaspoon salt
50 g/2 oz butter
50 g/2 oz lard
75 g/3 oz currants
Milk

Sift flour, baking powder and salt together and rub in fats until mixture is like fine breadcrumbs. Stir in currants and mix with enough milk to make a stiff paste. Roll into a large cake 1.25 cm/½ in thick (or cut into 7.5 cm/3 in rounds), prick top and put on a greased griddle or frying pan. Cook for about five minutes on each side until golden, split and butter.

Makes 12

YORKSHIRE FAT CAKES

350 g/12 oz plain flour
1 teaspoon baking powder
1 teaspoon salt
100 g/4 oz lard
15 g/½ oz fresh yeast
150 ml/¼ pint milk

Sift the flour, baking powder and salt into a basin. Rub in the lard. Make a well in the centre of the mixture. Cream the yeast with a little warm milk, and leave to stand for five minutes. Add to the flour mixture and then add the remaining warm milk. Mix to a soft dough. Divide into four pieces and roll these out in circles 1.25 cm/½ in thick. Put on to a greased baking sheet and bake at 375°F, 190°C, gas mark 5 for thirty minutes. While still hot, split and butter thickly.

Makes 4

SHROPSHIRE FRIED CAKES

225 g/8 oz self-raising flour
50 g/2 oz butter or lard
50 g/2 oz sugar
Milk to mix
Bacon fat for frying

Sieve the flour and rub in the fat. Add the sugar and mix with enough milk to make a firm dough. Turn the mixture on to a floured board and roll out 1.25 cm/½ in thick, and cut into rounds. Put into a smoking hot frying pan with plenty of bacon fat. Cook for about two minutes, until well risen and brown underneath. Turn over and cook the other side until brown. Eat while fresh.

Makes 12

SUFFOLK BROTHERLY LOVE

450 g/1 lb bread dough
25 g/1 oz lard
50 g/2 oz sugar

When making a batch of bread, take some of the dough weighing 450 g/1 lb and roll out in a rectangle 1.25 cm/½ in thick. Cut lard in thin flakes, and spread over the dough. Scatter the surface with the sugar. Roll up like a Swiss roll, and cut in 2.5 cm/1 in slices. Put on a greased baking sheet and bake at 425°F, 220°C, gas mark 7 for thirty minutes.

Makes 15 slices

SURREY LARDIES

225 g/8 oz bread dough
50 g/2 oz lard
50 g/2 oz sugar
25 g/1 oz currants

Roll the bread dough into a rectangle 5 mm/¼ in thick. Divide the lard and sugar into three portions. Spread dough with one portion of lard and one portion of sugar. Fold into three and roll again. Repeat the process twice, adding currants the last time. Roll out and cut into rounds. Score with a knife and put on a greased baking sheet. Leave to rise for twenty minutes in a warm place. Bake at 450°F, 230°C, gas mark 8 for twenty-five minutes.

Makes 10 slices

GLOUCESTER LARDY CAKE

450 g/1 lb basic bread dough which has
* risen once*
100 g/4 oz lard
100 g/4 oz brown sugar
75 g/3 oz sultanas
50 g/2 oz currants

Roll out the dough into a rectangle as for puff pastry. Spread one-third of the lard, sugar and fruit over two-thirds of the surface and fold into three. Repeat this twice more and then set aside to rest. Roll the dough mixture out again, roll up like a Swiss roll and cut into two. Place each half cut side down in a greased 12.5 cm/5 in diameter cake tin. Cover with a clean towel and leave in a warm place to prove. Bake at 400°F, 200°C, gas mark 6 for forty-five minutes. Turn out of tins immediately when cooked.

Makes two cakes

CORNISH HEAVY CAKE

2.25 kg/3 lb plain flour
850 g/1 lb 14 oz lard
850 g/1 lb 14 oz sugar
95 g/3½ oz baking powder
750 ml/1¼ pints milk
2.25 kg/3 lb mixed dried fruit and
* chopped peel*

Sift the flour, sugar and baking powder and lightly rub in the lard. Drop in the fruit and add the milk all at once, mixing lightly to a soft dough. Weigh out 550 g/1¼ lb of mixture for each 18 cm/7 in sponge tin. Brush the top with beaten egg and bake at 425°F, 220°C, gas mark 7 for thirty minutes.

Makes 10 cakes

WILTSHIRE SEED LARDY CAKE

450 g/1 lb bread dough
175 g/6 oz lard
175 g/6 oz sugar
15 g/½ oz caraway seeds

Roll out the dough into an oblong. Cut the lard into flakes. Put half the lard and half the sugar on to two-thirds of the dough. Fold dough into three, bringing up the bottom third first and folding the top third over it. Seal the ends with a rolling pin. Give a half turn and roll into an oblong. Repeat the process, scattering on the caraway seeds with the sugar. Roll to fit a baking tin and score across in diamonds. Leave to rise for thirty minutes in a warm place and bake at 400°F, 200°C, gas mark 6 for one hour. Leave to stand for five minutes so that the fat soaks into the cake.

Makes 12–15 slices

HARVEST BETSY CAKE

225 g/8 oz barley flour
225 g/8 oz plain flour
1½ teaspoons baking powder
½ teaspoon salt
100 g/4 oz butter
100 g/4 oz caster sugar
1 dessertspoon golden syrup
300 ml/½ pint milk
225 g/8 oz sultanas

Sift the two kinds of flour together with baking powder and salt. Cream butter and sugar, and add syrup. Add the flour mixture and the milk alternately, then fold in the sultanas. Put into a buttered 18 cm/7 in cake tin and bake at 350°F, 180°C, gas mark 4 for one and a half hours.

Makes one 18 cm/7 in cake

SUFFOLK RUSKS

225 g/8 oz self-raising flour
Pinch of salt
75 g/3 oz butter
1 egg
Milk or water to mix

Sieve the flour and salt together. Rub in the butter lightly and mix with the beaten egg and just enough milk or water to make a smooth dough. Roll out lightly to 2.5 cm/1 in thick and cut in 6.25 cm/2½ in rounds. Bake at 450°F, 230°C, gas mark 8 for ten minutes. Remove from the oven and split in half. Put on baking sheets with the cut sides upwards. Bake at 375°F, 190°C, gas mark 5 for about fifteen minutes until crisp and golden. Cool and serve with butter and cheese. These rusks store well in a tin.

Makes 30

SUFFOLK HARVEST CAKE

450 g/1 lb white flour
100 g/4 oz cornflour
2 teaspoons baking powder
½ teaspoon bicarbonate of soda
Pinch of powdered nutmeg
Pinch of powdered cinnamon
25 g/1 oz finely crumbled fresh yeast
450 g/1 lb sugar
225 g/8 oz lard
300 ml/½ pint milk
2 eggs
450 g/1 lb currants
100 g/4 oz chopped candied lemon peel

Sift together the flour, cornflour, baking powder, bicarbonate of soda, nutmeg and cinnamon. Rub in the crumbled yeast and stir in the sugar. Cut the lard into flakes and work into the dry ingredients. Beat together the eggs and milk and stir them into the other ingredients. Finally stir in currants and candied peel until the ingredients are well blended. Put into two greased and lined 25 cm/10 in round tins and leave in a warm place for thirty minutes to rise. Bake at 350°F, 180°C, gas mark 4 for two hours.

Makes two 25 cm/10 in cakes

POTATO BISCUITS

100 g/4 oz plain flour
1 level teaspoon salt
100 g/4 oz rolled oats
75 g/3 oz butter
100 g/4 oz cold mashed potatoes

Mix flour, salt and oats. Rub in the butter and then knead in the potatoes until a stiff dough is formed. Roll out thinly. Cut into 2 cm/¾ in rounds. Put on baking sheets and cook at 325°F, 170°C, gas mark 3 for 20–25 minutes until crisp and brown. Cool on a wire rack. These biscuits are excellent with cheese.

Makes 20

DERBYSHIRE OATCAKES

225 g/8 oz medium or fine oatmeal
225 g/8 oz plain flour
Pinch of salt
25 g/1 oz yeast
1 teaspoon sugar
300 ml/½ pint warm water

Sift the oatmeal and flour with the salt into a warm basin. Cream the yeast and sugar and gradually work in the warm water. Stir the yeast liquid into the flour mixture to form a thin batter, adding a little more warm water if necessary. Leave to stand in a warm place for thiry minutes until well risen. Heat a griddle, hotplate or heavy frying pan and grease it lightly. Pour small cupfuls of batter on to the griddle and cook for two minutes. Turn and bake the other side. Eat hot. These oatcakes can later be fried with bacon, or toasted and served with butter or dripping.

Makes 12

WELSH OATCAKES (BARA CEIRCH)

225 g/8 oz medium oatmeal
1 teaspoon bacon fat
300 ml/½ pint warm water

Put the oatmeal into a basin. Melt the bacon fat in the water and stir into the oatmeal to make a fairly stiff dough. Put on a board dusted with oatmeal and divide into small pieces. Make each into a ball and press down, then roll out very thinly, pressing with the fingers where neccesary to avoid cracks. Cook on a hot griddle, hotplate or frying pan. When the oatcakes start to curl at the sides, after about three minutes, turn them and bake to a pale biscuit colour.

Makes 15

CHAPTER SEVEN

TIME FOR TEA

Tea has always been a very important meal in a farmhouse, marking the end of the working day. It is therefore often served about 6 p.m., and combines supper dishes with cakes and a pot of tea, thus dispensing with a later, cooked evening meal. The farming family has instead a substantial bedtime snack of pies, sandwiches, cakes and hot drinks in the late evening.

A farmhouse tea or 'High Tea' can consist of cold meats or pies and salads, bread and butter, sandwiches, scones and teabreads, jams, cold sweets (such as stewed fruit, jellies or trifles), and a profusion of cakes and biscuits. Spice cakes, gingerbreads, fruit cakes and sponges are all popular, with iced sponges and cream-filled cakes on special occasions. Many of the plainer cakes appear again at the mid-morning break, or form part of next day's packed midday meal.

Use unsalted butter for sweet scones, cakes and biscuits if possible.

MORE SCONES, BREADS AND PLAIN CAKES

GINGER SCONES

225 g/8 oz self-raising flour
1 teaspoon ground ginger
¼ teaspoon bicarbonate of soda
½ teaspoon cream of tartar
1 dessertspoon caster sugar
40 g/1½ oz lard
1 egg
1 teaspoon golden syrup
5 tablespoons milk

Sift the dry ingredients. Rub in the lard until fine. Add beaten egg, combined with the syrup and milk, to the dry ingredients. Mix to a soft dough. Turn dough on to a floured board and knead very lightly. Divide into two; shape each piece into a round and roll gently to about 15 cm/6 in in diameter. Cut into half and each half into three, making six small triangular scones of each round. Bake near the top of the oven for ten minutes at 400°F, 200°C, gas mark 6. If not quite done in ten minutes, reduce the heat and move to a lower shelf in the oven for a further 5–10 minutes.

Makes 12

FAVOURITE SCONE RING

225 g/8 oz self-raising flour
Pinch of salt
50 g/2 oz butter
50 g/2 oz sugar
50 g/2 oz mixed dried fruit
1 egg
3 tablespoons milk

Sieve the flour and salt into a bowl and rub in butter. Add the sugar and dried fruit. Beat egg with the milk. Add most of the liquid to the mixture to make a fairly soft dough. Divide the dough into eight and lightly knead each piece into a round. Place scones overlapping to form a ring on a greased baking tray. Brush the tops only with the remaining milk and egg liquid. Bake at 425°F, 220°C, gas mark 7 for 20–25 minutes until golden-brown and cooked through. Cool on a wire tray.

Makes 8 individual scones

BARM BRACK

450 g/1 lb plain flour
¼ level teaspoon nutmeg
Pinch of salt
50 g/2 oz butter
20 g/¾ oz fresh yeast
50 g/2 oz sugar
300 ml/½ pint milk
2 well-beaten eggs
225 g/8 oz sultanas
225 g/8 oz currants
100 g/4 oz mixed chopped candied peel

Sieve the flour, nutmeg and salt together. Rub in the butter. Cream the yeast with a little of the sugar. Add remaining sugar to flour mixture. Warm the milk gently, and add to the liquid yeast and eggs (reserve a little egg for glazing the bread). Beat liquid into dry ingredients until batter is stiff but elastic. Fold in the dried fruit and peel, and turn into a buttered 20 cm/8 in cake tin. Cover with a cloth and put into a warm place for one hour. Brush with beaten egg and bake in a fairly hot oven, 400°F, 200°C, gas mark 6 for one hour. Brush over with one tablespoon sugar dissolved in two tablespoons boiling water, and return to the oven for three minutes. Turn out and cool on a wire rack, Serve in slices with butter. When stale, the bread can be toasted and buttered.

Makes one 20 cm/8 in cake

NORTH COUNTRY OVERNIGHT SPICE CAKE

450 g/1 lb plain flour
150 g/6 oz lard
50 g/2 oz unsalted butter
225 g/8 oz caster sugar
100 g/4 oz ground almonds
2 teaspoons mixed spice
2½ teaspoons bicarbonate of soda
225 g/8 oz currants
225 g/8 oz raisins
300 ml/½ pint milk

Rub the fat into the flour until the mixture resembles fine crumbs. Sift in the sugar, almonds, spice and soda. Scatter the currants and raisins over the mixture. Mix to a soft dough with the milk. Place the mixture in an 20 cm/8 in round cake tin, greased and lined with foil or parchment paper. Leave overnight. Next day, bake at 325°F, 170°C, gas mark 3 for one hour, then reduce the heat to 300°F, 150°C, gas mark 2 for a further one and a half hours or until the cake is springy and brown. Cool well on a wire rack before cutting.

Makes one 20 cm/8 in cake

FARMHOUSE TEA LOAF

100 g/4 oz mixed dried fruit
100 g/4 oz caster sugar
150 ml/¼ pint hot tea
2 tablespoons chunky marmalade
1 egg
225 g/8 oz self-raising flour

Place the fruit, sugar and tea in a bowl. Leave to stand for at least six hours, but preferably overnight. Add the marmalade and egg, sieve in the flour and then mix well. Turn the mixture into a greased and base-lined 450 g/1 lb-loaf tin and bake at 350°F, 180°C, gas mark 4 for 50–60 minutes, until cooked. Test with a skewer. Allow to cool, and serve thinly sliced and spread with butter.

Makes 450 g/1 lb loaf

SEED BREAD

225 g/8 oz plain flour
¼ teaspoon salt
1 teaspoon bicarbonate of soda
50 g/2 oz lard
50 g/2 oz sugar
1 egg
1 tablespoon caraway seeds
50 g/2 oz chopped mixed peel
150 ml/¼ pint hot water

Sieve the flour, salt and bicarbonate of soda into a bowl. Put the butter, sugar, peel and caraway seeds into another bowl and pour over them the hot water. Stir well and leave to cool. Beat up the egg and fold this into the liquid mixture. Add the sieved dry ingredients and beat very hard. Pour into a greased 450 g/1 lb-loaf tin, and bake at 375°F, 190°C, gas mark 5 for fifty minutes.

Makes 450 g/1 lb loaf

BARA BRIETH

150 ml/¼ pint milk
25 g/1 oz yeast
900 g/2 lb plain flour
225 g/8 oz butter
225 g/8 oz brown sugar
Pinch of salt
½ teaspoon mixed spice
350 g/12 oz mixed currants, sultanas, raisins
100 g/4 oz chopped mixed candied peel

Mix yeast with the warmed milk. Put the flour into a bowl and rub in butter. Add sugar, fruit and spice and mix in the warm liquid. Cover and leave to rise in a warm place for one and a half hours until double its size. Knead into a loaf shape and put into two 450 g/1 lb-loaf tins. Leave to rise for ten minutes. Bake at 400°F, 200°C, gas mark 6 for one hour. Cool, slice thinly and spread with butter.

Makes two 450 g/1 lb loaves.

BREAD PUDDING (CAKE)

8 slices bread (toast thickness)
300 ml/½ pint milk
350 g/12 oz mixed dried fruit
50 g/2 oz mixed chopped candied peel
1 apple
3 tablespoons brown sugar
2 tablespoons marmalade
3 tablespoons self-raising flour
2 eggs
Squeeze of lemon juice
1 teaspoon ground cinnamon
100 g/4 oz butter

Soak the bread in the milk until it is really soft. Add dried fruit and peel, grated peeled apple, sugar, marmalade, flour, eggs and cinnamon. Beat very thoroughly together. Melt the butter and pour half into the mixture. Beat and put into a greased meat tin. Pour on remaining butter. Bake at 300°F, 150°C, gas mark 2 for one and a half hours; then at 350°F, 180°C, gas mark 4 for thirty minutes. Leave until cold, sprinkle with icing sugar, and cut in slices like a cake.

Makes 20 pieces

COUNTRY TEA BREAD

200 g/7 oz mixed currants, sultanas
* and seedless raisins*
25 g/1 oz chopped peel
150 ml/¼ pint tea
100 g/4 oz clear honey
1 egg
225 g/8 oz self-raising flour
Salt
25 g/1 oz melted butter

Topping
Clear honey to taste
20 g/¾ oz chopped walnuts
7 g/¼ oz Demerara sugar

Put the fruit, peel, tea and 100 g/4 oz honey into a bowl, cover and leave overnight to allow the fruit to swell and absorb the tea flavour. Stir in the beaten egg, sifted flour and salt and melted butter, in that order. Transfer to a greased 450 g/1 lb-loaf tin and bake for about one hour ten minutes at 350°F, 180°C, gas mark 4. After fifty minutes remove the bread from the oven, brush with honey and sprinkle nuts and sugar on top. Trickle more honey over and return to the oven to finish cooking.

Makes one 450 g/1 lb cake

APPLE LOAF

450 g/1 lb plain flour, sifted
Pinch of salt
1 teaspoon baking powder
100 g/4 oz butter
100 g/4 oz lard
2 eggs, beaten
50 g/2 oz currants
50 g/2 oz raisins, seeded
1 cooking apple, peeled, cored and
* sliced*
Milk to mix
100 g/4 oz icing sugar, sifted
A little water
1 tart eating apple (red), cored and
* sliced*

Dip the fruit in a little lemon juice as soon as prepared, to prevent discoloration.

Sift together the flour, salt and baking powder. Rub in the fat, mix in the beaten egg, currants, raisins, cooking apple and milk. Mix well. Turn into a 450 g/1 lb, lined loaf tin, and bake in a moderate oven at 375°F, 190°C, gas mark 5 for 40–45 minutes, or until springy and browned. When cool, spread the loaf with a thin icing made with icing sugar and water, and decorate with sliced eating apple. Serve for high tea, especially when salads are scarce.

Makes 450 g/1 lb loaf

DRIPPING CAKE

225 g/8 oz mixed dried fruit and
    candied peel
75 g/3 oz clarified beef dripping
150 g/5 oz brown sugar
250 ml/8 fl oz water
225 g/8 oz wholemeal flour
1 teaspoon baking powder
Pinch of nutmeg
Pinch of cinnamon
Pinch of mixed spice
½ teaspoon bicarbonate of soda

Put the fruit in a heavy pan with dripping, sugar and water, bring to the boil and simmer for ten minutes. Leave to cool, then pour into the rest of the ingredients which have been sifted together. Blend well but do not beat. Put into a greased 15 cm/6 in cake tin and bake at 350°F, 180°C, gas mark 4 for 1¼–1½ hours.

Makes one 15 cm/6 in cake

CUMBERLAND BUTTERMILK CAKE

450 g/1 lb plain flour
75 g/3 oz lard
75 g/3 oz unsalted butter
100 g/4 oz caster sugar
225 g/8 oz chopped candied lemon peel
100 g/4 oz seedless raisins
2 tablespoons marmalade
1 teaspoon bicarbonate of soda
250 ml/8 fl oz buttermilk or sour milk

Sift the flour, and rub in the fats till the mixture resembles fine crumbs. Add the sugar. Scatter the peel and raisins over the surface. Mix the marmalade into the milk, warm to dissolve, then cool. Mix the soda into the milk mixture, and use it to mix the dry ingredients to a soft dough. Place in a lined and greased 20 cm/8 in cake tin, and bake at 325°F, 170°C, gas mark 3 for one hour. Lower the heat to 300°F, 150°C, gas mark 2, and bake for a further forty-five minutes or until the cake is springy and browned. Cool well before cutting.

Makes one 20 cm/8 in cake

VICTORIAN LUNCHEON CAKE

225 g/8 oz self-raising flour
100 g/4 oz beef dripping
100 g/4 oz soft brown sugar
1 egg
3 tablespoons milk
1 rounded teaspoon baking powder
225 g/8 oz currants

Butter and flour the sides and base of a 15 cm/6 in loose-bottomed cake tin. Cream the dripping thoroughly, add sugar, and cream again. Sift the flour and baking powder together. Add two tablespoons flour to dripping mixture, then the egg and whip again. Continue adding flour gradually with single spoonsful of milk until both ingredients are absorbed. Turn into the prepared tin. Flour the currants and shake off the surplus flour in a sieve. Turn on to the top of cake mixture and work in with a fork, being careful not to let the fork touch the base of the tin. Bake on middle shelf of oven at 325°F, 170°C, gas mark 3 for one hour plus 10–15 minutes.

Makes one 15 cm/6 in cake

DUNDEE CAKE

225 g/8 oz butter
225 g/8 oz sugar
8 eggs
225 g/8 oz self-raising flour
½ teaspoon nutmeg
350 g/12 oz mixed currants and
*   sultanas*
75 g/3 oz ground almonds
75 g/3 oz chopped glacé cherries
50 g/2 oz candied peel
50 g/2 oz split blanched almonds

Cream butter and sugar and add eggs one at a time, each with a sprinkling of flour to avoid curdling. Beat well after each addition. Stir in most of the flour and lastly the fruit lightly coated with the rest of the flour. Turn into a 22.5 cm/9 in cake tin lined with greased paper, smooth the top and arrange almonds on surface. Bake at 325°F, 170°C, gas mark 3 for 2–2½ hours.

Makes one 22.5 cm/9 in cake

LEMON CAKE

100 g/4 oz butter
175 g/6 oz caster sugar
175 g/6 oz self-raising flour
2 eggs
Pinch of salt
150 ml/¼ pint milk
Grated rind and juice of 1 lemon
1 heaped tablespoon caster sugar

Mix butter, sugar, flour, eggs, salt, milk and lemon rind together and bake in a 450 g/1 lb-loaf tin for one hour at 350°F, 180°C, gas mark 4. Combine the lemon juice and sugar and pour over the cake while still hot.

Makes 450 g/1 lb loaf

IRISH WHISKEY CAKE

2 tablespoons Irish whiskey
1 orange
175 g/6 oz sultanas
175 g/6 oz butter
3 eggs
225 g/8 oz plain flour
Pinch of salt
1 teaspoon baking powder

Put the whiskey into a small bowl. Peel the orange thinly and soak the rind in the whiskey for a few hours. Discard the peel. Leave the sultanas to soak in the whiskey while preparing the rest of the cake. Cream the butter and sugar. Add the eggs, one at a time, with a teaspoon of flour for each one, beating well between each addition. Sift flour, salt and baking powder together and fold into the egg mixture. Fold in the whiskey and sultanas. Line a greased 18 cm/7 in round cake tin with greased paper. Put in the mixture and bake in a moderate oven, 350°F, 180°C, gas mark 4 for 1¼ hours. Cool on a wire rack.

Makes one 18 cm/7 in cake

GRANNY'S GINGERBREAD

450 g/1 lb black treacle
175 g/6 oz butter
100 g/4 oz dark soft brown sugar
450 g/1 lb wholemeal flour
1 teaspoon baking powder
1 teaspoons ground ginger
A good pinch of salt
2 eggs
150 ml/¼ pint milk

Melt butter in a saucepan with the sugar and treacle, but do not allow the mixture to get too hot. Mix the flour, baking powder, ginger and salt together in a basin. Beat the eggs and milk lightly together. Beat in all the other ingredients. Pour into two greased 450 g/1 lb-loaf tins. Bake for one hour at 350°F, 180°C, gas mark 4. This gingerbread keeps for weeks in an airtight tin.

Makes two 450 g/1 lb cakes

LANCASHIRE GINGERBREAD

1 tablespoon bitter marmalade
450 g/1 lb butter
½ level teaspoon bicarbonate of soda
225 g/8 oz wholemeal flour
225 g/8 oz self-raising flour
2 teaspoons ground ginger
2 teaspoons mixed spice
Handful of sultanas
450 g/1 lb black treacle
175 g/6 oz dark soft brown sugar
3 eggs
300 ml/½ pint milk

Melt butter in a saucepan. Add treacle, sugar, milk and marmalade, and stir over a low heat until sugar has dissolved. While this mixture cools, measure into a large bowl the wholemeal and self-raising flours, spice, ginger, bicarbonate of soda and sultanas. Beat eggs and stir with flour mixture, gradually adding warm butter mixture from the saucepan. Pour the cake into a deep baking tin lined with buttered paper, and bake at 350°F, 180°C, gas mark 4 for about one and a half hours. Cool on a sieve and leave the cake until quite cold before cutting.

Makes 20 pieces

OLD-FASHIONED GINGERBREAD

225 g/8 oz plain flour
1 level teaspoon bicarbonate of soda
1 heaped teaspoon ground ginger
1 level teaspoon ground cinnamon
75 g/3 oz dark soft brown sugar
Pinch of salt
100 g/4 oz black treacle
75 g/3 oz lard
100 g/4 oz mixed cake fruit
1 egg
4–5 tablespoons milk

Line a 15 cm/6 in square tin with greaseproof paper. Heat the oven to 375°F, 190°C, gas mark 5. Put the treacle and the lard in a small saucepan and melt. Sieve all the dry ingredients together and add the sugar to them with the fruit. Beat up the egg in a separate basin and add the milk to it. Pour into the centre of the flour and stir all together with the melted lard mixture. Mix thoroughly and turn into the prepared tin. Bake in the centre of the oven for 30–40 minutes, reducing heat slightly after the first fifteen minutes.

Makes 9 pieces

GRANNY'S HIGH TEA CAKE

225 g/8 oz self-raising flour
1 rounded teaspoon mixed spice
1 level teaspoon grated nutmeg
Pinch of salt
150 g/5 oz butter
6 level tablespoons golden syrup
100 g/4 oz chopped stoned dates
225 g/8 oz stoned raisins
225 g/8 oz currants
100 g/4 oz sultanas
100 g/4 oz chopped mixed peel
150 ml/¼ pint and 2 tablespoons milk
2 eggs
½ level teaspoon bicarbonate of soda

Put the butter, syrup, fruit, peel and milk into a saucepan. Heat slowly until butter is melted, then simmer gently five minutes, stirring once or twice. Remove and cool. Beat eggs lightly. Make a well in the centre of the dry ingredients. Add the eggs but do not stir. Stir bicarbonate of soda quickly into cooled mixture, add to dry ingredients and mix thoroughly, beating well. Put into a 18 cm/7 in cake tin lined with greaseproof paper and brushed inside with melted butter. Bake for one and three quarter hours on the middle shelf at 325°F, 170°C, gas mark 3. Cool on wire tray.

Makes one 18 cm/7 in cake

OVERNIGHT CAKE

450 g/1 lb plain flour
225 g/8 oz currants
225 g/8 oz sultanas
225 g/8 oz sugar
50 g/2 oz mixed peel
175 g/6 oz lard
1 tablespoon golden syrup
2 teaspoons bicarbonate of soda

Mix all dry ingredients and mix in the melted lard and syrup, together with the bicarbonate of soda dissolved in a little milk and 300 ml/½ pint water. Put into a greased 20 cm/8 in tin and leave overnight. Bake at 325°F, 170°C, gas mark 3 for one and three quarter hours.

Makes one 20 cm/8 in cake

DEVONSHIRE SAFFRON CAKE

½ teaspoon saffron strands
25 g/1 oz fresh yeast
900 g/2 lb plain flour
225 g/8 oz sugar
¼ teaspoon mixed spice
Pinch of salt
100 g/4 oz lard
100 g/4 oz butter
300 ml/½ pint milk
350 g/12 oz mixed dried fruit
50 g/2 oz chopped mixed peel

Prepare the saffron by cutting up the stamens finely and putting them into 50 ml/2 fl oz warm water. Leave this mixture overnight. Mix the yeast with two tablespoons of the flour. Mix with 75 ml/3 fl oz warm water and one teaspoon sugar. Put in a warm place and leave for thirty minutes. Put the flour into a bowl and mix with the sugar, spice and salt. Rub in the lard and butter until the mixture is like fine breadcrumbs. Add the risen yeast mixture. Warm the milk to lukewarm and stir in the saffron liquid and pieces of saffron. Pour this into the flour mixture, and add the dried fruit and peel. Mix well and leave in a warm place covered with a cloth

for four hours. Put into two 450 g/1 lb-loaf tins and bake at 425°F, 220°C, gas mark 7 for forty minutes.

Makes two 450 g/1 lb loaves

DORSET APPLE CAKE

100 g/4 oz lard or butter
225 g/4 oz plain flour
Pinch of salt
1½ teaspoons baking powder
225 g/8 oz peeled, cored and chopped
  apples
100 g/4 oz sugar
1 egg

Rub the lard or butter into the flour and salt. Stir in the baking powder. Mix the apples with the sugar and stir into the flour mixture. Mix to a dough with the beaten egg. Put into a greased 20 cm/8 in cake tin, spreading the mixture about 2.5 cm/1 in thick. Bake at 350°F, 180°C, gas mark 4 for fifty minutes. Cut open while still hot and spread with butter. A few currants or raisins can be added to the mixture.

Makes one 20 cm/8 in cake

PLUM LOAF

225 g/8 oz self-raising flour
50 g/2 oz lard
50 g/2 oz butter
50 g/2 oz sugar
2 tablespoons treacle
100 g/4 oz currants
50 g/2 oz sultanas
50 g/2 oz raisins
Milk

Put flour into bowl and rub in the butter and lard. Add sugar, treacle and fruit. Mix with milk into a stiff mixture. Put into a greaseproof lined 450 g/1 lb-loaf tin, and place on low oven shelf at 300°F, 150°C, gas mark 2 for two hours.

Makes one 450 g/1 lb loaf

SEED CAKE

225 g/8 oz plain flour
Pinch of salt
1 teaspoon baking powder
150 g/5 oz butter
150 g/5 oz caster sugar
2 eggs
2 tablespoons milk
3 teaspoons caraway seeds
50 g/2 oz chopped mixed peel

Sieve together the flour, salt and baking powder. Cream the butter and sugar together. Separate the eggs. Beat the yolks and stir them into the creamed butter mixture, then fold in the flour mixture, and stir in the milk. Add the caraway seeds and the peel. Whisk the egg whites very stiffly, and fold them into the cake mixture. Put into a greased 18 cm/7 in tin, and bake on the middle shelf of the oven at 350°F, 180°C, gas mark 4 for one hour. Leave in the tin for five minutes before turning out to cool.

Makes one 18 cm/7 in cake

POUND CAKE

275 g/10 oz plain flour
¼ teaspoon salt
1 teaspoon baking powder
225 g/8 oz butter
225 g/8 oz sugar
4 eggs
100 g/4 oz sultanas
100 g/4 oz currants
Grated rind of one lemon
50 g/2 oz chopped mixed peel
75 ml/3 fl oz brandy

Sieve together the flour, salt and baking powder. Cream the butter and sugar. Add the eggs to the creamed mixture alternately with some of the flour mixture. When incorporated, add the sultanas, currants, lemon rind and mixed peel, stirring but not beating. Stir in the brandy. Put into a greased 20 cm/8 in tin and bake at 350°F, 180°C, gas mark 4 for one and three quarter hours.

Makes one 20 cm/8 in cake

SWEETER CAKES

LIGHT CREAM CHOCOLATE CAKE

4 eggs
115 g/4½ oz caster sugar
60 g/2½ oz plain flour
25 g/1 oz drinking chocolate powder
150 ml/¼ pint double cream

Whip the eggs and sugar together until light and fluffy. Carefully fold in the flour and drinking chocolate powder sifted together. Bake in two 18 cm/7 in greased sponge tins at 400°F, 200°C, gas mark 6 for fifteen minutes. Cool on a wire cake tray. Whip the cream with about one tablespoon sugar, and use to sandwich the cakes together when they are quite cold.

Makes one 18 cm/7 in cake

MOIST CHOCOLATE CAKE

225 g/8 oz butter
175 g/6 oz light soft brown sugar
175 g/6 oz black treacle
4 eggs
175 g/6 oz self-raising flour
50 g/2 oz cocoa

Cream together the butter, sugar and treacle. Gradually beat in the eggs, adding a tablespoon of sieved flour with the last amount of egg. Sieve together flour and cocoa and fold into the creamed mixture. Turn into two greased and bottom-lined 20 cm/8 in sponge sandwich tins and bake at 350°F, 180°C, gas mark 4 for fifty minutes. Turn out. When cold sandwich together with fresh cream or buttercream and top with chocolate glacé icing.

Makes one 20 cm/8 in cake

SPECIAL DAY COCOA CAKE

3 large eggs
150 g/3 oz caster sugar
150 g/3 oz plain flour
1 level teaspoon baking powder
A few drops of vanilla essence
1 level tablespoon cocoa
175 g/6 oz butter
275 g/10 oz sifted icing sugar
3 tablespoons cocoa
50 g/2 oz grated plain chocolate

Grease a tin measuring 35 × 25 cm/14 × 10 in and a 20 cm/8 in round tin, and line with grease-proof paper. Whisk the eggs and sugar together in a bowl placed over a pan of hot water, until really thick. The whisk should leave a good trail. Sieve the flour with a pinch of salt and the baking powder, and fold carefully into the mixture with the vanilla essence, leaving no pockets of dry flour. Place a good half of the mixture into the prepared rectangular tin. Gently shake the tin to level off the surface. Sieve the one table-spoon cocoa and fold into remaining mixture. Place in the round cake tin, levelling off the sur-face again. Bake the cakes one above the other at 400°F, 200°C, gas mark 6 for 10–15 minutes, until cooked and springy to the touch. The bottom cake may take a little longer to cook. Turn out on to a wire tray to cool.

To assemble the cake: cream together the icing sugar and butter to make a buttercream. Keep out one tablespoon of the plain buttercream for the top. Blend the three tablespoons cocoa with a little boiling water and beat into remaining buttercream. Cut the rectangular cake length-ways into five 35 cm/14 in even-sized strips. Split the chocolate cake in half, spread the cut surfaces with chocolate buttercream. Spread the strips of cake with buttercream and form into a circle, placing it on a round of chocolate cake as you do so. Use all the plain sponge to make a complete spiral. Place the remaining chocolate cake on top. Cover with chocolate buttercream, coat the sides with grated chocolate, then lift on

to a plate. Soften the plain buttercream with a little hot water; pipe straight lines about an inch apart on the top of the cake. Make a 'feather' pattern by drawing a skewer in alternate direc-tions across the lines.

Makes 12 slices

ICED MARMALADE CAKE

175 g/6 oz butter
175 g/6 oz caster sugar
3 eggs
275 g/10 oz self-raising flour
3 level tablespoons chunky marmalade
50 g/2 oz chopped mixed peel
Grated rind of one orange
3 tablespoons water

Icing
100 g/4 oz icing sugar
Juice of one orange
2–5 slices crystallised orange

Line and grease a 18 cm/7 in round cake tin. Beat butter and sugar together until light and creamy. Beat in the egg yolks, one at a time, then one tablespoon of the flour. Stir in marmalade, peel, orange rind and water. Fold in the remaining flour. Whisk the egg white until just stiff and fold into the cake mixture. Turn into the pre-pared tin and bake at 350°F, 180°C, gas mark 4 for one and a quarter hours until risen and firm to the touch. Cool.

Icing: Blend icing sugar with sufficient orange juice to give a stiff coating consistency. Pour over cake and allow icing to trickle down sides. Leave to set. Cut slices of crystallised orange in half and use to decorate the top.

Makes on 18 cm/7 in cake

LEMON SLICES

175 g/6 oz butter
175 g/6 oz caster sugar
3 eggs
175 g/6 oz self-raising flour
Grated rind of one lemon
Grated rind of one orange
3 drops vanilla essence
Juice of half lemon
Juice of half orange
Icing sugar

Cream together the butter and sugar. Gradually work in the beaten eggs, alternately with the flour. Add the grated fruit rinds and the essence, and pour into a greased rectangular tin. Bake at 375°F, 190°C, gas mark 5 for thirty minutes. Cool and ice with the fruit juices mixed with enough icing sugar to make a spreading consistency. Cut in squares to serve.

Makes 16 slices

OLD-FASHIONED SPONGE CAKE

3 eggs
75 g/3 oz caster sugar
3 teaspoons hot water
75 g/3 oz plain flour
3 drops vanilla essence

Put the eggs, sugar, water and essence into a bowl and put them over a saucepan which has been half-filled with boiling water. Whisk the mixture well over this heat for five minutes. Put the saucepan over heat, and continue whisking for five minutes. Take the bowl from the saucepan and whisk until the mixture is cold and thick. Fold in the sifted flour very carefully. Pour into a 20 cm/8 in greased and lined cake tin, and bake at 400°F, 200°C, gas mark 6 for twenty-five mintues. Cool on a wire cake tray. When the cake is cold, split with a sharp knife and fill with jam or lemon curd. Dust the top with icing sugar.

Makes one 20 cm/8 in cake

TARTS AND BISCUITS

BLACKBERRY BAKESTONE TART

350 g/12 oz blackberries
225 g/8 oz shortcrust pastry
25 g/1 oz butter
50 g/2 oz brown sugar

Clean the fruit. Roll out the pastry into a circle and put the fruit in half of it. Fold over the pastry and seal the edges. Bake at 375°F, 190°C, gas mark 5 for forty minutes. Take from the oven and just before serving, gently lift the top and insert small pieces of butter and sprinkle in the brown sugar.

Serves 4

This is a Welsh dish which used to be cooked on a warm greased bakestone, and turned half-way through cooking. It is easier, now, to bake the tart, but it can be cooked in a thick frying pan instead.

RASPBERRY TART

225 g/8 oz puff pastry
450 g/1 lb raspberries
175 g/6 oz caster sugar
3 large eggs

Line a 20 cm/8 in pie plate with the pastry. Mix the raspberries with half the sugar and put them in the pastry case. Beat the eggs roughly with the remaining sugar and pour over the fruit. Bake at 375°F, 190°C, gas mark 5 for thirty minutes.

Serves 4–6

WELSH BUTTER TARTS

225 g/8 oz shortcrust pastry
60 g/2½ oz butter
175 g/6 oz light soft brown sugar
2 tablespoons milk or cream
100 g/4 oz raisins
1 egg
1 teaspoon vanilla essence

Line small tartlet tins with the pastry. Melt the butter and mix all the other ingredients together. Fill the pastry cases and bake at 350°F, 180°C, gas mark 4 for twenty-five minutes.

Makes 12–15 tarts

BERWICK MAY DAY TARTS

150 g/5 oz plain flour
25 g/1 oz lard
40 g/1½ oz salted butter
50 g/2 oz unsalted butter, softened
50 g/2 oz caster sugar
1 egg, beaten
25 g/1 oz ground almonds
25 g/1 oz chopped candied peel
50 g/2 oz currants
Almond essence or rose-water to taste
Lemon glacé icing

Rub the lard and salted butter into the flour, and mix to a stiff pastry dough with cold water. Roll out, and line twelve 6.25 cm/2½ in tartlet pans, well greased. Cream together the unsalted butter and sugar, and beat in the egg. Sift in the almonds, add the peel, currants and flavouring, and mix thoroughly. Fill the pastry shell with the mixture. Trim the pastry edges and use any scraps to make a decorative design on each tartlet. Bake the tartlets at 400°F, 200°C, gas mark 6 for seven minutes, then reduce the heat to 350°F, 180°C, gas mark 4, for a further fifteen minutes. While still slightly warm, trickle the icing over the tartlets.

Makes 12

STRAWBERRY TARTLETS

350 g/12 oz shortcrust pastry
450 g/1 lb ripe strawberries
60 g/2½ oz icing sugar
4 eggs

Roll out the pastry and line sixteen tartlet tins with it. Crush the strawberries and mix them with the sugar. Whisk the eggs and gradually add them to the strawberry mixture. Beat the mixture until well blended and pour into the pastry cases. Bake at 375°F, 190°C, gas mark 5 for twelve minutes.

Makes 16

BISCUITS FOR THE DIGESTION

100 g/4 oz porridge oats
150 g/5 oz self-raising flour
50 g/2 oz lard
½ teaspoon bicarbonate of soda
25 g/1 oz sugar
1 tablespoon syrup
Pinch salt

Mix together the dry ingredients. Melt lard, sugar, syrup and bicarbonate of soda in a pan and add to dry ingredients. Roll out very thin, cut out and place on a greased tray. Bake at 350°F, 180°C, gas mark 4 for ten minutes.

Makes 20

NORFOLK SHORTCAKES

225 g/8 oz plain flour
½ teaspoon baking powder
100 g/4 oz butter or lard
40 g/1½ oz granulated sugar
40 g/1½ oz currants
5 tablespoons water

Sieve the flour with the baking powder and rub in 50 g/2oz fat. Divide the rest of the fat into three portions; also the currants and sugar. Mix the flour into a pliable paste with the cold water and roll it out into a long strip. Spread this with dabs of fat and sprinkle with sugar and currants. Fold into three layers, give the paste a half turn and repeat this process twice more. Roll out to about 5 mm/¼ in thick, cut into twenty-four 6.25 cm/2½ in rounds or squares and bake at 400°F, 200°C, gas mark 6 for fifteen minutes until golden-brown. Dredge with caster sugar when cooked.

Makes 24

ALMOND HONEY BISCUITS

175 g/6 oz butter
2 tablespoons honey
A few drops of vanilla essence
200 g/7 oz plain flour
25 g/1 oz icing sugar
50 g/2 oz blanched almonds

Filling
40 g/1½ oz softened butter
1 tablespoon honey
75 g/3 oz icing sugar

Beat together the butter and honey until well blended. Add the vanilla essence and carefully stir in flour and icing sugar. Beat until the mixture is smooth. Leave to chill for thirty minutes. Roll into 20–24 equal-sized balls, about 2 cm/¾ in in diameter. Place on a floured baking sheet, spacing out well. Press lightly to flatten to 5 mm/¼ in thickness. Sprinkle chopped almonds on half the biscuits. Bake at 325°F, 170°C, gas mark 3 for 18–20 minutes until lightly browned.

Leave to cool for five minutes before removing from the tray. Beat filling ingredients together until creamy. Spread a little of the filling on the biscuits without the nuts and sandwich with the nut-topped biscuits.

Makes 10–12

NORFOLK GINGERS

100 g/4 oz brown sugar
100 g/4 oz butter
2 teaspoons ground ginger
½ teaspoon mixed spice
1 small teaspoon bicarbonate of soda
225 g/8 oz plain flour
About 2 tablespoons milk
1 egg

Sift the flour, spices and sugar into a basin and rub in butter. Dissolve the bicarbonate of soda in warm milk. Add the egg and beat until blended. Stir into the dry ingredients, and knead until smooth. Flour the hands lightly, and roll equal-sized small portions of dough into balls. Place well apart on a greased baking sheet. Press each ball lightly on top. Bake in a moderate oven, 350°F, 180°C, gas mark 4 for twenty-five minutes. Leave on the baking sheet until they cool.

Makes 24–30

HUNTER NUTS

225 g/ 8 oz plain flour
1 level teaspoon ground ginger
75 g/3 oz butter
175 g/6 oz sugar
1 small egg
75 g/3 oz black treacle

Sift the flour and ginger. Rub in the butter. Stir in the sugar and bind with beaten egg and treacle. Form into small balls about the size of marbles and place on a greased baking sheet, a little way apart. Bake in a slow oven, 325°F, 170°C, gas mark 3 for thirty minutes.

Makes 24

OLD SPICE BISCUITS

175 g/6 oz plain flour
½ level teaspoon bicarbonate of soda
½ level teaspoon ginger
1 level teaspoon mixed spice
1 level teaspoon cinnamon
75 g/3 oz butter
50 g/2 oz caster sugar
2 tablespoons black treacle

Sift together the dry ingredients. Put butter, sugar and treacle into a pan and melt slowly over a low heat. Remove from the heat and stir in the sifted dry ingredients. Work with fingertips until well blended. Roll the mixture into small balls and transfer to greased baking trays, allowing plenty of room between each for spreading. Press flat with a knife or the prongs of a fork. Bake in the centre of the oven, at 350°F, 180°C, gas mark 4 for 10–15 minutes. Cool on a wire tray, then store in an airtight container.

Makes 20

CORNISH FAIRINGS

100 g/4 oz flour
Pinch of salt
¼ teaspoon ground ginger
¼ teaspoon mixed spice
¼ teaspoon cinnamon
1½ teaspoons bicarbonate of soda
50 g/2 oz butter
50 g/2 oz caster sugar
2½ level tablespoons golden syrup

Sift the flour, salt, ground ginger, cinnamon, spice and bicarbonate of soda into a basin. Rub the butter into the dry ingredients. Mix in the sugar. Melt the syrup and stir it into the mixture, to make a soft dough. Roll the mixture between the hands into balls about the size of marbles and place them on greased baking trays with a space between them to allow them to spread. Bake the fairings at 350°F, 180°C, gas mark 4 for ten minutes. Take the tray out of the oven and hit it on a solid surface to make the fairings crack and spread. Then put them back into the oven for another five minutes to finish baking.

Makes 15

GINGER SHORTIES

175 g/6 oz self-raising flour
4 level teaspoons ground ginger
100 g/4 oz butter
75 g/3 oz caster sugar
1 egg
2 tablespoons ginger marmalade
100 g/4 oz sifted icing sugar
Crystallised ginger

Sieve the flour with the ginger and rub in the butter. Add the sugar and enough beaten egg to bind the mixture together. Turn on to a lightly floured surface, divide mixture in half and knead lightly. Roll into two 18 cm/7 in circles to fit a shallow cake tin. Place one circle in the tin, spread over the ginger marmalade and then place the other circle on top. Bake at 350°F, 180°C, gas mark 4 for fifty minutes until golden-brown. Turn the shortcake on to a wire tray to cool. Stir a little water into the icing sugar, to make a soft icing. Pour on to the shortcake and decorate with pieces of ginger. Cut in wedges to serve.

Makes 8 wedges

SAVOURY HIGH TEA DISHES

COLD PRESSED BEEF

3.25 kg/7 lb salt beef brisket
2 carrots
1 onion
1 turnip
20 peppercorns
6 cloves

Peel or scrape the carrots, peel the onion and turnip, and cut up all the vegetables so that they are in even-sized pieces. Place them, with the salt brisket, peppercorns and cloves, in a thick-based saucepan of warm water and cook very slowly for six or seven hours, until the meat will come away from the bone and a fork pierces it easily. When the meat is tender, remove from the pan. Take out the bone carefully, put the meat into a cloth and pat it into a good shape. Press between two plates and tie together with string. Put very heavy weights on top of the plates and leave until next day.

Serves 20

CIDER-BAKED HAM

2–2.25 kg/4–5 lb ham in a piece
2 onions
3 carrots
3 sticks celery
12 cloves
Demerara sugar
300 ml/½ pint cider

Soak the ham in cold water overnight. Drain, and put into a pan with enough water to cover, and the vegetables cut into pieces. Simmer gently, allowing twenty-five minutes per 450 g/lb but subtracting forty minutes from the total. At the end of the time, remove the pan from the heat and leave for thirty minutes. Lift the ham from the liquid, place in a baking tin, remove the skin and stud the fat with the cloves. Spread thickly with Demerara sugar and pour the cider over the ham. Bake at 350°F, 180°C, gas mark 4 for forty minutes, basting three times with the cider during this period. Lift on to a rack to cool. Stand the rack on a dish and baste a further two or three times as the ham cools.

Serves 12

BUBBLE AND SQUEAK

450 g/1 lb cold boiled beef
1 cabbage
1 onion
1 carrot
50 g/2 oz butter
Salt and pepper
A little beef stock

The beef is best if slightly underdone. It should be cut in thin pieces. Boil the cabbage, onion and carrot until just tender. Drain very well, and mince finely. Melt the butter and put in the beef to warm, taking care it does not dry up. Remove the meat and put in the vegetables and cook them until very hot, moistening with a little stock. Add salt and pepper and dish the vegetables with the meat in a shallow dish, moistening with a little more stock.

Serves 4–6

Bubble and squeak is usually thought of as fried leftover vegetables, most often potatoes and cabbage or sprouts. The original dish always included boiled beef, either fresh or salt. This version comes from a handwritten family cookery book dated 1847.

POACHER'S ROLL

350 g/12 oz puff pastry
175 g/6 oz streaky bacon
450 g/1 lb pork sausagemeat
50 g/2 oz mushrooms
1 small onion
½ teaspoon chopped fresh sage
Salt and pepper

Beaten egg for glazing. Roll the pastry into a rectangle 32.5 × 25 cm/13 × 10 in. Chop the bacon finely and mix with the sausagemeat. Chop the mushrooms and onion finely and add to the meat with the sage and plenty of seasoning. Form into a fat sausage shape and place along the centre of the pastry. Fold over the pastry to enclose the meat and put join downwards on a baking sheet. Brush well with beaten egg. Bake at 425°F, 220°C, gas mark 7 for 20 minutes, then at 375°F, 190°C, gas mark 5 for 40 minutes. Serve hot or cold.

EGG AND APPLE BREAD

8 apples
50–75 g/2–3 oz butter
60 g/2½ oz granulated sugar
4–5 tablespoons water
3 eggs
3 tablespoons milk
8 slices bread
Bacon as required

Core the apples and cut them into half-inch slices without peeling them. Heat 25 g/1 oz butter and fry the apple rings golden-brown on one side. Sprinkle with sugar, turn, and fry. Sprinkle with water and simmer three minutes.

Heat the remaining butter in another frying pan.

Combine the eggs and milk and dip the bread slices in it. Fry the bread until light brown on both sides, turning once. To serve, place a slice of this fried French toast on each plate, top with equal portions of fried apples, and surround with hot, crisp bacon.

Serves 8

JELLIED BEEF

900 g/2 lb shin beef
225 g/8 oz bacon
Bunch of mixed fresh herbs
Pepper
Ground nutmeg
450 ml/¾ pint water or beef stock

Cut the beef into neat cubes. Remove the rinds from the bacon, but do not discard them. Chop the bacon and mix with the beef. Put into a casserole and arrange the bunch of herbs on top. Season well with pepper and nutmeg and pour in the water or stock. Arrange the bacon rinds on top. Cover and cook at 300°F, 150°C, gas mark 2 for 3 hours. Discard the herbs and bacon rinds. Spoon the beef, bacon and liquid into a 900 ml/1½ pint bowl and leave in a cold place for 24 hours before serving.

Serves 6–8

CRUMBLED BACON AND LETTUCE SALAD

2–3 round lettuces
A few small dandelion leaves
  (optional)
6 rashers lean rindless bacon, minced
3 tablespoons lemon juice
3 teaspoons granulated sugar
½ teaspoon salt
¼ teaspoon dry mustard

Separate and wash the leaves. Drain, dry thoroughly, and tear into shreds. Toss the minced bacon in a hot pan until crisp, then drain on soft kitchen paper.

Add the lemon juice, sugar, salt and mustard to the bacon fat remaining in the frying pan. Heat for 2–3 minutes, or until the sugar is dissolved. Arrange the lettuce leaves in a salad bowl, pour the hot dressing over, and toss gently.

Serve immediately, topped with the crumbled bacon.

Serves 4–6

YORKSHIRE PLOUGHMAN'S SALAD

1 lettuce
Small bunch of chives
1 saltspoon salt
1 saltspoon pepper
2 tablespoons vinegar
1 tablespoon black treacle

Wash the lettuce and drain and dry it well. Shred the lettuce and add it to the chives chopped very finely. Mix the salt, pepper, vinegar and treacle, and toss the lettuce and chives in this dressing.

Serves 3–4

JELLIED PORK LOAF

450 g/1 lb lean pork
450 g/1 lb pork sausagemeat
Salt and pepper
Pinch of ground nutmeg
½ teaspoon chopped fresh basil
½ teaspoon chopped fresh marjoram
600 ml/1 pint water
25 g/1 oz gelatine

Chop the pork finely and put into a saucepan with the sausagemeat. Season well with salt, pepper and nutmeg, and add the herbs and water. Bring to the boil, cover and simmer for 1 hour. Strain off the liquid. Put the gelatine with 2 tablespoons water into a cup and stand the cup in a small saucepan of hot water. Heat and stir until the gelatine is syrupy. Stir the gelatine into the cooking liquid and leave until cold. Skim off any fat and stir the meat mixture into the liquid. Pour into a 900 g/2 lb loaf tin or dish and leave until cold. Serve in slices with salad or in sandwiches.

Serves 4–6

CHAPTER EIGHT

MEALS IN THE FIELD

Solid packed meals are always needed in the country since workers are out in the fields at midday, and children often have a long, cold walk to school. Sportsmen, too, need easily-eaten, concentrated food; and picnic meals are popular for race meetings, agricultural shows and the like.

All such meals must be easy to carry, tasty and nourishing. Pies and pasties are always popular, and so are sandwiches filled with pressed or potted meats or herb-flavoured brawn. (These meats are also liked for High Tea when everyone comes home.) Often, the packed meal is completed with a hard-boiled egg, an apple, or a chunk of cheese with a wedge of gingerbread or rich fruit cake.

SPICED AND JELLIED MEATS

MEAT LOAF

225 g/8 oz ham
225 g/8 oz rump steak
100 g/4 oz soft white breadcrumbs
1 egg
Salt and pepper
¼ teaspoon mace
¼ teaspoon allspice
¼ teaspoon thyme

Mince the ham and beef, add the breadcrumbs and bind with the egg. Add salt and pepper, spices and thyme. Put into a greased 600 ml/1 pint basin covered with foil, and steam for three hours. This is very good to eat with cold poultry.

Serves 4–6

MIXED MEAT SAUSAGE SHAPE

450 g/1 lb beef sausage meat
450 g/1 lb pork sausage meat
450 g/1 lb cooked ham or tongue
1 dessertspoon chopped pickles
1 teaspoon mixed spice
Pinch of freshly-ground black pepper
1 tablespoon sweet stout
1 tablespoon Worcestershire sauce
Pinch of rosemary
Salt
Stock

Mix together the sausage meats and finely-chopped ham or tongue. Add pickles, spice, pepper, stout, Worcestershire sauce, rosemary and salt to taste. Tie in a cloth, and cook very slowly in stock for two hours. Lift out and press between two dishes under heavy weights until cold. This loaf can be used for sandwiches, or may be glazed when cold to serve with salad.

Serves 7–8

DORSET SAUSAGE

450 g/1 lb lean beef
450 g/1 lb bacon
175 g/6 oz soft white breadcrumbs
½ teaspoon ground nutmeg
½ teaspoon ground mace
2 eggs
Salt and pepper

Mince the beef and bacon together coarsely. Mix with all the other ingredients. Put into a damp cloth and tie up in a sausage shape. Bake the sausage in a tin at 350°F, 180°C, gas mark 4 for one and a half hours. Remove from the oven and leave until cold under weights. The sausage may be finished with a light aspic glaze, or it may be scattered with crisp brown breadcrumbs.

Serves 6

LIVER LOAF

225 g/8 oz liver
50 g/2 oz rindless streaky bacon
100 g/4 oz pork sausage meat
1 medium-sized onion
50 g/2 oz soft white breadcrumbs
1 teaspoon Worcestershire sauce
1 egg
150 ml/¼ pint water
Salt and pepper

Fry the liver lightly in a little butter or bacon fat. Put the liver through a coarse mincer with the bacon and onion. Mix with the sausage meat, breadcrumbs, sauce, egg and seasoning. Add enough of the water to make a soft mixture. Put into a greased loaf tin or terrine and cover with a lid or foil. Bake at 400°F, 200°C, gas mark 6 for forty-five minutes. Cool and serve in slices. A little sage is nice added to this mixture if the sausage meat is not highly seasoned.

Serves 4

PRESSED CHICKEN

1.75 kg/4 lb chicken
1 medium carrot
1 medium onion
1 bunch fresh mixed herbs
Salt and pepper

Put the chicken and giblets (except liver) into a pan and cover with water. Add the peeled carrot, onion and herbs. Bring to the boil, skim, cover and simmer for 2–3 hours until the meat is ready to fall from the bones. Leave the chicken to cool in the liquid, and then remove to a plate. Remove skin and bones and return to the saucepan. Take the chicken flesh from the bones in small pieces and put into a bowl or 900 g/2 lb loaf tin.

Bring the cooking liquid to the boil and then simmer until reduced by half. Strain and season well with salt and pepper. Pour over the chicken flesh and stir until well mixed. Leave in a cold place until set and firm. Cut in slices to serve.

LINCOLNSHIRE HASLET

900 g/2 lb lean pork
1 small onion
225 g/8 oz stale bread
15 g/½ oz salt
1 teaspoon white pepper
1 teaspoon sage, chopped

Mince the meat coarsely with the onion. Cut the bread into cubes and soak in a little water. Squeeze out the moisture, and mix the bread with the meat. Season with the salt and pepper and the finely chopped sage. Put into a loaf tin or casserole, and bake at 350°F, 180°C, gas mark 4 for one hour. Cool in the tin or casserole before turning out. Cut in slices to serve with salad, or use in sandwiches.

Serves 6

BACON AND MUSHROOM LOAF

1 small 'tin' loaf white bread
100 g/4 oz butter
4 rashers back bacon
225 g/8 oz chicken livers
100 g/4 oz mushrooms
1 small onion
Salt and pepper

Cut a 'lid' from the bread and keep on one side. Scoop out the soft centre and save the bread to make crumbs for another dish. Leave about 3.75 cm/1½ in wall all round the loaf. Melt 75 g/3 oz butter and fry the outside of the loaf and lid until crisp and golden, and leave to cool. Chop the bacon, chicken livers, mushrooms and onion finely.

Add the remaining butter to any fat left in the frying pan and cook the bacon for 1 minute. Add the onion and cook until transparent. Add chicken livers and mushrooms. Season well with salt and pepper and cook for 3 minutes, stirring well. Pack the mixture into the loaf, including all the cooking juices. Wrap in foil and chill for 2 hours. Cut into slices to serve.

Serves 4

SHOOTING SANDWICH

1 sandwich loaf
1 large thick rump steak
100 g/4 oz mushrooms
Salt and pepper
50 g/2 oz butter

Cut off one end of the loaf and scoop out the centre of the soft crumb, leaving a 'wall' of crumb at top and bottom. Grill the steak medium rare. Chop the mushrooms coarsely, season well and cook in the butter until just soft. Put the steak into the loaf and top with the mushrooms and butter. Put back the end crust, and wrap the loaf in greaseproof paper and then in foil. Tie into a parcel with string and then put under heavy weights for 6 hours. Carry out in the foil and do not unwrap and slice.

SUFFOLK OXTAIL BRAWN

1 oxtail
25 g/1 oz butter
1 onion
3 cloves
Bunch of mixed herbs
Salt and pepper
3 tablespoons vinegar
1 hard-boiled egg, sliced

Wash the oxtail and cut it into joints. Dry it well and dust it lightly with a little flour. Melt the butter and fry the oxtail, turning it so that it is brown all over. Add the onion stuck with the cloves, the bunch of herbs, salt and pepper and the vinegar, and cover with cold water. Bring to the boil and simmer for four hours until the meat leaves the bones. Cool slightly and then chop the meat. Grease a mould lightly with butter and decorate it with slices of hard-boiled egg. Put the meat into this mould. Return the oxtail bones to the saucepan and boil rapidly until the liquid is reduced to 300 ml/½ pint. Cool slightly and then fill the mould. Turn out when cold.

Serves 6

MEAT PIES AND PASTIES

SAUSAGE AND EGG ROLL

450 g/1 lb pork sausage meat
225 g/8 oz shortcrust pastry
2 hard-boiled eggs, chopped
3 shallots
Sage, salt and pepper
Grated Double Gloucester cheese

Press sausage meat flat on a floured board or table. Cover with chopped hard-boiled egg and finely-chopped shallot. Sprinkle with some dried or fresh sage and season to taste. Roll up as for a Swiss roll. Roll out the pastry and put the sausage in the middle. Bring up the sides and seal well. Brush with milk and pat on some grated cheese. Bake at 400°F, 200°C, gas mark 6 for about forty-five minutes.

Serves 6

HAND-RAISED PORK PIE

350 g/12 oz self-raising flour
½ teaspoon salt
100 g/4 oz lard
150 ml/¼ pint water
1 egg

Filling
575 g/1¼ lb shoulder pork
½ teaspoon powdered sage
Salt and pepper

Jelly
450 g/1 lb pork bones or a trotter
1.1 litre/2 pints water
1 onion
Seasoning
1 teaspoon gelatine

Sieve the flour and salt into a bowl. Boil the lard and the water in a pan. When dissolved, pour into the centre of the flour while hot. Work all together until a smooth dough is obtained. Cut off a third of the dough and reserve for the lid. Work the remainder on a floured board, gradu-ally moulding to form a bowl shape. (A cake tin can be used as a guide.) Put on a greased baking sheet and fill the centre with the diced pork, sage and seasoning. Roll out the reserved third for the lid, brush edges of the pie with beaten egg and seal on the lid. Use trimmings to form leaves for decoration. Make a hole in the top and brush the pie all over with the egg. Bake at 400°F, 200°C, gas mark 6 for thirty minutes, then reduce heat to 350°F, 180°C, gas mark 4 for a further one and a half hours. Make a jelly from the bones, water, onion and seasoning by boil-ing for about two hours. Strain, and add the dissolved gelatine. Allow to cool but not set. Pour enough into the hole in the lid when the pie is cool to fill it; leave to set before cutting.

Serves 6

CORNISH PASTIES

450 g/1 lb plain flour
1 teaspoon salt
175 g/6 oz lard
4 tablespoons finely-grated suet
Water to mix
2 large potatoes
1 small turnip
1 onion
350 g/12 oz lean chopped chuck steak
Salt and pepper

Mix the flour and salt, rub in the lard and add the suet. Mix to a stiff paste with water, and roll out to quarter-inch thickness. Cut into six rounds, using a 16.25 cm/6½ in plate to cut the size. Slice the potatoes, turnip and onion finely, and place a mixture down the centre of each round, sea-soning well. On top put the chopped meat. Damp the edge of each round, and close each pasty across the top, sealing the edges firmly. Pinch the edges between finger and thumb to give a fluted top. Put on a baking sheet and bake in a very hot oven, 450°F, 230°C, gas mark 8 for ten minutes. Reduce heat to moderate, 350°F, 180°C, gas mark 4 and continue cooking until the meat is tender (about forty-five minutes).

Serves 6

CORNISH PASTY

Shortcrust pastry
100 g/4 oz plain flour
50 g/2 oz fat
Pinch of salt
Water to mix to a firm dough

Filling
Potato, finely sliced (not diced)
Onion and/or turnip, finely cut
100 g/4 oz chuck or skirk steak
Seasoning

Roll pastry into four rounds. Pile up sliced potato on about half the pastry. Put onion and/or turnip on potato. Cut meat in small pieces and spread over. Season with salt and pepper. Place a few thin pieces of potato on top to save the meat drying. Damp edges of pastry. Fold over to semi-circle and crimp edges. (Crimp by pinching the pastry with the left hand and fold over with right hand, forming a rope-like effect on the side of the pastry.) Place on an unfloured baking sheet and bake at 425°F, 220°C, gas mark 7 for 10–15 minutes; reduce the heat to 350°F, 180°C, gas mark 4 for a further thirty minutes.

Serves 4

SAUSAGE AND ONION PIE

225 g/8 oz shortcrust pastry
225 g/8 oz sausage meat
1 onion
1 egg, beaten
Mixed herbs

Roll out the pastry and cut into two circles to fit a 17.5 cm/7 in pie plate. Line the plate with one round of pastry. Mix the sausage meat, chopped onion, beaten egg and plenty of chopped fresh herbs. Cover with the pastry lid. Bake at 425°F, 220°C, gas mark 7 for thirty minutes.

Serves 4

BACON PASTIES

350 g/12 oz shortcrust pastry
225 g/8 oz minced raw steak
175 g/6 oz rindless streaky bacon
100 g/4 oz lamb's kidneys
1 large onion
Salt and pepper
½ teaspoon Worcestershire sauce
Egg for glazing

Roll out the pastry and cut out six 17.5 cm/7 in rounds. Chop the bacon, kidney and onion, and mix with the steak, seasoning and sauce. Put mixture on half of each round and fold over pastry. Pinch edges together. Put on to a wet baking sheet. Bake at 425°F, 220°C, gas mark 7 for fifteen minutes; then at 350°F, 180°C, gas mark 4 for forty-five minutes. Serve hot or cold.

Serves 6

BACON AND EGG PIE

175 g/6 oz shortcrust pastry
4 thick lean rindless bacon rashers
4 eggs
Salt and pepper
Beaten egg

Line a 17.5 cm/7 in sponge tin with pastry, leaving enough for a lid. Cut the bacon into small pieces and arrange them in the tin. Break the four eggs on top of the bacon, leaving them whole. Season with salt and pepper and cover with the remaining pastry. Brush the pastry well with milk or a little beaten egg. Bake at 400°F, 200°C, gas mark 6 for ten minutes. Lower heat to 350°F, 180°C, gas mark 4 for thirty minutes. A little chopped parsley is a pleasant addition to this pie.

Serves 4

CHICKEN AND EGG PIE

*1.4–1.5 kg/3–3½ lb roasting or boiling
  chicken
300 ml/½ pint water
1 bay leaf
Salt and pepper
25 g/1 oz butter
1 onion
175 g/6 oz button mushrooms
1 teaspoon mixed herbs
4 hard-boiled eggs*

*275 g/10 oz plain flour
¼ teaspoon salt
60 g/2½ oz butter
60 g/2½ oz lard
3–4 tablespoons water
Beaten egg for glazing*

Place the chicken in a pan with water, bay leaf and seasoning. Bring slowly to the boil, cover tightly and simmer very gently until the meat is tender; it will take fifty minutes if using a roasting chicken, or two and a half hours if using a boiling chicken. Remove the chicken meat from the carcass and chop it roughly. Skim the fat from the pan, remove the bay leaf and reserve the stock. Melt the butter in a pan and fry the chopped onion gently for five minutes. Add the chopped mushrooms and cook for a further two minutes. Add the chicken meat and herbs, and season to taste. Cool.

For the pastry, sift together the flour and the salt and rub in the fats until the mixture resembles fine breadcrumbs. Add the water and mix to a firm dough. Turn on to a floured surface, and knead lightly until smooth. Roll out into a circle approximately 28 cm/13 in diameter. Cut out a section representing quarter of the circle and reserve for the lid. Line a round cake tin 18 cm/7 in diameter and 7.5 cm/3 in deep with the larger piece of pastry, joining cut edges. Spoon half of the chicken mixture into the tin the press down.

Arrange the hard-boiled eggs on top and cover

with the remaining chicken mixture, pressing it down between the eggs to fill the spaces. Spoon over four tablespoons of the chicken stock. Damp the edges of the pastry. Roll out the remaining pastry for the lid and cover the pie. Trim off excess pastry, press edges together and flute. Roll out trimmings and cut leaves to decorate centre of pie. Brush with glaze and make a hole in the centre of the pie. Bake at 400°F, 200°C, gas mark 6 for thirty minutes. Reduce heat to 350°F, 180°C, gas mark 4 for a further thirty minutes. Leave to cool in the tin. Remove from the tin and pour stock through the hole in the centre until the pie is full. Leave to set.

Serves 6

PASTIES WITH FRUIT

APPLE TURNOVERS

*350 g/12 oz shortcrust or flaky pastry
675 g/1½ lb cooking apples
4 tablespoons light soft brown sugar
25 g/1 oz raisins
50 g/2 oz butter*

Roll out the pastry and cut into six 10 cm/4 in circles (cut round a saucer for the shape). Peel and slice the apples and cook gently with the sugar, raisins and butter until soft. If you like a pinch of cloves or cinnamon, add them during the cooking. Put a spoonful of mixture on to half of each circle, fold over and press edges together, damping them a little first. Bake at 425°F, 220°C, gas mark 7 for twenty-five minutes.

Makes 6

BEDFORDSHIRE CLANGER

For the savoury filling
1 small onion, finely-chopped
1 tablespoon lard
225 g/8 oz minced pork
1 teaspoon dried sage
1 cooking apple, peeled, cored and
* chopped*
50 g/2 oz cooked peas
Seasoning

For the sweet filling
2 dessert apples, cored and chopped
Grated rind and juice of one orange
2 tablespoons caster sugar
50 g/2 oz stoned dates, chopped
50 g/2 oz sultanas

For the covering
450 g/1 lb shortcrust pastry
1 egg, beaten
Granulated or crushed lump sugar

This is an old 'packed meal' containing both a savour and a sweet filling; it was taken by the men to the fields when the work was too heavy or too far from home for them to return at midday.

First make the savoury filling. Fry the chopped onion in the lard until soft. Add the pork and sage and cook gently for ten minutes, stirring often. Add the chopped apple after five minutes. Stir in the peas after ten minutes and remove from the heat. Leave aside. Make the sweet filling by mixing all the ingredients together thoroughly.

Roll out the pastry and cut into two 25 cm/10 in circles. Using trimmings, cut a 25 cm/10 in strip or roll of pastry and lay it across the centre of one circle. Make it hold with a little beaten egg. Brush the edge of the circle with beaten egg likewise. Hold the pastry circle with both hands grasping the ends of the dividing roll. Lift the two edges and pinch together, pinching the dividing roll too, to make a wall of pastry across the centre of the pastry. Fill one side with half the savoury filling, the other side with half the sweet filling. Pinch the pastry edges firmly over them, forming a conventional pasty shape. Glaze with beaten egg, and sprinkle with sugar. Make a second pasty in the same way, and bake at 425°F, 220°C, gas mark 7 for 15–20 minutes or until crisp and golden.

Serves 2

BUCKINGHAMSHIRE CHERRY BUMPERS

450 g/1 lb black cherries
75 g/3 oz sugar
225 g/8 oz shortcrust pastry

Stone the cherries and sprinkle them with sugar. Roll out the pastry about 5 mm/¼ thick. Cut into four 10 cm/4 in rounds. Heap the centre of each with cherries. Damp the edges of the pastry, fold them over and seal them by pinching together with the fingers. Bake at 400°F, 200°C, gas mark 6 for twenty-five minutes. Dredge with sugar.

Serves 4

OLD-FASHIONED

PUDDINGS

Country families have always been fond of sweet puddings to follow their main meat, poultry or fish dish. These puddings serve a double purpose, providing sweetness which gives energy for heavy outdoor work, and also adding bulk to an often frugal main course. The ingredients most commonly used are those which are always to hand in the country – flour, bread, suet, milk and cream, soft fruit in season, or easily-stored apples and pears. Spices, dried fruits and home-made jams from the store cupboard provide a little extra sparkle for the simple recipes.

Steamed puddings, batters and pastry tarts and pies are the popular hot sweets; cool creams, fools and flummeries provide a delicious ending to lighter summer meals.

PUDDINGS USUALLY SERVED HOT

APPLE-SAUCE PUDDING

100 g/4 oz butter
75 g/3 oz light soft brown sugar
3 tablespoons thick unsweetened apple
  sauce or purée
1 egg
175 g/5 oz self-raising flour
1 teaspoon bicarbonate of soda
1 teaspoon ground cinnamon
75 g/3 oz sultanas
75 g/3 oz chopped dates

Cream together the butter and brown sugar until light and fluffy. Beat in the egg and apple sauce. Stir in the dry ingredients and the dried fruit to make a thick batter. Turn into a greased 1.1 litre/2 pint pudding dish and bake at 350°F, 180°C, gas mark 4 for one hour. Serve with custard or cream.

Serves 4–6

UNCLE TOBY

175 g/6 oz white breadcrumbs
75 g/3 oz unsalted butter
100 g/4 oz caster sugar
600 ml/1 pint creamy milk
2 eggs
Grated rind of 1 lemon
5 tablespoons medium sherry

Put the breadcrumbs into a large bowl. Cut the butter into thin flakes and mix with the crumbs and sugar. Bring the milk to the boil and pour over the crumbs. Mix well and leave until just cold. Beat the eggs, lemon rind and sherry together and beat them into the crumb mixture. Pour into a greased 900 ml/1½ pint pie dish and bake at 350°F, 180°C, gas mark 4 for 40 minutes. Serve hot or cold with pouring cream.

Serves 4–5

BAKEWELL PUDDING

225 g/8 oz puff pastry
Strawberry jam
100 g/4 oz butter
175 g/6 oz caster sugar
Yolks of 5 eggs
Whites of 3 eggs
Almond essence

Line an 18 cm/7 in flan ring or baking tin with the pastry, and spread with jam. Melt together the butter and sugar, and mix in the egg yolks and whites and the essence. Bake at 375°F, 190°C, gas mark 5 for about twenty-five minutes.

Serves 4–6

BROWN BREAD PUDDING

175 g/6 oz brown breadcrumbs
300 ml/½ pint milk
*50 g/2 oz raisins (or chopped candied
   peel)*
Grating of nutmeg
1 teaspoon cinnamon
Pinch of salt
75 g/3 oz butter
100 g/4 oz sugar
3 eggs

Put the breadcrumbs in a bowl and pour on the hot milk. Add the spices, raisins, and salt. Cream the butter and sugar, and add the eggs one at a time. Gradually work in the breadcrumb mixture. Put into a well-buttered 900 ml/1½ pint mould, cover with foil or buttered paper and steam for two hours. Serve with jam, fruit syrup or custard.

Serves 4–6

FULBOURN APPLE PUDDING

225 g/8 oz self-raising flour
Pinch of salt
100 g/4 oz shredded suet
6 large eating apples
50 g/2 oz butter
Grated rind of one lemon
175 g/6 oz sugar
225 g/8 oz apricot jam

Sift the flour and salt together. Stir in the suet and mix with enough cold water to make a firm dough. Roll out this dough and line a 900 ml/1½ pint pudding basin, leaving enough for a lid. Peel and core the apples and cut them into slices. Put them into a saucepan with the butter, lemon rind, sugar and jam and heat gently until the apples soften but do not break up. Cool, then put the apple mixture into the pudding basin. Cover with a lid of the suet pastry and cover with greased paper and foil. Steam for two hours. (This recipe is about 150 years old, but has been slightly adapted to suit modern ingredients. In the original recipe, the method of cooking apples was also recommended when making Apple Charlotte, or serving apples with rice or whipped cream.)

Serves 4–6

COTTAGE PUDDING

60 g/2½ oz shredded suet
225 g/8 oz plain flour
100 g/4 oz seeded raisins
100 g/4 oz sugar
½ tablespoon cream of tartar
Pinch of salt
4 tablespoons milk
¼ teaspoon bicarbonate of soda
1 egg

Mix the suet, flour, raisins, sugar, cream of tartar and salt together. Dissolve the soda in the milk, add it to the well-beaten egg, mix well, and stir into the dry ingredients. The mixture must be rather stiff. Turn into a greased roasting tin, and bake at 350°F, 180°C, gas mark 4 for forty minutes. Cut the pudding into squares, and serve, after dusting it over with white sugar.

Serves 4–6

DRIPPING PUDDING

150 g/5 oz plain flour
1 dessertspoon baking powder
75 g/3 oz caster sugar
75 g/3 oz dripping
1 egg
150 ml/¼ pint milk
Jam or stiffly-whipped egg white

Sift together the flour and baking powder, and stir in the sugar. Mix in the dripping with your fingers until it is well blended with the flour and sugar. Stir in the beaten egg and milk and pour into a greased 600 ml/1 pint pie dish. Bake at 350°F, 180°C, gas mark 4 for forty-five minutes. To serve, cover with jam, or with stiffly-whipped egg white quickly browned in the oven.

Serves 4

DORSET STIR-IN PUDDING

450 g/1 lb self-raising flour
200 g/7 oz lard
½ teaspoon salt
225 g/8 oz sugar
350 g/12 oz fresh fruit
Milk

Rub together the flour, salt and lard to make fine crumbs. Stir in the sugar. Stir in prepared gooseberries, chopped apple, halved plums or chopped rhubarb. Mix with sufficient milk and water to make a soft dough which will drop easily into a greased 1.1 litre/2 pint basin. Cover with greased paper, then foil. Steam for two hours. Serve with fresh cream or smooth, creamy custard.

Serves 6

SUSSEX POND PUDDING

450 g/1 lb plain flour
225 g/8 oz shredded suet
½–1 teaspoon salt
1 egg, mixed with milk (or plain cold water)
1 lemon
75 g–100 g/3–4 oz Demerara sugar
Pinch each grated nutmeg and ground allspice
½ tablespoon firm, chilled butter

Sift the flour into a basin, add the suet, salt, a little grated lemon rind and 2–3 teaspoons of the sugar. Make a well in the centre of the mixture, trickle in the egg and milk or water, and work with the hand into a soft dough. Place the dough in a greased 1.1 litre/2 pint pudding basin, and make a hole in the centre with your fist. Work the dough up the sides, so that there is plenty of room in the hole; then place in it the lemon cut in quarters, the sugar and spice and the butter cut in flakes. Close up the hole, make sure that the dough seals it over completely without cracks. Have ready a large saucepan two-thirds full of boiling water. Cover and seal the basin,

and boil for 2–2½ hours. Serve with a lemon-flavoured custard, or a sauce of hot golden syrup flavoured with lemon juice.

Serves 6

HAMPSHIRE SIX-CUP PUDDING

100 g/4 oz self-raising flour
100 g/4 oz soft white breadcrumbs
100 g/4 oz suet
175 g/6 oz brown sugar
250 ml/8 fl oz milk
100 g/4 oz mixed raisins, sultanas and currants
1 teaspoon bicarbonate of soda

Mix all the dry ingredients together except the bicarbonate of soda. Warm the milk and dissolve the bicarbonate of soda in it. Leave to cool. Add the milk to the other ingredients. Place in a greased 1.1 litre/2 pint bowl and steam for four hours.

Serves 6

GOOSEBERRY PUDDING

225 g/8 oz self-raising flour
Pinch of salt
100 g/4 oz shredded suet
25 g/1 oz butter
450 g/1 lb gooseberries
100 g/4 oz sugar

Rub the suet and butter into the flour and salt and add enough cold water to make a firm dough. Roll out the dough and line a greased 900 ml/1½ pint pudding basin, leaving enough for the lid. Top and tail the gooseberries and fill the basin, adding the sugar. Cover with the suet pastry lid and seal the edges. Cover with greased paper and foil, and steam for two and a half hours. Turn out and serve with cream or custard. This pudding is particularly good served with hot apricot jam and cream.

Serves 6

OLD-FASHIONED RHUBARB PUDDING

25 g/1 oz butter
Light soft brown sugar
225 g/8 oz self-raising flour
1 teaspoon salt
75 g/3 oz suet
150 ml/¼ pint water
675 g/1½ lb young rhubarb
25 g/1 oz chopped candied peel
50 g/2 oz currants
Rind and juice of half lemon
100 g/4 oz sugar
Pinch of ground cinnamon
75 ml/3 fl oz water

Butter a 1.1 litre/2 pint pudding basin thickly and sprinkle plentifully with brown sugar. Make a suet crust by sieving together the flour and salt and working in the suet and water. Knead the pastry until smooth and cut off one-third pastry for lid. Line the basin with the larger portion of suet crust pastry. Cut the rhubarb into 2.5 cm/ 1 in pieces and put half into the basin. Sprinkle over the peel, currants, lemon rind and juice, half the sugar, and the cinnamon. Add the rest of the rhubarb and sugar, and pour in the water. Cover with a suet crust lid, and a greased paper on top. Bake at 350°F, 180°C, gas mark 4 for one and a quarter hours. Turn out to serve, and hand round cream or egg custard.

Serves 6

KENTISH WELL PUDDING

225 g/8 oz plain flour
1 teaspoon baking powder
Pinch of salt
100 g/4 oz suet
Milk or water to mix
100–175 g/4–6 oz dried fruit
75 g/3 oz butter
100 g/4 oz light soft brown sugar

Mix all the dry ingredients and mix to an elastic dough with milk or water. Turn on to a floured board and roll into a neat round about nine inches wide. Take the butter and brown sugar and place in the middle of the pastry. Gather the edges together at the top and make secure. Tie in a cloth or place in a greased basin and boil for two hours. Serve on a large dish deep enough to catch the filling which comes out once the pudding has been cut.

Serves 4

PANCAKES

100 g/4 oz plain flour
Pinch of salt
300 ml/½ pint milk
2 eggs
Sugar
Lemon wedges

Sift flour and salt, and beat in milk and egg lightly. Beat with a fork till the mixture bubbles. Heat a frying pan well greased with lard and pour in a little batter. Tilt the frying pan at various angles quickly, to spread the batter all over the pan's bottom. Cook till light brown underneath, then turn and cook briefly on the other side. Lift on to a plate and fold in three like an envelope or lay flat with a circle of greasproof paper on top. Keep warm while you cook the rest of the pancakes. If folded, serve at once with lemon wedges and sugar. If flat, the pancakes can wait in a warm (not hot) oven if an extra one is stacked on top and discarded before serving. Pancakes also freeze perfectly if packed flat between paper circles.

Serves 4

BAK⋯HERRY BATTER

450 g/1 lb black cherries
100 g/4 oz sugar
50 g/2 oz plain flour
3 tablespoons milk
50 g/2 oz caster sugar
150 ml/¼ pint double or clotted cream
Pinch of mace
Grated rind of one lemon
3 eggs

Simmer the cherries with the sugar and a little water until tender. Cool and take out the cherry stones. Mix the flour, milk, sugar, cream and mace and heat to lukewarm. Add the beaten egg yolks and lemon rind. Whisk the egg whites stiffly and fold into the mixture. Butter a 1.1 litre/2 pint ovenproof dish and put in a layer of cherries. Add a layer of batter and then more cherries. Continue the layers until the dish is full. Cover with a piece of greased paper or foil and bake at 350°F, 180°C, gas mark 4 for forty-five minutes. Sprinkle with caster sugar and serve hot with cream or egg custard.

Serves 6

CHERRY BATTER PUDDING (BOILED)

3 tablespoons plain flour
600 ml/1 pint milk
25 g/1 oz butter
2 eggs
Pinch of salt
450 g/1 lb black cherries

Put the flour into a bowl and mix to a smooth paste with a little of the milk. Gradually work in the remaining milk, melted butter, lightly-beaten eggs and salt. When the mixture is smooth, stir in the stoned cherries. Put into a buttered basin and cover with foil, greaseproof paper or a cloth. Put into a pan of boiling water, and boil for two hours. Serve quickly, sprinkled with caster sugar.

Serves 4–6

YORKSHIRE SUMMER BATTER

150 g/5 oz plain flour
600 ml/1 pint milk
2 eggs
100 g/4 oz sugar
225 g/8 oz summer fruit
   (blackcurrants, redcurrants,
   gooseberries or raspberries)

Mix the flour smoothly with 150 ml/¼ pint milk. Boil the remaining milk and add this gradually to the flour mixture. Return to the pan, and boil the mixture for five minutes, stirring all the time. Leave until lukewarm, then beat in the eggs and sugar. Beat thoroughly and stir in the fresh fruit. Put into a buttered 1.1 litre/2 pint pudding basin. Cover with greaseproof paper, and foil or a pudding cloth. Put into a saucepan of boiling water, and boil for one and a half hours. Turn out and sprinkle with sugar. Serve with cream or custard.

Serves 4

NORTHALLERTON BATTER PUDDING

100 g/4 oz plain flour
1 egg
1 tablespoon caster sugar
300 ml/½ pint milk
2 drops vanilla essence
25 g/1 oz lard

Sieve the flour into a mixing bowl. Make a well in the centre, add the egg and sugar and gradually beat the egg into the flour, adding a little milk to make a smooth paste. Add the vanilla essence and beat in the remining milk until small bubbles rise to the surface. Leave to stand for thirty minutes. Heat the lard in a baking dish until smoking, add batter and bake at 425°F, 220°C, gas mark 7 for thirty minutes. Serve with golden syrup and cream.

Serves 4

NORFOLK APPLE PIE

350 g/12 oz shortcrust pastry
900 g/2 lb cooking apples
25 g/1 oz butter
1 tablespoon granulated sugar
2 tablespoons orange marmalade
1 tablespoons currants

Line a deep 20 cm/8 in pie plate with half the pastry. Peel, core and slice the apples and cook them without any water, adding the small knob of butter to prevent burning. When they are soft, stir in the sugar and beat them to a pulp. Pour half of this into the pastry case, spread the marmalade over, and sprinkle on the currants. Spread the remaining apple pulp on the top. Make a lid from the other piece of pastry and put on top. Trim and decorate the edges. Bake at 400°F, 200°C, gas mark 6 for fifteen minutes, then reduce heat to 350°F, 180°C, gas mark 4 for twenty-five minutes more.

Serves 6

COUNTRY GRAPE PIE

225 g/8 oz shortcrust pastry
450 g/1 lb small, tart green grapes
150 g/5 oz caster sugar
3 tablespoons flour
1 tablespoon lemon juice
1 tablespoon unsalted butter

Use half the pastry or a little more to line a 20 cm/8 in greased pie plate. Halve the grapes and take out the pips with a knife-point. Mix half the flour and sugar together; sprinkle the bottom of the pastry shell with the remaining flour, then scatter over it the flour and sugar mixed. Mix the grapes and lemon juice and fill the shell. Mound them high since they shrink in cooking. Cover with the remaining sugar and flakes of butter. Cover with the remaining pastry. If you like, reserve a little sugar to sprinkle on the outside crust. Bake at 350°F, 180°C, gas mark 4 for 20–30 minutes until the

pastry is 'set' and golden. Serve hot with single cream or custard.

If this seems a curious recipe for a farmhouse, remember that in the past many great houses had their own vines. Small tart fruit were picked off to give the remainder room and strength, and, if not wanted for making a flavouring or pickles, were thrown away or given to the farm hands for sweet dishes. Many a cottage garden had its own vine too, and used the fruit for the same purposes.

Serves 6

RAISED GOOSEBERRY PIE

Make this unusual pie exactly like a raised pork pie, using the same pastry but slightly sweetened instead of with salt and pepper seasoning. Fill it with well-drained green gooseberries. When baked and cooled, fill with warmed melted apple jelly and allow to cool again completely before serving. It can then be cut like a pork pie.

OATMEAL RAISIN PIE

350 g/12 oz shortcrust pastry
2 tablespoons oatmeal
2 tablespoons black treacle
75 g/3 oz raisins

Roll out the pastry thinly and use half to line an 18 cm/7 in pie plate. Cover with the oatmeal and pour on the treacle. Sprinkle the raisins evenly over the tart. Moisten the edges of the tart with water and cover with the rest of the pastry. Press the edges together to seal, and trim off any surplus pastry. Flute the edges. Bake at 425°F, 220°C, gas mark 7 for twenty-five minutes. Serve hot or cold.

Serves 6

TREACLE CUSTARD PIE

175 g/6 oz shortcrust pastry
1 dessertspoon coarse semolina or
*   rolled oats*
1 tablespoon black treacle
300 ml/½ pint milk
2 eggs
25 g/1 oz caster sugar

Roll out the pastry and with it line a 18 cm/7 in heatproof pie plate. Sprinkle the base with semolina or oats, then pour in the treacle. Combine the milk and eggs and beat until well blended. Stir in the sugar, then pour the custard into the lined pie plate. Bake in the centre of the oven at 425°F, 220°C, gas mark 7 for ten minutes; then at 325°F, 170°C, gas mark 3 for thirty minutes.

Serves 6

NORFOLK MARROW TART

225 g/8 oz shortcrust pastry
50 g/2 oz jam
450 g/1 lb vegetable marrow
1 egg
Pinch of ground nutmeg
1½ tablespoons sugar

Line an 18 cm/7 in flan tin with the pastry, keeping the trimmings to decorate the top of the tart. Spread with a thin layer of jam. Boil the marrow until soft, and place in a colander to remove all the liquid. When cold, add a well-beaten egg, and nutmeg. Beat together with a fork and put in the bottom of the flan. Sprinkle a little more nutmeg over the top. Decorate with strips of pastry. Bake at 400°F, 200°C, gas mark 6 for 10–15 minutes until turning brown. Continue at 350°F, 180°C, gas mark 4 for ten minutes until the pastry is golden. Serve hot or cold.

Serves 6

NORFOLK TREACLE TART

175 g/6 oz shortcrust pastry
1 egg
2 tablespoons golden syrup
Rind and juice of half lemon

Line an 18 cm/7 in pie plate with the pastry. Beat the egg lightly until mixed. Warm the syrup and beat the egg into it, and add the lemon rind and juice. Pour this mixture into the pastry case and bake at 375°F, 190°C, gas mark 5 for thirty-five minutes. Eat cold.

Serves 6

MARMALADE TART

225 g/8 oz puff pastry
50 g/2 oz butter
50 g/2 oz sugar
1 egg
2 tablespoons marmalade

Line an 18 cm/7 in dish with the pastry. Cream together the butter, sugar, well beaten egg and marmalade, and fill the pastry case. Bake at 375°F, 190°C, gas mark 5 for thirty-five minutes.

Serves 6

KENTISH APPLE TART

175 g/6 oz shortcrust pastry
2 large cooking apples
75 g/3 oz sugar
1 egg
50 g/2 oz softened butter
Rind and juice of one lemon

Line an 18 cm/7 in pie plate with the pastry. Peel the apples, and grate the flesh into a basin. Add the sugar, beaten egg, butter, lemon rind and juice and mix well. Put this mixture into the pastry case and bake at 375°F, 190°C, gas mark 5 for thirty-five minutes.

Serves 6

MATRIMONY CAKE

225 g/8 oz shortcrust pastry
4 tablespoons brown breadcrumbs
4 large apples
50 g/2 oz mixed raisins and currants
½ teaspoon mixed ginger and nutmeg
Juice of one lemon
2 tablespoons sugar
2 tablespoons golden syrup
1 large slice lemon

Line a greased 20 cm/8 in flan ring with half the pastry. Put the breadcrumbs on the bottom of the pastry case. Peel and core the apples and cut them in rings. Put the apple rings into the pastry case and cover with the remaining ingredients, putting the lemon slice on top. Cover with the remaining pastry. Brush with milk and bake at 350°F, 180°C, gas mark 4 for forty-five minutes until golden-brown. Eat hot with thick cream.

Serves 6

BAKED APPLE DUMPLINGS

225 g/8 oz shortcrust pastry
4 small cooking apples
25 g/1 oz raisins
20 g/¾ oz light soft brown sugar
20 g/¾ oz butter
¼ teaspoon ground cinnamon

Roll out the pastry and cut four circles round a saucer. Peel and core the apples and put one in the centre of each piece of pastry. Fill the centre of the apples with a mixture of raisins, sugar, butter and cinnamon. Enclose the apples completely in pastry and invert on to a baking sheet.

Brush the pastry with egg or milk and bake at 425°F, 220°C gas mark 7 for twenty-five minutes. Sprinkle with caster sugar as they come out of the oven, and serve hot or cold with cream.

Serves 4

FEN COUNTRY APPLE CAKE

675 g/1½ lb cooking apples
Juice of half lemon
25 g/1 oz butter
50 g/2 oz caster sugar
2 rounded tablespoons semolina
225 g/8 oz shortcrust or puff pastry
25 g/1 oz currants
3 tablespoons black treacle

Peel, core and slice the apples. Put apples, lemon juice and butter into a pan, cover, and simmer slowly until pulpy. Add sugar and semolina, and bring slowly to the boil. Cook gently for five minutes or until the mixture has thickened. Remove from the heat and leave until completely cold. Divide the pastry into two pieces. Roll out one portion and with it line an 18 cm/7 in heatproof plate. Spread with half the apple-filling to within 1.25 cm/½ in of edges. Sprinkle with currants and add treacle, and then top with the remaining filling. Roll out the rest of pastry into an 20–22.5 cm/8 in round, moisten edges with water and cover the pie. Press the edges well together to seal, and knock up with the back of a knife. Brush the top with beaten egg or milk and then bake towards the top of the oven set at 425°F, 220°C, gas mark 7 for 25–30 minutes or until pale gold.

Serves 6

Right: A baked pudding served with cream or custard makes the perfect ending to an autumn or winter meal.
Over: Devonshire Junket flavoured with nutmeg makes a light pudding.

RHUBARB TANSY

450 g/1 lb rhubarb
100 g/4 oz butter
50 g/2 oz sugar
2 egg yolks, beaten
150 ml/¼ pint double cream
2 tablespoons lemon juice
Caster sugar to taste

Prepare and chop the rhubarb into 2.5 cm/1 in pieces. Simmer gently in the butter until cooked. Add the beaten egg yolks and the lightly-whipped cream; sweeten to taste. Boil the mixture gently until it is barely firm. Turn out immediately into a serving dish. Sprinkle with caster sugar and lemon juice. Serve hot or cold.

Serves 4

SOMERSET APPLE CAKE

4 apples
75 g/3 oz butter
150 ml/¼ pint milk
2 eggs
50 g/2 oz plain flour
3 tablespoons sugar

Peel and slice apples and fry them in hot butter. Mix the milk, eggs and flour. Stir in the apples and butter. Put in a greased 18 cm/7 in sponge sandwich tin and bake at 375°F, 190°C, gas mark 5 for twenty minutes. Turn out, sprinkle with sugar, and brown in the oven or under the grill.

Serves 4

CIDER-BAKED PEARS OR QUINCES

900 g/2 lb hard pears or quinces
100 g/4 oz caster sugar or honey
300 ml/½ pint cider
300 ml/½ pint water
Shredded blanched almonds
A piece of lemon peel

Peel the pears or quinces leaving the stems on, and arrange them upright in a deep casserole. Add sugar or honey, pour over the cider and water and add the lemon peel. Cook at 300°F, 150°C, gas mark 2 until the pears or quinces are tender and can be pierced with a fork. Leave to cool in the juice, then remove the fruit and reduce the juice by heating until thick and syrupy. Spike the fruit with almonds, and serve with thick cream. The quinces are best flavoured with honey.

Serves 4

SOMERSET BLACKBERRY AND APPLE CHARLOTTE

225 g/8 oz blackberries
3 large cooking apples
50 g/2 oz butter
¼ teaspoon cinnamon
100 g/4 oz soft white breadcrumbs
100 g/4 oz Demerara sugar

Peel, core and slice the apples thinly. Wash the blackberries. Melt the butter in a pan. Mix the breadcrumbs with cinnamon and sugar and throw into the hot butter. Sprinkle a thin layer of well-stirred crumbs on to the bottom of a lightly greased 900 ml/1½ pint pie dish. Cover with a layer of apple, then a layer of crumbs. Repeat this twice. Then cover with blackberries, then crumbs, apple and lastly crumbs. Bake at 325°F, 170°C, gas mark 3 for about one hour until the top is golden-brown. Serve with cream or creamy custard.

Serves 4

Left: Surplus fruit and vegetables can be transformed into pickles and chutneys which add zest to cold meats, cheese and pies.
Page 139: Delicious Cooked Mincemeat, with a generous lacing of brandy, complements shortcrust pastry to make perfect mince pies.

FRIAR'S OMELET (HOT OR COLD)

450 g/1 lb apples
100 g/4 oz light soft brown sugar
3 cloves
100 g/4 oz butter
2 tablespoons lemon juice
2 egg yolks, beaten
100 g/4 oz soft white breadcrumbs
A little extra butter
A little water

Peel, core and slice the apples. Simmer the slices with the sugar and cloves in just enough water to prevent them from sticking to the pan. When thoroughly pulped, remove from the heat and beat well with a wooden spoon. Add the butter and lemon juice and set aside until cold. Take out the cloves. When ready to cook, stir in the beaten egg yolks. Butter a deep fireproof dish and cover the bottom and the sides with a generous layer of breadcrumbs. Put in the apple mixture and cover the top with the rest of the breadcrumbs. Bake at 375°F, 190°C, gas mark 5 for twenty-five minutes. Serve hot or cold. If to be served cold, turn out when cool and sprinkle the top with caster sugar.

Serves 4

PUDDINGS SERVED COLD

APPLE TANSY

2 medium-sized tart cooking apples
2 dessertspoons unsalted butter
3 eggs, separated
2 dessertspoons triple-strength rose-water
¼ teaspoon grated nutmeg
2 dessertspoons caster sugar

Peel, core and slice the apples. Heat the butter in a frying pan, and fry the apple slices very gently until just softening. Beat the egg yolks in a basin with two dessertspoons water and the rose-water, nutmeg and sugar. Beat the egg whites separately until stiff (but not dry), then fold the whites into the yolk mixture. Tip this mixture very gently over the apples, and fry until the underside is set. While it cooks, heat the grill, and as soon as the omelette is set underneath, slide the pan under the grill flame to brown the top.

The difficult part of making this light tansy is to fold it with the cooked apple inside. The best way is to have a sheet of warmed foil or grease-proof paper ready, and to invert the whole pan on to it. Then tip up one side of the sheet, to fold the omelette. Dredge the omelette with caster sugar before serving it.

Serves 4

NORFOLK SYLLABUB

Scant 140 ml/¼ pint white wine
1 tablespoon sherry
2 tablespoons brandy
1 lemon or one bitter (Seville) orange
50 g/2 oz caster sugar
300 ml/½ pint double cream

Put the wine, sherry and brandy into a basin. Peel the lemon or orange very thinly and squeeze out the juice. Put the peel and the juice into the wine mixture. Leave overnight, and removes the peel. Stir in the sugar until it dissolves. Add the cream and whip until the mixture forms soft peaks. Put into four tall glasses. This syllabub will hold its shape for twelve hours.

Serves 4

WHIPPED SYLLABUB

300 ml/½ pint double cream
300 ml/½ pint white wine
2 tablespoons grape brandy or cream
*   sherry*
100 g/4 oz caster sugar
Grated rind of one lemon

Put the cream into a deep bowl and pour in the wine from a height. Traditionally, cider or raisin wine was used, but white wine came to be used most often, with two tablespoons brandy or sherry included. Add the sugar and the lemon rind, and whip the mixture briskly. As the cream rises, remove the top with a slotted spoon or fish slice. Place the light and fluffy cream in small glasses or custard cups, and set aside in a cool larder or a refrigerator. Sometimes, this kind of syllabub is served with crisp almond or shortbread biscuit, dipped in brandy, placed in each glass.

Originally the syllabub was made by milking the cow into the wine mixture, and skimming off the froth which arose into serving glasses.

Serves 4

BLACKCURRANT FLUMMERY

450 g/1 lb blackcurrants
600 ml/1 pint water
1 dessertspoon cornflour
100 g/4 oz caster sugar
2 teaspoons lemon juice
2 eggs

Remove the stalks and wash the currants. Stew gently in the water until tender, and then sieve them. Mix the cornflour to a smooth paste with a tablespoonful of the blackcurrant purée. Put the rest of the purée on to boil with the sugar. When boiling, add the blended cornflour and the lemon juice, and cook for two minutes, stirring all the time to prevent the mixture sticking. Leave to cool. Separate the eggs, beat the yolks, and add to the cooled blackcurrant mixture, mixing well. Whip the egg whites to a stiff foam and fold into the mixture when cold. Pour into a serving bowl. Serve with cream.

Serves 4

APPLE BARLEY FLUMMERY

4 tablespoons pearl barley
1.1 litre/2 pints water
675 g/1½ lb eating apples
40 g/1½ oz caster sugar
Juice of one lemon
3 tablespoons double cream

Put the barley into the water, and bring to the boil. When boiling, add peeled and sliced apples, and cook until the barley and apples are soft. Put the mixture through a sieve, and return to the saucepan. Stir in the sugar and lemon juice and bring to the boil. Cool and stir in the cream and pour into a serving dish. Serve very cold.

Serves 4

GLOUCESTER GOOSEBERRY MOULD

675 g/1½ lb gooseberries
15 g/½ oz gelatine
Sugar to taste
300 ml/½ pint water

Soak the gelatine for one hour in 150 ml/¼ pint water. Cook the fruit in the rest of the water until tender. Add the sugar and dissolve. Bring fruit again to the boil, stirring all the time. Beat in the softened gelatine and when quite dissolved, turn the mixture into a wetted mould or basin and leave to set. Turn on to a plate and serve with cream.

Serves 4

GOOSEBERRY FLUMMERY

450 g/1 lb gooseberries
225 g/8 oz sugar
1 teaspoon lemon juice
300 ml/½ pint milk
4 tablespoons fine semolina

Simmer the gooseberries with the sugar and very little water in a covered pan until the skins burst and the fruit is pulpy. Remove from the heat and add the lemon juice. Warm the milk, and sprinkle on the semolina. Bring just to the boil, then simmer for three minutes. Take off the heat and stir in the gooseberries. Tint with a little green vegetable colouring if liked. Pour into a bowl and serve chilled, with thick cream.

Serves 4

RICE FLUMMERY

600 ml/1 pint milk
Strip of lemon peel
2.5 cm/1 in cinnamon stick
50 g/2 oz caster sugar
75 g/3 oz ground rice
25 g/1 oz butter
4 drops almond essence

Heat the milk just to boiling point with the lemon peel and cinnamon. Remove the peel and cinnamon stick, and stir sugar into the milk. Mix the ground rice with a little cold milk and then stir in the hot milk with the butter and essence. Cook gently, stirring all the time, until the mixture thickens and leaves the sides of the saucepan. Pour into a wetted mould and leave until cold. Turn out and serve with fresh fruit, jam or cream.

Serves 4

DAMASK JUNKET

600 ml/1 pint single cream
1 blade of whole mace
1 cracked cinnamon stick
Sifted icing sugar
Triple-strength rose-water
Small pinch of salt
Rennet
More single cream and icing sugar
*Deep pink rose petals or one crimson
    rosebud*
Plain or almond biscuits

Pour the single cream into a saucepan, add one blade of mace and one cracked cinnamon stick, and heat the mixture gently, well under the boil, until it is well flavoured. Remove the pan from the heat, take out the spices, and add sifted icing sugar and triple-strength rose-water to taste, with a small pinch of salt. Pour the mixture into its serving dish, and cool it to blood heat if necessary. Then set it with rennet, using the amount directed for 600 ml/1 pint milk.

When it is cold and firm, pour over it, very, very gently, enough single cream flavoured with rose-water to cover it to a depth of about quarter inch. Sprinkle more sifted icing sugar on top. Strew deep pink rose petals round the edge of the dish, or place one crimson rosebud in the centre. Serve at once, with thin plain or almond biscuits.

Serves 4

PORT WINE JELLY

600 ml/1 pint port
100 g/4 oz caster sugar
25 g/1 oz gelatine
150 ml/¼ pint water
1 teaspoon lemon juice
Pinch of ground nutmeg
Pinch of ground cinnamon

Put half the port into a pan with the sugar and heat gently until the sugar has dissolved. Put the gelatine and water into a cup and stand the cup in a small pan of hot water. Heat gently, stirring the gelatine until it is syrupy. Stir into the hot port with the lemon juice and spices. Mix very well and strain into a bowl. Stir in the remaining port. Leave in the bowl or pour into individual glasses. Leave until cold and set, but do not chill. Serve with whipped cream and small sweet biscuits.

Serves 6

LEMON SOLID

900 ml/1½ pints milk
300 ml/½ pint single cream
25 g/1 oz gelatine
2 lemons
150 g/3 oz granulated sugar

Put gelatine to stand in 600 ml/1 pint milk. Put remaining milk and cream in a pan with the sugar. Warm until the sugar has melted and bring to near boiling point. Add the rind of the lemons. Pour in the other milk and slowly stir in the juice of the lemons. It should slightly curdle. Pour into a mould, set and turn out.

Serves 6

RICH GOOSEBERRY FOOL

450 g/1 lb gooseberries
225 g/8 oz sugar
1 dessertspoon orange-flower water
450 ml/¾ pint single cream

Simmer the gooseberries with the sugar in 150 ml/¼ pint water until pulpy. Put through a sieve and cool. Mix with the orange-flower water and cream. Chill before serving in a stemmed glass bowl; decorate with candied orange peel or angelica strips.

Serves 4

STONE CREAM

225 g/8 oz apricot, plum, or strawberry
  jam
600 ml/1 pint single cream
50 g/2 oz icing sugar
7 g/¼ oz gelatine

Cover the bottom of a glass dish about 2.5 cm/1 in thick with the jam. Put the cream into a thick pan with the sugar and bring only just to the boil. Mix the gelatine with a tablespoon of water and stand it in a bowl of hot water until the gelatine is syrupy. Stir this into the cream. Strain the mixture and when it is nearly cold, stir it well and pour it gently over the jam.

This dish was first mentioned in the seventeenth century. It should be made the day before it is needed. Isinglass gives the best result, but is little used now, so gelatine will suffice. Sometimes the juice and grated rind of a lemon, and a wineglass of white wine were poured over the jam before the cream was added and the dessert used to be prettily decorated. Apricot jam is recommended, but other kinds will do. The cream should not be stiff.

Serves 6

SWEETMEATS

The sweetmeats best known and loved by the country child were until lately those made from homely ingredients in their mother's kitchens. They were mostly simple boiled mixtures of butter, sugar and milk, made into toffees and fudges both wholesome and delicious. Sugar thermometers were not known, but the cooking time could be tested by dropping a little of the mixture into cold water. This is still the method used most. The varying degrees of hardness show whether the mixture will remain soft or become brittle when it cools.

HONEYCOMB

175 g/6 oz sugar
2 tablespoons golden syrup
25 g/1 oz butter
2 tablespoons water
½ teaspoon vinegar
1 teaspoon bicarbonate of soda

Put the sugar, syrup, butter and water into a heavy pan, and stir over a low heat until the sugar has melted. Boil steadily until a little of the mixture forms a firm ball when dropped into cold water. Take off the heat and stir in the vinegar and then the bicarbonate of soda. The mixture will froth up in the pan. Pour into an oiled tin and break into pieces when cold. This toffee does not store well and is best eaten quickly.

Makes 225 g (8 oz)

BUTTERSCOTCH

450 g/1 lb soft brown sugar
75 ml/3 fl oz water
225 g/8 oz butter

Dissolve the sugar over a low heat in the water. Stir in the butter and boil until the mixture is thick. When it is thick, stir very well so that it does not 'catch' on the bottom of the pan, and cook until a little dropped into cold water is brittle. Pour into a buttered shallow tin and mark into small squares before it sets.

Makes 675 g (1½ lb)

BARLEY SUGAR

450 g/1 lb loaf sugar
150 ml/¼ pint water
1 dessertspoon strained lemon juice
Rind of one lemon
A little yellow food colouring

Put the sugar, water and lemon juice into a heavy pan, together with the thinly peeled lemon rind. Stir over a gentle heat until the sugar has dissolved. Bring to the boil, and boil quickly. Take out the lemon rind just after the mixture begins to boil. Continue boiling until a little of the mixture is very brittle when dropped into cold water. Remove from the heat, stir in a little yellow colouring, and leave to cool slightly. When the mixture is cool enough to handle, roll on an oiled surface into long thin strips. Twist up, and leave to set.

Makes 450 g (1 lb)

HUMBUGS

450 g/1 lb Demerara sugar
150 ml/¼ pint water
50 g/2 oz butter
2 drops oil of peppermint
Pinch of cream of tartar

Put all the ingredients into a heavy pan and boil until a little of the mixture will form a fine thread when dropped into cold water. Remove from the heat, cool for one minute and pour on to an oiled surface. When it is cool enough to handle, pull the mixture into long strips. Pull half the mixture until it becomes much paler than the other pieces. Twist the two colours together, and cut into short pieces.

Makes 550 g (1¼ lb)

SIMPLE TOFFEE

100 g/4 oz butter
225 g/8 oz granulated sugar
2 tablespoons vinegar
2 tablespoons golden syrup

Put the butter into a heavy pan and let it start melting over a low heat. Add the remaining ingredients and stir until the sugar has melted. Bring to the boil; boil quickly, only stirring occasionally, until the mixture is golden-brown and a little dropped into cold water is brittle. Pour into a greased shallow tin and mark into squares just before it sets.

Makes 350 g (12 oz)

BONFIRE TOFFEE

450 g/1 lb granulated sugar
50 g/2 oz butter
250 ml/8 fl oz can sweetened condensed
  milk
1 tablespoon golden syrup
1 teaspoon lemon juice

Put sugar, butter and syrup into a large heavy pan and stir over a low heat until they have melted together. Bring to the boil, add the milk and lemon juice, and boil until a little dropped in cold water forms a firm ball. Take the pan off the fire and leave to stand until the toffee stops bubbling, then pour into a well-greased tin. Mark into squares when nearly set.

Makes 675 g (1½ lb)

TREACLE TOFFEE

*275 g/10 oz black treacle or golden
    syrup
100 g/4 oz brown sugar
15 g/½ oz butter
2 teaspoons vinegar
½ teaspoon bicarbonate of soda
1 teaspoon lemon juice*

Mix the treacle, sugar, butter and vinegar in a saucepan, and boil without stirring until a few drops in cold water are brittle. Add the bicarbonate of soda to the mixture. Boil again for about eight minutes, pour out on to a greased tin, and sprinkle the lemon juice on top. When it is cool enough to handle, smear a scrap of butter on the hands and roll the toffee into small balls. Leave to harden.

Makes 450 g (1 lb)

ALMOND TOFFEE

*150 g/5 oz whole almonds
450 g/1 lb sugar
300 ml/½ pint water
Pinch of cream of tartar
3 drops almond essence*

Blanch the almonds, skin them and cut them in half crosswise. Put them on a baking tray and dry them in the oven without browning. Dissolve the sugar in the water, add the cream of tartar, and boil until the syrup becomes dark in colour. A little dropped in cold water will be brittle. Stir in the almonds and essence and pour into a greased tin to set. Mark in squares or irregular shapes just before setting.

Makes 675 g (1½ lb)

TOFFEE APPLES

*Apples
450 g/1 lb Demerara sugar
100 g/4 oz butter
5 tablespoons vinegar*

Use small crisp apples for these; spear them on wooden sticks about four inches long. Do not peel them, but wash them well and wipe them very dry. Put the butter and sugar into a heavy pan and stir over a low heat until the sugar has melted. Add the vinegar and boil the mixture quickly until it becomes dark brown and is brittle when a little is dropped into cold water. Put the apples ready with their sticks, and as soon as the toffee is ready, dip quickly into the toffee so they are completely coated. Twirl them in the air, and put them on a tin to set.

Makes 10

PULLED TOFFEE

*675 g/1½ lb granulated sugar
5 tablespoons vinegar
15 g/½ oz butter
1 teaspoon vanilla essence
150 ml/¼ pint water*

Pour the vinegar and water into a clean pan, add the sugar and boil for fifteen minutes. Add the butter in little bits, and boil for another fifteen minutes. Have ready a plate greased with butter, turn out the toffee on it and sprinkle on the vanilla essence. Turn the edges inward (as if folding them) when cool enough to handle, smear the fingers with butter and hang the mixture over a hook. Pull the toffee lengthways, then hang it up again and again for 8–10 minutes until it is all white, or streaked with white. Then twist in sticks about 2 cm/¾ in thick, and before it can set, cut into 1.25 cm/½ in and 2.5 cm/1 in lengths with a pair of scissors. Place on greased paper to harden.

Makes 675 g (1½ lb)

PULLED TREACLE CANDY

450 g/1 lb black treacle
350 g/12 oz dark soft brown sugar
50 g/2 oz butter
1 tablespoon vinegar
1 teaspoon bicarbonate of soda

Put the treacle, sugar, butter and vinegar into a pan and boil until a few drops harden at once when dropped into cold water. Dissolve the bicarbonate of soda in a very little boiling water, and stir into the candy. Pour into a greased tin. As the edges begin to cool, turn them in with a knife. As soon as the candy is cool enough to be handled, put it on to a marble slab and pull it out until it hardens. Twist it into sticks and cut it into short lengths.

Makes 675 g (1½ lb)

RUSSIAN TOFFEE

225 g/8 oz cube sugar
100 g/4 oz butter
150 ml/¼ pint cream
1 tablespoon redcurrant jelly

Put the sugar, butter and cream into a thick pan, and stir on a very low heat until the mixture thickens and leaves the sides of the pan. Add the redcurrant jelly, stir and pour into a greased tin. Cut into squares when cold.

Makes 450 g (1 lb)

CREAM TOFFEE

450 g/1 lb sugar
150 ml/¼ pint water
225 g/8 oz golden syrup
40 g/1½ oz butter
250 ml/8 oz can condensed milk

Heat the water and sugar gently until the sugar has dissolved. Stir in the syrup, butter and con-densed milk. Boil until a little of the mixture forms a hard ball when dropped in cold water. Pour into a greased tray and mark in squares when it is cooling.

Makes 900 g (2 lb)

NUT BRITTLE

225 g/8 oz nuts (almonds, hazelnuts or peanuts)
450 g/1 lb sugar
150 ml/¼ pint water
Few drops almond essence

Skin the nuts by pouring hot water over them and leaving them for a few minutes until the skins can be rubbed off. Dry carefully, and spread the nuts on a baking sheet. Brown, but do not over-brown, in a moderate oven 350°F, 180°C, gas mark 4. Put the sugar and water into a thick pan and put over a low heat. When it begins to boil, add the nuts. Boil hard until the syrup becomes pale brown, stirring well. Take off the heat. Add a few drops of almond essence and stir well. Put tablespoons of the mixture on to an oiled tin to set.

Makes 675 g (1½ lb)

EASY FUDGE

450 g/1 lb sugar
300 ml/½ pint milk
25 g/1 oz cocoa
½ teaspoon cream of tartar
50 g/2 oz butter
½ teaspoon vanilla essence

Dissolve the sugar in the milk over a gentle heat. Add the cocoa and cream of tartar and boil until a little of the mixture forms a soft ball in cold water. Remove from the heat and add the butter and the vanilla essence. Beat until creamy and smooth and pour into a greased tin. Cut into squares when cold.

Makes 675 g (1½ lb)

CHOCOLATE FUDGE

450 g/1 lb sugar
2 tablespoons milk
25 g/1 oz butter
225 g/8 oz plain chocolate

Mix the sugar and milk and cook in a double saucepan until it is a thick paste. Add the butter and chocolate broken into small pieces. Now put the saucepan directly on the heat and cook very gently until the sugar and chocolate are completely melted. The reason for using the double boiler is that, if the fudge is boiled before this stage, it will crystallise. Boil for five minutes, stirring all the time. Take off the heat, and beat hard until the fudge is thick. Pour into a greased tray, and cut into squares before it is completely cold.

Makes 675 g (1½ lb)

NUT FUDGE

150 ml/¼ pint milk
550 g/1¼ lb granulated sugar
50 g/2 oz butter
225 g/8 oz nuts (hazelnuts or walnuts)

Put the milk and sugar into a saucepan and leave to soak for forty-five minutes. Add the butter and heat gently, stirring very occasionally until the sugar has dissolved. When the sugar has dissolved, bring the mixture to the boil and boil quickly, sometimes stirring so the mixture does not stick on the bottom of the pan, for about fifteen minutes, until a little of the mixture forms a soft ball when dropped into a cup of cold water. Add the chopped nuts and beat until the fudge is thick and creamy. Pour into a greased tin. Just before it sets, mark into squares.

Makes 900 g (2 lb)

SCOTS TABLET

900 g/2 lb granulated sugar
400 ml/14 oz single cream
Flavouring

Put the sugar and cream into a heavy pan. Bring gradually to boiling point, stirring all the time. Boil for a few minutes, but do not boil hard. Test for setting, until the mixture forms a soft ball when a little is dropped into cold water. Add the chosen flavouring. Put the pan into a basin of cold water and stir quickly with a spoon, scraping down the edges of the pan as the mixture begins to solidify round the edge. When the mixture is looking a little grained, pour it into a buttered tin. This is a little tricky and practice will make perfect. If the mixture is too highly grained, it will not pour out flat, and if it is too thin, the tablet will be sticky. When firm, mark into bars with a knife or cut into circles with a pastry cutter.

Favourite *tablet flavourings* are: cinnamon; desiccated coconut; chopped dried figs; ground and chopped preserved ginger; lemon essence; orange juice and rind; peppermint oil; vanilla essence; chopped walnuts.

Makes 1 kg (2.2 lb)

BLACKBERRY PASTE CANDIES

900 g/2 lb blackberries
Sugar
Water

Heat the fruit in just enough water to cover until it is soft. Drain through a jelly bag and weigh the juice, and use an equal quantity of sugar. Stir together over gentle heat until the miture is thick and dry. Pour this thick mixture into a baking tin and sprinkle it with caster sugar. When the paste is cold and hard, cut it into pieces, dip them in caster sugar, and store in a wooden box lined with waxed paper. These candies are also good made with redcurrants, as Redcurrant Paste Candies.

Makes 450 g (1 lb)

COCONUT ICE

900 g/2 lb cube sugar
300 ml/½ pint water
275 g/10 oz desiccated coconut

Put the sugar and water in a strong saucepan and stand it over a gentle heat until the sugar is dissolved. Bring to the boil, and continue boiling rapidly for ten minutes, stirring all the time. Remove from the heat, stir in the coconut and mix well. Pour half the mixture into an oiled rectangular tin. Colour the remainder lightly with cochineal and press on top of the white ice. Mark into twelve bars when partly cool and finish cutting when cold.

Makes 800 g (1¾ lb)

PEPPERMINT CREAMS

1 egg white
450 g/1 lb icing sugar
Oil of peppermint

Beat the egg white until it is frothy but not stiff. Sieve the icing sugar and mix it gradually into the egg white until the mixture is a firm paste. Add peppermint to taste (oil of peppermint gives the best flavour, although pepperemint essence can be used). Knead the mixture until it is smooth, and then roll it out on a board dusted with icing sugar. Cut into small circles. If preferred, the mixture can be rolled into small balls with the hands and then flattened with a fork. Leave overnight to become firm. When firm, these peppermint creams can be dipped into melted plain chocolate if liked.

Makes 450 g (1 lb)

CHAPTER ELEVEN

THE STILLROOM

In the days before refrigeration, every country housewife had her store cupboard full of preserved foods to see her through the winter. In the larger houses and more prosperous farmhouses, there was a special stillroom for storing jams, jellies and syrups, dried fruits and vegetables, pickles, chutneys and sauces, smoked and salted meat and fish, and potted meats or fish for short-term storage. In the cottages, there was little room for more than a jam cupboard, but there were hooks for ham and bacon, and vegetables could be 'clamped' in the garden plot or stored in an outhouse. With these varied preserving methods, the housewife kept her surplus produce, and provided some stimulating flavours, at least to vary an otherwise boring winter diet.

JAMS AND JELLIES

APPLE, PEAR AND PLUM JAM

675 g/1½ lb cooking apples
675 g/1½ lb ripe pears
675 g/1½ lb plums
1.75 kg/3¾ lb sugar
15 g/½ oz root ginger

Peel and core the apples and pears. Skin and stone the plums. Put the fruit into a pan, and add the bruised root ginger tied into a muslin bag. Simmer until the fruit is soft but not broken, adding a little water if necessary to prevent burning. Stir in the sugar until dissolved, then boil quickly to setting point. Remove the ginger, and pour into hot jars. This is sometimes called *Mock Apricot Jam*.

Makes 2.7 kg (6 lb)

BLACKBERRY AND APPLE JAM

675 g|1½ lb blackberries
675 g|1½ lb apples
150–300 ml|¼–½ pint water
1.4 kg|3 lb sugar

Prepare the fruit, and simmer gently with water until soft. Add sugar, and cook rapidly until setting point is reached. Pour into warm jars and cover.

Makes 1.8 kg (4 lb)

PEAR MARMALADE

2.75 kg|6 lb pears
600 ml|1 pint sweet cider
1.75 kg|4 lb sugar
Juice of one lemon
Pink colouring

Do not peel or core the pears, but cut into small pieces. Heat the cider and then add the pears and simmer gently until tender. Put through a sieve. Return to the pan with the sugar and lemon and stir until the sugar is dissolved. Boil moderately fast, stirring constantly, until setting point is reached. Tint lightly with pink colouring and pour into hot jars. Cover as usual.

Makes 3.5 kg (8 lb)

BLACKCURRANT AND CHERRY JAM

900 g|2 lb blackcurrants
900 g|2 lb black cherries
600 ml|1 pint water
1.4 kg|3 lb sugar

Simmer the blackcurrants in the water for one hour, and put through a jelly bag. Simmer stoned cherries in the blackcurrant juice for twenty minutes. Stir in the sugar until dissolved, then boil quickly to setting point. Pour into hot jars, cover and seal when cold.

Makes 2.7 kg (6 lb)

CHERRY AND GOOSEBERRY JAM

1.4 kg|3 lb Morello cherries
675 g|1½ lb red gooseberries
7 g|¼ oz tartaric acid
1.75 kg|4 lb sugar

Stone the cherries, and top and tail the gooseberries. Put into a pan and heat until the juice flows. Add the acid and simmer until the fruit is soft. Stir in the sugar until dissolved, then boil quickly to setting point. Pour into hot jars, cover and seal when cold.

Makes 2.7 kg (6 lb)

MARROW JAM

1.75 kg|4 lb diced marrow
2.25 kg|5 lb sugar
Ground ginger (optional)
600 ml|1 pint apple juice (made from
*   windfalls, cores, skins and all, and*
*   as little water as possible)*

Overnight, in a big bowl, stand the diced marrow covered with 1.75 kg/4 lb sugar. Next morning add the apple juice, and the remaining sugar. Boil until the marrow is cooked and slightly transparent (about forty-five minutes). Pour into jars and cover as usual.

Makes 3 kg (7 lb)

RASPBERRY AND RHUBARB JAM

1.4 kg|3 lb raspberries
1.4 kg|3 lb rhubarb
600 ml|1 pint water
2.75 kg|6 lb sugar

Cut the rhubarb into pieces and simmer in the water until soft. Add the raspberries and cook until soft. Stir in the sugar until dissolved, then boil rapidly to setting point. Pour into hot jars, cover and seal when cold.

Makes 4.5 kg (10 lb)

RHUBARB AND FIG JAM

900 g/2 lb rhubarb
225 g/8 oz dried figs
1.4 kg/3 lb sugar
Juice of one lemon

Cut rhubarb and figs finely, combine with sugar and lemon juice, and leave to stand for twenty-four hours. Bring to boil, and boil rapidly until a little sets when tested on a cool plate. Leave to stand for thirty minutes before filling jars. Cover, then secure and seal when cold.

Makes 1.8 kg (4 lb)

ROSE-PETAL AND RHUBARB JAM

100 g/4 oz dark red rose petals
450 g/1 lb rhubarb
Juice of one lemon
450 g/1 lb sugar

Clean and cut up the rhubarb and leave it to stand overnight with the lemon juice and sugar. Cut the white tips off the rose petals, then cut the petals in pieces and add to the mixture. Bring to the boil, and then boil to setting point. Pour into small hot jars and cover. This is delicious with scones or rusks.

Makes 675 g (1½ lb)

WHOLE STRAWBERRY JAM

1.75 kg/4 lb strawberries
1.75 kg/4 lb sugar

Put the strawberries into a bowl with the sugar in layers and leave overnight. Put into a pan and bring to the boil. Boil for five minutes and return to the bowl. Leave overnight, then boil to setting point. Cool for fifteen minutes, stir well, and pour into hot jars. Cover and seal in the usual way.

Makes 2.7 kg (6 lb)

TOMATO JAM

2.75 kg/6 lb ripe tomatoes
6 lemons
2.75 kg/6 lb granulated sugar
1 teaspoon salt
1 tablespoon ground ginger

Skin the tomatoes. Grate the lemon rind and put the rind and juice into a pan with the chopped tomatoes. Cook gently until the mixture is reduced to a pulp. Remove from the heat and carefully stir in the sugar, salt and ground ginger. Return to the heat and boil until setting point is reached. Pour into warmed jam jars, allow to cool, seal, and store carefully.

Makes 3.5 kg (8 lb)

RHUBARB PRESERVE

1.5 kg/3½ lb rhubarb
1.5 kg/3½ lb sugar
1 lemon
50 g/2 oz blanched split almonds

Peel the rhubarb and cut it into neat pieces. Put over a low heat until the juice runs. Add warm sugar, grated rind and juice of the lemon, and split almonds. Stir until sugar is dissolved, and boil for forty-five minutes until thick and brown. Pour into hot jars and cover.

Makes 2.25 kg (5 lb)

RASPBERRY PRESERVE

1.4 kg/3 lb raspberries
1.4 kg/3 lb sugar
25 g/1 oz butter

Warm a pan and rub it with the butter. Put in the raspberries and heat very slowly until the juice runs. Warm the sugar in the oven. Add the warm sugar to the raspberries and beat over a low heat for thirty minutes. Pour into hot jars and cover.

Makes 2.25 kg (5 lb)

PEAR CONSERVE

1.4 kg/3 lb firm eating pears
1½ lemons
150 ml/¼ pint water
550 g/1¼ lb sugar

Peel and core the pears and cut the flesh into neat pieces. Peel the lemons thinly and squeeze out the juice. Boil the pear peel and cores and the lemon peel in 150 ml/¼ pint water for ten minutes, and strain. Put the liquid into a pan with the pears and lemon juice, and simmer until tender. Add the sugar and stir until dissolved. Bring to the boil, and boil to setting point. Pour into hot jars and cover.

Makes 1.8 kg (4 lb)

QUINCE CONSERVE

1.25 kg/2½ lb quinces
1.5 litre/2¾ pints water
1.25 kg/2½ lb sugar

Peel and core the quinces and cut the flesh into small cubes. Put the cubes into 1.2 litre/2 pints water and bring to the boil. Add the sugar, remove from the heat and stir until the sugar dissolves. Return to the heat and cook gently until the fruit is soft but not broken. Meanwhile put the cores and peel into the remaining water and cook until the pulp is reduced by half. Strain the liquid into the quinces. Boil hard to setting point. Cool a little and stir before putting into warm pots. This gives a clear red jelly with small cubes of quince.

Makes 2.25 kg (5 lb)

MARIGOLD CONSERVE

150 g/5 oz marigold petals
450 g/1 lb sugar
Lemon juice

Pound the petals (using a pestle and mortar, or a blender on slow speed). Make them very small,

adding a little lemon juice to aid the process if necessary. Gradually work in the sugar until it is thoroughly absorbed. Put into small jars and cover. (This conserve was originally valued as a cure for melancholy.)

Makes 450 g (1 lb)

CONSERVE OF FLOWERS

1.75 kg/4 lb cooking apples
1.1 litre/2 pints water
225 g/8 oz flower petals (carnations, jasmine, primrose, violets, roses)
Sugar

Choose the flowers according to the season of the year. Cut the fruit in pieces and put into preserving pan with water and flower petals. Simmer until the fruit is pulpy, and strain through a jelly bag. Measure the juice and allow 450 g/1 lb sugar to each 600 ml/1 pint of juice. Stir in the sugar until dissolved, and boil rapidly to setting point.

Makes 900 g (2 lb)

APPLE AND ELDERBERRY JELLY

1.4 kg/3 lb cooking apples
1.75 kg/4 lb elderberries (weighed off stalks)
Rind of one orange
½ cinnamon stick
1.2 litre/2 pints water
Sugar

Wash the apples, cut into pieces and put into a pan with the elderberries. Add water, cover the pan, and simmer to a pulp. Leave to drip through a jelly bag. Measure the juice and allow 450 g/1 lb sugar to 600 ml/1 pint juice. Put into a pan, stir well and put in orange rind and cinnamon tied in musling. Boil rapidly to setting point, remove the orange peel and cinnamon, put into warm jars and cover. This jelly is nice if soft and not too firm.

Makes 1.35 kg (3 lb)

BRAMBLE JELLY

1.75 kg/4 lb blackberries
450 ml/¾ pint water
Sugar
Juice of one lemon

Wash the blackberries and put them into a pan with the water. Bring to the boil and simmer gently until the juice runs from the fruit. Strain and leave the juice to drip through a jelly bag. Allow 450 g/1 lb sugar to each 600 ml/1 pint of juice. Heat gently together until the sugar dissolves, and then bring to the boil and add the lemon juice. Boil rapidly for twenty minutes until setting point is reached. Put into warm pots and cover.

Makes 1.35 kg (3 lb)

BLACKBERRY AND SLOE JELLY

1.75 kg/4 lb blackberries
450 g/1 lb sloes
Sugar

Put the blackberries into a pan with the sloes which have been pricked with a needle. Cover with water and simmer until tender. Strain through a jelly bag and measure the juice. Allow 450 g/1 lb sugar to each 600 ml/1 pint of juice. Heat the juice gently, stirring in the sugar until dissolved. Boil hard to setting point and pour into hot jars. Cover.

Makes 1.35 kg (3 lb)

BLACKCURRANT JELLY

1.75 kg/4 lb ripe blackcurrants
1.4 litre/2½ pints water
Sugar

Simmer the fruit in 900 ml/1½ pints water, mash well. Strain through a clean, scalded jelly bag, or

closely woven linen tea towel for ten minutes. Put pulp from the cloth back into the pan, add 60 ml/1 pint of water and simmer for thirty minutes. Strain the pulp again and mix together the two extracts. Add 350 g/12 oz sugar to each 600 ml/1 pint of juice and cook for five minutes. Pour into jars and seal as usual.

Makes 1.35 kg (3 lb)

CRAB-APPLE JELLY

1.75 kg/4 lb crab-apples
1.1 litre/2 pints water
6 cloves
Sugar

Do not peel or core the fruit. Cut into quarters and put into a pan with the water and the cloves. Bring to the boil, and then simmer until the apples are very soft. Add a little more water if the fruit is boiling dry. Strain through a jelly bag and measure the juice. Allow 450 g/1 lb sugar to each 600 ml/1 pint of juice. Heat the juice gently and stir in the sugar until dissolved. Boil hard to setting point and pour into hot jars. Process as usual.

Makes 1.35 kg (3 lb)

CRAB-APPLE AND GERANIUM JELLY

2 good pressed down handfuls of
scented rose geranium leaves
1.4 kg/3 lb crab-apples

Shred the leaves and cut up the apples. Cover with water and boil until the fruit is soft. Strain through a jelly bag. To each 600 ml/1 pint of juice, add 450 g/1 lb sugar. Stir to dissolve, then bring to the boil, and boil to setting point. Process as usual.

Makes 900 g (2 lb)

FIVE FRUIT JELLY

225 g/8 oz each strawberries,
raspberries, cherries, redcurrants,
gooseberries
450 ml/¾ pint water
Sugar

Wash the fruit, cover with the water and simmer gently until soft (probably about 30–40 minutes). Turn into a jelly bag or cloth and leave to drip until thoroughly drained. Measure the juice, making up to an even 600 ml/1 pint or 300 ml/½ pint if necessary. Bring to the boil, take off the heat and stir in and thoroughly dissolve 450 g/1 lb sugar to each 600 ml/1 pint of juice. Bring to a good rolling boil and boil until setting point is reached (about 10–15 minutes). Process as usual.

Makes 675 g/1½ lb)

MEDLAR JELLY

900 g/2 lb medlars
Sugar
1 lemon

Peel very ripe medlars, remove the pips, and slice the flesh into a pan with enough water to cover the fruit. Simmer with the cut-up lemon until soft. Strain the juice through a jelly bag. Allow 350 g/12 oz sugar to each 600 ml/1 pint of juice and stir until dissolved. Boil fast for ten minutes until transparent. Skim well and cool slightly before pouring into jars and sealing. This can be eaten with bread and butter, or served with game.

Makes 675 g (1½ lb)

MINT JELLY

2.75 kg/6 lb apples
1.1 litre/2 pints mint leaves
1.75 kg/4 lb sugar

Quarter the apples, leaving the skins on and the cores in. Chop mint leaves roughly. Put apples and mint into a large saucepan. Cover with cold water and bring to the boil. Simmer until thoroughly cooked. Put the mixture into a jelly bag over a large basin and drain overnight. Measure the liquid and add 450 g/1 lb sugar for every 600 ml/1 pint. Turn into a large saucepan, add sugar and bring to the boil. When sugar is dissolved, boil rapidly until the jelly reaches setting point when tested on a cold saucer. To improve colour, a few drops of green colouring may be stirred well in at this stage. Pour the jelly into clean, hot jars. Leave until cold then cover and seal.

Makes 2.25 kg (5 lb)

RASPBERRY AND REDCURRANT JELLY

900 g/2 lb raspberries
900 g/2 lb redcurrants
600 ml/1 pint water

Put the fruit into the water and simmer gently until the fruit is very soft. Strain through a jelly bag and measure the juice. Allow 450 g/1 lb sugar to each 600 ml/1 pint of juice. Heat the juice gently, stirring in the sugar until dissolved. Boil quickly to setting point, and pour into small jars. Cover and seal. This makes an excellent glaze for cakes and flans.

Makes 900 g (2 lb)

ROSEHIP JELLY

Rosehips
Sugar

The rosehips should be left until they are ripe and soft. Take off the tops, cut up the hips and put them into a pan with just enough water to cover. Bring to the boil and then reduce the heat and simmer to a pulp. Squeeze through a coarse jelly bag or cheese cloth, and then pass through an ordinary jelly bag. Allow 450 g/1 lb sugar to each 600 ml/1 pint of juice. Put together in a preserving pan and stir until the sugar is dissolved. Boil for twenty minutes to setting point. Put into small jars. This jelly is very good with hare or turkey.

SPICED REDCURRANT JELLY

1.4 kg/3 lb redcurrants
600 ml/1 pint water
150 ml/¼ pint white vinegar
3 cloves
½ stick cinnamon
Sugar

Simmer the redcurrants with the water and vinegar. Put the spices in a muslin bag and suspend in the pan. When the fruit is soft, remove the spice bag. Strain through a jelly bag and measure the juice. Allow 450 g/1 lb sugar to each 600 ml/1 pint of juice. Heat the juice gently, stirring in the sugar until dissolved. Boil rapidly to setting point and pour into hot jars. Cover and seal. This is excellent with roast lamb or with game.

Makes 900 g (2 lb)

ROWANBERRY JELLY

1.75 kg/4 lb rowanberries
5 tablespoons lemon juice
900 ml/1½ pints water
Sugar

Use ripe rowanberries. Remove them from their stems and put into a pan with the lemon juice and water. Simmer for forty-five minutes until the fruit is soft. Strain through a jelly bag and measure the juice. Allow 450 g/1 lb sugar to each 600 ml/1 pint of juice. Heat the juice gently, stirring in the sugar until dissolved. Boil rapidly to setting point and pour into hot jars. Cover and seal as usual. This jelly is good with venison, game and roast lamb or mutton.

Makes 1.35 kg (3 lb)

OTHER FRUIT PRESERVES

BLACKBERRY AND APPLE CURD

450 g/1 lb apples
900 g/2 lb blackberries
Juice of two lemons
225 g/8 oz butter
1.25 kg/2½ lb caster sugar
4 eggs

Peel and core the apples, and cook with the blackberries in very little water until soft. Put through a sieve. Cook in a double saucepan with lemon juice, butter and sugar. When the butter and sugar have melted, add the well-beaten eggs and cook until the mixture thickens, stirring well. Pour into hot jars and cover. This will keep for about two months.

Makes 1.8 kg (4 lb)

LEMON CURD

450 g/1 lb caster sugar
225 g/8 oz butter
4 lemons
4 eggs

Put the sugar and butter into a double saucepan over hot water. Grate the lemon rind, and squeeze out the juice. Add rind and juice to the sugar, together with lightly beaten eggs. Cook gently, stirring often, until the mixture is smooth, thick and creamy. Put into small pots and cover. Keep in a cool place, and use within four weeks.

Makes 900 g (2 lb)

Variation
To make *Lemon Curd with Honey*

4 lemons
100 g/4 oz butter
450 g/1 lb clear honey
4 eggs and 2 egg yolks

Grate the lemon rinds, and squeeze and strain the juice. Put into a double saucepan with the butter and honey. Beat the eggs and the egg yolks and strain them into the mixture. Cook and stir over a gentle heat until thick and creamy. Pour into hot jars and cover. This will keep two months.

Makes 675 g (1½ lb)

SPICY APPLE BUTTER

2.75 g/6 lb apples
1.2 litres/2 pints water
1.2 litres/2 pints cider
1 teaspoon ground cloves
1 teaspoon ground cinnamon
1 teaspoon nutmeg
Granulated or soft brown sugar

Do not peel the apples, but cut them into large pieces. Simmer in water and cider until soft and put through a sieve. Weigh the pulp and simmer until thick. Add 350 g/12 oz sugar to each 450 g/1 lb of weighed apples. Stir sugar and spices into apples, and cook gently, stirring frequently, until no surplus liquid remains. Pour into hot jars and cover. This is particularly good made with equal quantities of differently flavoured apples; six different kinds could be used for this recipe. The best apple butter is slightly sharp-flavoured. The same recipe can be used with crab-apples, to make *Crab-Apple Butter*.

Makes 3 kg (7 lb)

APPLE AND PLUM BUTTER

1.4 kg/3 lb apples
450 g/1 lb plums
350 g/12 oz sugar to each 600 ml/1 pint
of pulp

Peel and core the apples and cut them in slices, and cook in very little water until soft. Add stoned plums and cook until soft. Put through a sieve, measure and add sugar. Boil to setting point and put into warm jars. This is a stiff 'butter'. It may be used with bread and butter, or if put into straight-sided jars, it can be turned out, sliced and eaten with cream as a 'spoon sweet'.

Makes 1.8 kg (4 lb)

CHERRY BUTTER

1.75 kg/4 lb cherries
1 lemon
900 g/2 lb sugar

Take the stones from the cherries. Remove the kernels from a few of them, blanch and skin. Put the cherries in layers in a bowl with the sugar and the grated rind and juice of the lemon. Leave overnight.

Simmer for twenty minutes, add the kernels and then boil quickly until very thick, stirring well. Pour into small hot jars and cover. Use within six weeks.

Makes 1.35 kg (3 lb)

FRUIT BLACK BUTTER

Redcurrants
Blackcurrants
Gooseberries
Strawberries
Sugar

A mixture of some or all of the fruits can be used. For each 900 g/2 lb fruit, allow 450 g/1 lb sugar. Prepare and mix the fruits and heat gently in a pan until the juices start to run. Stir in sugar until dissolved, and boil until very thick. Pour into small hot jars and cover. Use within four weeks.

DAMSON CHEESE

Damsons
Sugar

Wash the damsons and just cover them with water. Simmer until the fruit is soft. Put through a sieve and weigh the pulp. Add 350 g/12 oz sugar to each 600 ml/1 pint of damson pulp. Stir the sugar into the pulp until it is dissolved and then cook and stir for about forty-five minutes until the mixture is thick enough to hold the impression of a spoon. Pour into hot jars and cover. Keep for several weeks before use. It should be firm enough to slice and eat on bread with cheese.

GOOSEBERRY CHEESE

1.4 kg/3 lb green gooseberries
300 ml/½ pint water
Sugar

Top and tail the gooseberries and simmer them in water until soft. Put through a sieve and weigh the pulp. Allow 350 g/12 oz sugar to each

450 g/1 lb pulp. Stir the sugar until dissolved and bring to the boil. Cook gently, stirring all the time, until the mixture is very thick. Pour into hot jars and cover. Keep for some months before use if possible. This is then very good as a spread; or it can be sliced and eaten with cold meat, particularly lamb.

Makes 900 g (2 lb)

APPLE HONEY

2.25 kg/5 lb apples
900 g/2 lb sugar
Grated rind of one lemon
1 tablespoon lemon juice
25 g/1 oz butter

The best apples are those which 'fluff' quickly while cooking. Peel and core the apples and cut into small pieces. Put into a pan with a tight-fitting lid and very little water, and cook gently to a fine pulp. Stir the apples occasionally to prevent burning. Add the sugar, lemon rind and juice, and butter. Bring to the boil, and then simmer for fifteen minutes. Pour into hot jars and seal. This will keep for 2–3 months.

Makes 1.8 kg (4 lb)

TOMATO HONEY

450 g/1 lb red tomatores
450 g/1 lb sugar
1 lemon

Chop the tomatoes and put them into a pan with the grated rind of the lemon. Simmer until soft, and put the mixture through a sieve. Put the pulp into the pan with the sugar and juice of the lemon, and stir until the sugar has dissolved. Boil rapidly until thick. This is a delicious and unusual filling for tarts.

Makes 450 g (1 lb)

PARSLEY HONEY

100 g/4 oz fresh parsley
750 ml/1¼ pints water
450 g/1 lb sugar
1 dessertspoon vinegar

Wash the parsley well and chop it up roughly, including the stalks. Put it into a pan with the water and bring to the boil. Boil gently until the liquid has been reduced to one pint. Strain the liquid and put it into a clean saucepan with warm sugar. Stir well and when the sugar has dissolved, bring to the boil. Add the vinegar and boil slowly for about thirty minutes until the mixture is like clear honey. Pour into pots and cover. Keeps well, like jam.

Makes 450 g (1 lb)

WELSH MINCEMEAT

225 g/8 oz butter
450 g/1 lb currants
450 g/1 lb sultanas
450 g/1 lb raisins
100 g/4 oz peel
225 g/8 oz skinned, chopped, almonds
675 g/1½ lb dark soft brown sugar
900 g/2 lb apples
350 ml/12 fl oz rum or brandy

Put all the ingredients except sugar and currants through a mincer. Mix well, stand overnight, re-mix and put into jars.

Makes 2.7 kg (6 lb)

MINCEMEAT

1.75 kg/4 lb apples
1.25 kg/2½ lb shredded suet
1.5 kg/3½ lb dark soft brown sugar
1.4 kg/3 lb currants
1 kg/2¼ lb raisins
675 g/1½ lb finely-chopped peel
2 teaspoons salt
1 tablespoon mixed spice
2 teaspoons ground nutmeg
2 teaspoons ground cloves

Peel and core the apples, and simmer them in very little water until soft. Leave overnight. Mix with all the other ingredients and put in jars.

Makes 5.5 kg (12 lb)

COOKED MINCEMEAT

450 ml/¾ pint apple juice (see method)
450 g/1 lb seedless raisins
450 g/1 lb currants
450 g/1 lb shredded suet
675 g/1½ lb light soft brown sugar
2.75 kg/6 lb cooking apples
450 g/1 lb chopped mixed peel
½ teaspoon ground mace
1½ teaspoons ground cinnamon
75 ml/3 fl oz brandy

Make the apple juice by mincing a large quantity of apples, and squeezing them in muslin to get a clear juice. Put the juice in a large pan, and bring it rapidly to the boil. Add the dried fruit, suet, brown sugar, chopped apples, peel and spices. Simmer slowly for one hour. Stir in the brandy and put into screw-topped jars. This mincemeat will keep for one year.

Makes 4 kg (9 lb)

GINGERED PEARS

3.5 kg/8 lb pears
1.75 kg/4 lb sugar
100 g/4 oz stem ginger
4 lemons

Peel, quarter and core the pears. Cut the quarters into small slices, add sugar, chopped ginger and the strained juice of the lemons. Cut the lemon rind into long thin strips, and add to the fruit and mix. Cover and allow to stand in a cool place overnight. Stir over moderate heat until the sugar has dissolved, and then bring quickly to boil. Cook very slowly for three hours until clear and thick. Pour into jars and cover.

Makes 3.5 kg (8 lb)

BRANDIED PEARS

2.75 kg/6 lb hard pears
3 lemons
8 cloves
2 kg/4½ lb sugar
10 cm/4 in cinnamon stick
6 tablespoons brandy

Peel the pears, quarter them and take out the cores. Grate the rind off the lemons and squeeze out the juice. Layer the pears, sugar and lemon rind in a large bowl and sprinkle the lemon juice over the top. Cover the bowl and leave overnight. Transfer the pears to a large casserole, covering them with the juice which has formed during the night. Add cinnamon and cloves. Cover with a lid and bake at 275°F, 140°C, gas mark 1 for six hours until the pears are tender and golden. Leave to cool, and then stir in the brandy. Remove the cinnamon stick and cloves, and transfer the pears to jars, screwing them down for storage.

Makes 2.7 kg (6 lb)

APPLE GINGER

1.75 kg/4 lb apples
1.75 kg/4 lb sugar
1.75 litre/3 pints water
50 g/2 oz ground ginger

Peel and core apples and cut them into thin slices. Dissolve the sugar in the water and boil syrup until thick. Add the apple slices and boil until transparent. Stir in ginger, boil for five minutes, pour into jars and cover. This is very good for filling tarts.

Makes 2.7 kg (6 lb)

EVERLASTING RUM-POT

1 bottle light or dark rum
Granulated sugar
Strawberries, cherries, apricots,
*   raspberries, plums, redcurrants,*
*   peaches, grapes, melon*

The fruit should be sound, whole and ripe. The rum-pot should not be over-loaded with fruit and it is best to preserve a little at a time, using only the choicest fruits. Citrus fruits, apples, bananas and pears should not be used. Gently wipe the fruit, and do not peel or stone (except for melon which should be peeled, seeded and cut into large chunks). Put fruit into a large stone crock with its own weight of sugar, and cover with rum. Cover the crock tightly with waxed paper and a lid and keep in a cool place. You can then continue adding fruit to the rum-pot throughout the season, and replacing any you use.

The fruit and syrup can be used as a 'spoon' sweet by serving small quantities with cream or yoghurt. It can also be used with a fresh fruit salad of oranges, apples and nuts, or put into a pastry case.

PRESERVED QUINCES

2.25 kg/5 lb quinces
900 ml/1½ pints cold water
1.4 kg/3 lb sugar

Peel, quarter and core the quinces, dropping them into cold water to prevent discoloration. Cook the peelings and cores in boiling water to cover for fifteen minutes, then strain off the liquid. Add the quinces to the liquid and cook slowly until tender. Remove the quinces to a basin with a perforated spoon so that the liquid runs back into the pan. Add the sugar. Stir until dissolved, and then bring quickly to the boil. Add the quinces and cook until clear. Turn into heated jars and cover.

Makes 2.7 kg (6 lb)

FRUIT SYRUP

Syrups are best stored in lever-stoppered bottles with a china cap and rubber washer, or in screw-topped bottles; ordinary bottles tend to burst. The full bottles should be sterilised by putting them in a deep pan filled with cold water to cover them. The water should be heated slowly so that it reaches simmering point within an hour, and it should then remain at this temperature for thirty minutes. When the bottles have been cooled, they should be stored in a cool dark place. To avoid the problems of sterilisation and storage, the syrups can be poured into freezer containers, leaving room for expansion, and frozen solid. Colour and flavour remains perfect by this method.

Use single fruits or a mixture for syrups. They can be made from raspberries, strawberries, elderberries, blackberries and blackcurrants. Fruit should be clean and ripe, and should not be washed if possible. A little water should be added to the fruit (about 150 ml/¼ pint to 1.4 kg/3 lb raspberries or strawberries, but 300 ml/½ pint to the same weight of blackcurrants). Simmer the fruit gently for an hour, crushing the fruit at intervals. Strain through a jellybag and allow 100 g/4 oz sugar to each 600 ml/1 pint of juice. Stir until dissolved, and then strain and bottle or freeze. In the past, syrups were often used as soothing medicine for coughs and colds. Syrups are good, diluted, as winter drinks; or they can be used as sauces for puddings.

CANDIED FRUIT AND CRYSTALLISED FLOWERS

Few farmers' wives in time past had the leisure or inclination for the elaborate processes of candying and crystallising for decoration; but they knew the value of saving the delicate flavour of flowers, herbs and the rare and treasured citrus fruit for special occasions in simple preserves. Sometimes they reduced the thick fruit pulp left from jelly-making and cooked it with sugar to make chewy sweetmeats, or candied the homely marrow too.

PRESERVED ORANGE PEEL

Peel from oranges
Sugar

Wipe orange skins and remove as much white pith as possible. Cut the peel into pieces a little thinner than a matchstick. Put a layer of peel about 1.25 cm/½ in thick in a jar and sprinkle lightly with sugar. Continue with these layers until the jar is full, put on a lid, and shake well. During the first week, shake the jar daily, and occasionally stand the jar upside down. Store in a cool dark place.

This orange peel lasts for years and is good for flavouring cakes and puddings. The longer it is kept, the richer the flavour. The jar can be topped up from time to time with fresh layers of peel and sugar.

FRUIT PASTES

Apple, pear, quince, plum and apricot pastes are made with pulped cooked fruit, cooked again with an equal quantity of sugar to make a thick paste; they are rather like the fruit butters or cheeses.

CRYSTALLISED ANGELICA

Young angelica stems
600 ml/1 pint water
100 g/4 oz salt
675 g/1½ lb sugar

Use young stems, which are best cut in April. Cut them into 10 cm/4 in lengths and put them into a glass or china bowl. Pour on a solution of boiling water and salt, and leave under cover for twenty-four hours. Lift out the pieces, drain them, peel them and wash them in cold water. Make a syrup with the sugar and 900 ml/1½ pints fresh water and boil for ten minutes. Put the angelica stems into the boiling syrup for twenty minutes. Lift them out and drain them on a rack for four days. Re-boil again for twenty minutes in the same syrup. Leave to cool in the syrup, lift out and drain for four days. Toss in sugar and store in airtight jars. Angelica is delicious cooked with rhubarb, and used in rhubarb jam, as well as for cake decoration.

CRYSTALLISED FLOWERS

Spring or summer flowers
Gum arabic crystals
Rose or orange flower water
Caster sugar

The most suitable flowers are primroses, violets, polyanthus, roses, carnation petals, forget-me-nots, mimosa, cowslips, sweet peas and fruit blossom. Flowers from bulbs should not be eaten. Use three teaspoons gum arabic crystals to three tablespoons rose or orange flower water. Mix them in a screw-topped jar and leave them for three days, shaking occasionally until the mixture is like sticky glue. Use a small paint brush to paint the flowers (or petals of large flowers) with this solution. Coat the petals completely, as bare spots will shrivel and will not keep. Dredge lightly and put on a rack covered with sugared, greaseproof paper. Dry in an airing cupboard or very cool oven for twenty-four hours. Store in tins between waxed paper.

PICKLES, CHUTNEYS AND SAUCES

NOTE: *Use malt vinegar for the recipes in this section.*

PICKLED BEETROOT WITH MUSTARD

1.75 kg/4 lb beetroot
600 ml/1 pint vinegar
6 teaspoons sugar
2 teaspoons dry mustard powder
2 teaspoons salt

Boil the beetroot until tender. Peel and slice into a jar. Put the vinegar and dry ingredients into a saucepan and bring slowly to the boil. Boil for five minutes, then pour over the beetroot. Cover when cool.

Makes 1.8 kg (4 lb)

PICKLED BEETROOT WITH HORSERADISH

8 medium-sized beetroot
7 g/¼ oz whole black peppercorns
1 small root horseradish (grated)
1.1 litre/1 quart malt vinegar
7 g/¼ oz whole allspice berries
1 teaspoon rock or sea salt

Bake the beetroot in the oven for 1½–2 hours. When cool, skin and slice, and place in jars. Boil the vinegar, horseradish, salt, pepper and spice together. When cool, pour over the beetroot. Store in a dry place.

Makes 675 g (1½ lb)

PICKLED EGGS

16 hard-boiled eggs
15 g/½ oz black peppercorns
15 g/½ oz whole allspice berries
15 g/½ oz root ginger
1.1 litre/2 pints white vinegar

The eggs are best if boiled for ten minutes. Simmer the vinegar with the peppercorns, allspice and bruised ginger for five minutes. Peel the eggs and put them into a jar. Pour the boiling vinegar over the eggs and cover. Store in a cool dry place. These eggs can be eaten within two weeks, but they will keep indefinitely.

PICKLED GREEN TOMATOES

1.25 kg/2½ lb green tomatoes
225 g/8 oz onions
225 g/8 oz sugar
600 ml/1 pint white vinegar

Slice the tomatoes and the onions. Sprinkle generously with salt. Leave for twenty-four hours, then drain off the salt liquid completely. Make a syrup with the sugar and vinegar and put in the tomatoes and onions. Simmer until tender, pour into preserving jars and cover while hot.

Makes 1.35 kg (3 lb)

PICKLED ONIONS

Small button onions
Vinegar to cover
To each 1.1 litre/2 pints of vinegar
*   allow 2 teaspoonfuls allspice and 2*
*   teaspoonfuls whole black*
*   peppercorns*

Peel onions into clean dry jars, boil vinegar with spices, and immediately or when cold pour it over to fill jars completely; cover with parchment paper and store in a dry place. They will be ready in two weeks if the vinegar is used cold, but much earlier if it is used while hot.

PICCALILLI WITH CAULIFLOWER

2.25 kg/5 lb cauliflower
450 g/1 lb onions
Salt
75 g/3 oz dry mustard powder
275 g/10 oz sugar
25 g/1 oz turmeric powder
25 g/1 oz ground ginger
8 chillies
8 cloves
2.25 litre/4 pints vinegar

Cut the vegetables into small pieces and put into a pan. Sprinkle with salt and allow to stand overnight. Mix the remining ingredients. Put the vegetables into a saucepan, pour on the mixture, and boil until tender. When cold, the pickle is ready for use. The vegetables can be varied; make *Marrow Piccalilli* or *Green Tomato Piccalilli* instead of cauliflower.

Makes 2.7 kg (6 lb)

MILITARY PICKLE

1 marrow
1 cauliflower
450 g/1 lb beans
450 g/1 lb onions
450 g/1 lb Demerara sugar
7 chilies
25 g/1 oz turmeric powder
25 g/1 oz ground ginger
100 g/4 oz plain flour
2.25 litre/4 pints vinegar

Cut the vegetables into small pieces and cover with salt. Allow to stand overnight, and then drain. Put into a saucepan, add the vinegar and boil for five minutes. Add the sugar and chillies. Mix the remaining ingredients to a smooth paste with a little vinegar and add while boiling. Boil for thirty minutes. Stir well to prevent burning. Bottle when cold.

Makes 2.25 kg (5 lb)

BEAN PICKLE (CUMBERLAND)

2.75 kg/6 lb runner beans
6 large onions
1.1 litre/2 pints white vinegar
100 g/4 oz plain flour
50 g/2 oz dry mustard powder
450 g/1 lb sugar
1 teaspoon black pepper
1 teaspoon turmeric powder

Slice the beans and onions thinly and cook in a little water until tender. Drain thoroughly. Moisten the flour with a little vinegar, then mix together in a saucepan the vinegar, flour, mustard, sugar, pepper and turmeric. Bring to the boil and continue stirring all the time until the mixture is thick. Add beans and onions and continue stirring until the mixture boils again. Put into jars, and cover while hot.

Makes 2.7 kg (6 lb)

PICKLED CABBAGE

1 large firm red cabbage
Salt
Cayenne pepper
Vinegar

Cut the cabbage into quarters and remove the stalk. Cut the leaves into very thin slices and put them on a large flat dish. Sprinkle with plenty of salt and leave overnight. Next morning, stir well to mix in the salt, and then drain the cabbage. Fill clean bottles with the cabbage, and sprinkle quarter teaspoon Cayenne pepper on top of each one. Cover with cold vinegar, tie down securely and store. This cabbage can be eaten within two or three days.

Makes 900 g (2 lb)

BLACKBERRY CHUTNEY

2.75 kg/6 lb blackberries
900 g/2 lb apples
900 g/2 lb onions
25 g/1 oz salt
50 g/2 oz dry mustard powder
50 g/2 oz ground ginger
2 teaspoons ground mace
1 teaspoon Cayenne pepper
1.1 litre/2 pints vinegar
900 g/2 lb light soft brown sugar

Wash the blackberries and put them into a pan. Peel and chop the apples and onions. Add them to the blackberries together with all the remaining ingredients except the sugar. Cook gently for one hour. Put through a sieve and add the sugar to the pulp. Cook until thick and pour into jars. Cover as usual.

Makes 3.5 kg (8 lb)

ELDERBERRY CHUTNEY

675 kg/1½ lb elderberries
1 onion
50 g/2 oz Demerara sugar
300 ml/½ pint vinegar
15 g/½ oz ground ginger
A few cloves
1 teaspoon salt
¼ teaspoon pepper
¼ teaspoon mace
50 g/2 oz stoned raisins

Pass berries through sieve, chop the onion finely, and boil with the other ingredients for fifteen minutes. Pot as usual.

Makes 450 g (1 lb)

GREEN TOMATO CHUTNEY (1)

675 g/1½ green tomatoes
450 g/1 lb apples
225 g/8 oz sugar
350 g/12 oz sultanas
100 g/4 oz onions
1 teaspoon salt
25 g/1 oz mixed spice
600 ml/1 pint vinegar
Pinch of dry mustard powder

Use an enamelled pan or casserole. Chop all the ingredients and cook slowly together until the colour deepens; this takes 1½–2 hours. Put into jars, and seal.

Makes 900 g (2 lb)

GREEN TOMATO CHUTNEY (2)

450 g/1 lb green tomatoes
3 large apples
3 large onions
600 ml/1 pint cider vinegar
450 g/1 lb sugar
½ teaspoon Cayenne pepper
1 teaspoon ground cloves
1 teaspoon ground cinnamon

Peel the tomatoes, slice and put in a bowl with a sprinkling of salt. Allow to stand overnight. Next day, turn into a strong pan, add peeled, sliced apples and onions, vinegar, sugar, Cayenne and spices. Bring to the boil and simmer for about one hour until the sugar is dissolved and the fruit and vegetables tender. Turn into warmed jars, allow to cool, then cover tightly and store in a cool, dark place.

Makes 900 g (2 lb)

PLUM CHUTNEY

900 g/2 lb plums, weighed after stoning
450 g/1 lb carrots
600 ml/1 pint vinegar
450 g/1 lb stoned raisins
450 g/1 lb light soft brown sugar
25 g/1 oz chopped garlic
25 g/1 oz chillies
25 g/1 oz ground ginger
40 g/1½ oz salt

Mix the plums with minced carrots and vinegar and simmer until soft. Add the other ingredients, and simmer until the mixture is thick. Put into jars and cover tightly.

Makes 1.5 kg (3 lb)

RHUBARB CHUTNEY

900 g/2 lb chopped rhubarb
900 g/2 lb brown sugar
450 g/1 lb sultanas
25 g/1 oz crushed garlic
25 g/1 oz finely-chopped shallots
25 g/1 oz salt
25 g/1 oz bruised root ginger
600 ml/1 pint vinegar
½ teaspoon Cayenne pepper
Grated rind and juice of 1 lemon

Put all the ingredients into a thick pan and boil together until thick and dark brown. Remove the root ginger, and put chutney into pots.

Makes 2.25 kg (5 lb)

MINT CHUTNEY

450 g/1 lb sugar
600 ml/1 pint vinegar
450 ml/¾ pint mint leaves, pressed
    down lightly
225 g/8 oz sultanas
6 small onions
225 g/8 oz red or green tomatoes
450 g/1 lb cooking apples
2 teaspoon salt
2 teaspoons made English mustard

Mince together the onions, apples, tomatoes and mint leaves. The sultanas can be minced or left whole as preferred. Heat the vinegar, and add and dissolve the sugar, salt and mustard. Mix in the minced ingredients and boil for twenty minutes. Bottle and seal.

Makes 1.2 kg (2½ lb)

BEETROOT CHUTNEY

900 g/2 lb onions
1.4 kg/3 lb beetroot
600 ml/1 pint vinegar
675 g/1½ lb apples
450 g/1 lb sugar
½ teaspoon salt
1 teaspoon ground ginger

Boil and chop the onions and beetroot. Put into a pan with the vinegar, the peeled and chopped apples, sugar, salt and ginger. Boil to a thick chutney consistency, which will take about one hour. Pot as usual.

Makes 2.25 kg (5 lb)

RIPE TOMATO CHUTNEY

450 g/1 lb ripe tomatoes
225 g/8 oz onions
100 g/4 oz sour apples
450 g/1 lb stoned raisins
100 g/4 oz light soft brown sugar
7 g/¼ oz salt
7 g/¼ oz ground ginger
Pinch of Cayenne pepper
300 ml/½ pint vinegar

Skin the tomatoes and peel and core the apples. Chop the tomatoes, onions, apples and raisins. Mix all the ingredients and boil to a mash. This will take an hour or more. Put into small jars, cover, and seal when cold.

Makes 675 g (1½ lb)

MRS HAWKYARD'S DRIED FRUIT CHUTNEY

2.25 kg/5 lb apples
300–600 ml/½–1 pint vinegar
1 tablespoon salt
225 g/8 oz stoned dates
225 g/8 oz raisins or sultanas
1 small tablespoon ground ginger
225 g/8 oz onions, minced
450 g/1 lb Demerara sugar
6 chillies

Peel and core the apples. Put the salt, ginger, chopped chillies and sugar into a pan with some of the vinegar. Add the apples and minced onions and bring to the boil. Add the chopped dates and whole raisins or sultanas and simmer until thick and brown, adding more vinegar as required (the apples make a lot of juice, and the chutney should not be runny). Put into warm jars and cover well.

Makes 1.8 kg (4 lb)

NORWICH APPLE CHUTNEY

1.25 kg/2½ lb apples
225 g/8 oz onions
225 g/8 oz light brown sugar
100 g/4 oz sultanas
15 g/½ oz salt
450 ml/¾ pint vinegar
1 tablespoon pickling spice
½ tablespoon dry mustard powder
1 teaspoon coriander seeds
2 pieces root ginger

Peel the apples and onions. Mince or chop them finely. Simmer with half the quantity of vinegar until tender. Add sugar, sultanas, salt, pickling spice, mustard, coriander seeds, ginger and remainder of the vinegar. Simmer for about twenty minutes until thick. Remove the ginger and turn into heated jars while hot and put on glass lids, if used, firmly. If ordinary jars are used, a cover should be put on to stop the vinegar evaporating, i.e. good corks or a layer of thick, waxed, vinegar-proof paper, then a metal lid and clip; the clip can be removed when the chutney is cold.

Makes 900 g (2 lb)

PICKLED PEARS

2.75 kg/6 lb hard pears
1.4 kg/3 lb sugar
300 ml/½ pint vinegar
25 g/1 oz cinnamon stick
24 cloves
24 peppercorns

Peel the pears and cut in half if they are large. Put them in cold salted water to keep a good colour. Dissolve the sugar in the vinegar and add the spices tied in a muslin bag. When hot, add the pears and simmer gently until the pears are tender but not broken. Put the pears into warm jars, pour the syrup over, and cover firmly.

Makes 1.8 kg (4 lb)

SPICED VINEGAR APPLES

900 g/2 lb apples
15 g/½ oz whole cloves
15 g/½ oz stick cinnamon
15 g/½ oz whole allspice
600 ml/1 pint vinegar
900 g/2 lb sugar
½ teaspoon salt

Put the sugar, vinegar and salt into a saucepan, with the spices tied in a muslin bag. Bring to the boil and add the peeled, cored and sliced apples. Cook gently until the apples are tender, then take out the fruit, drain carefully and pack into warm jars. Boil the syrup until it thickens, take out the spice bag, pour over the apples and seal tightly.

Makes 900 g (2 lb)

PICKLED BLACKBERRIES

1.4 kg/3 lb blackberries
450 g/1 lb sugar
300 ml/½ pint vinegar
½ teaspoon each ground cinnamon and
*   ground cloves*

Simmer the vinegar, sugar and spices together for five minutes. Add the blackberries and simmer for fifteen minutes. Bottle and seal down while very hot.

Makes 900 g (2 lb)

SPICY PICKLED PLUMS

1.25 kg/2½ lb firm plums
600 ml/1 pint vinegar
675 g/1½ lb sugar
2.5 cm/1 inch cinnamon stick
1 teaspoon cloves
Blade of mace
10 allspice berries

Prick the plums with a needle. Boil the vinegar, sugar and spices and pour over the plums. Leave overnight. Drain off the syrup and boil it for ten minutes. Pour over the fruit again and leave for twelve hours. Bring to the boil with the plums. Remove the spices and put the plums into hot preserving jars. Boil up the syrup, pour over the plums, and screw on the tops immediately.

Makes 1.35 kg (3 lb)

SWEET PICKLED DAMSONS

1.75 kg/4 lb large damsons
600 ml/1 pint vinegar
675 g/1½ lb sugar
25 g/1 oz mixed pickling spice

Prick the damsons with a large needle. Put the vinegar, sugar and spice in a pan and heat until the sugar has dissolved. Add the damsons, cook until soft but not broken, and then lift carefully into jars. Reduce the vinegar to a syrup by boiling, remove the spices and pour the syrup over the fruit. Cover tightly. These are good with poultry or cold meat, particularly goose.

Makes 1.8 kg (4 lb)

PICKLED GOOSEBERRIES WITH GARLIC

900 g/2 lb gooseberries
225 g/8 oz light soft brown sugar
1.1 litre/2 pints white wine vinegar
1 tablespoon dry mustard
2 whole garlic heads
350 g/12 oz raisins
15 g/½ oz Cayenne pepper

Cook together the gooseberries, sugar and half the vinegar until they are soft. Stir in the mustard, crushed garlic, raisins and Cayenne pepper. Add the remaining vinegar, stir well and put into preserving jars. Seal at once. Keep for six months before using.

Makes 1.35 kg (3 lb)

GOOSEBERRY RELISH

900 g/2 lb gooseberries
350 g/12 oz seedless raisins
450 g/1 lb onions
225 g/8 oz brown sugar
1 teaspoon dry mustard
1 tablespoon ground ginger
2 tablespoons salt
¼ teaspoon Cayenne pepper
2 teaspoons turmeric
600 ml/1 pint vinegar

Top and tail the gooseberries and put them through a mincer with the raisins and the onions. Add the sugar, mustard, ginger, salt, Cayenne pepper, turmeric and vinegar. Bring slowly to the boil, and then simmer for forty-five minutes. Put through a coarse sieve. Reheat thoroughly and pour into bottles.

Makes 900 g (2 lb)

WORCESTER SAUCE

600 ml/1 pint brown malt vinegar
2 shallots
2 tablespoons anchovy essence
3 tablespoons walnut ketchup
2 tablespoons soy sauce
A little salt

Mix all the ingredients together and put into a bottle. Cork firmly and shake the bottle twice a day for a fortnight. Strain and bottle.

Makes 600 ml (1 pint)

TOMATO SAUCE

1.75 kg/4 lb ripe tomatoes
4 large onions
450 g/1 lb Demerara sugar
25 g/1 oz salt
50 g/2 oz peppercorns
15 g/½ oz cloves
2 teaspoons Cayenne pepper
600 ml/1 pint vinegar

Slice the tomatoes and onions and mix with the other ingredients. Simmer gently for two hours, stirring occasionally. Rub through a fine sieve, leaving nothing but spice, seeds and skin in the sieve. Bring to the boil and boil for five minutes. Bottle when cold.

Makes 1.2 litres (2 pints)

SWEET-SOUR PLUM SAUCE

1.75 kg/4 lb plums or damsons
225 g/8 oz onions
600 ml/1 pint vinegar
25 g/1 oz salt
15 g/½ oz each ground ginger, allspice,
*   nutmeg and dry mustard powder*
225 g/8 oz sugar

Cut up plums and onions and cook with the vinegar, salt and spices for thirty minutes. Sieve, stir in the sugar and bring to the boil. Simmer for one hour, stirring occasionally, and bottle while still warm.

Makes 1.2 litres (2 pints)

POTTED PRODUCTS

Potted meats, fish and even vegetables and cheeses were often prepared in country households before the days of refrigerators. 'Potting' under a coating of clarified lard or butter was a useful way of preserving such products for a few days when supplies were plentiful. These 'potted' preserves were put up in very small jars, as they had to be eaten quickly once the seal of fat was broken. The flesh was usually minced or pounded, making them rather like pastes, so they can be sliced and eaten with salad, or can be used on toast or in sandwiches.

Whole game birds were sometimes 'potted' too; but the term only indicated that they had been cooked for a long time in a slow oven just with some butter and their own juices. Thereafter, the recipe might be for a hot pot-roast dish or for a whole bird preserved in fat.

CLARIFIED BUTTER

Place the desired quantity of unsalted butter in a saucepan and place over low heat. Skim off the foam from the surface as the butter heats. One half pound of butter will take 15–20 minutes; a larger quantity can take as long as an hour. When the butter becomes very clear, particles of sediment sink to the bottom of the pan, and foam stops rising to the surface, remove it from the heat and strain it through an extremely fine sieve or through several thicknesses of cheesecloth, leaving any excess sediment in the bottom of the pan. Allow the butter to cool to lukewarm before using it. Clarified butter can be stored in the refrigerator for several weeks, or can be frozen and stored for up to six months.

Right: Chutney combines well with fresh mackerel to make a tasty supper.
Over: Potted cheese formed part of meals in the fields and was served for high teas and snacks.

LET THE WEALTHY AND
ROLL IN SPLENDOUR AND
I ENVY THEM NOT, I DECLARE
I EAT MY OWN
MY OWN CHICKEN
I SHEAR MY OWN FLEECE AND
I HAVE LAWNS, I HAVE BOWERS
I HAVE FRUITS, I HAVE FLOWERS
THE LARK IS MY MORNING ALARMER
SO JOLLY BOYS NOW
HERE'S GOD SPEED THE PLOUGH
LONG LIFE AND SUCCESS TO THE
FARMER

INDUSTRY   PRODUCETH   WEALTH

POTTED SHRIMPS

450 g/1 lb shrimps, cooked and shelled
275 g/10 oz butter
½ teaspoon ground mace
½ teaspoon ground nutmeg
Pinch of Cayenne pepper

Prepare the shrimps. Put 100 g/4 oz butter into a saucepan, and melt it slowly. Skim off foam and remove butter from heat. Spoon the clear butter into a bowl, and discard the milky solids at the bottom of the pan. Melt the remaining butter over moderate heat. Stir in the spices and add the shrimps. Stir them so they are coated in the butter. Pour into individual dishes or one large one. Pour the clarified butter over them and leave until cold.

Serves 4–6

POTTED MEAT

Put any kind of cooked meat twice through the mincer, or rub through a sieve; season to taste, not forgetting nutmeg or cinnamon, if liked. Mix well with butter and press into pots; pour melted clarified butter over to preserve it.

POTTED BEEF

450 g/1 lb shin of beef
1 teaspoon salt
⅛ teaspoon pepper
100 g/4 oz clarified butter, melted

Wash and dry the meat and cut into very small pieces. Season and place in a stone jam jar or in a basin; cover with aluminium foil or greased greaseproof paper and stand in a pan of water. Cover the pan and simmer for two and a half hours. Strain the liquid into a bowl and add 75 g/3 oz of the butter. Mince the meat several times till very fine. Mix with the liquid. Put into a clean jar or bowl and pour over it the remaining melted clarified butter. Keep in a cool place and use within two days.

Serves 4–6

POTTED RABBIT

1 jointed rabbit
50 g/2 oz butter
1 lump of sugar
1 onion
12 cloves
12 allspice
6 peppercorns
Ground nutmeg to taste
225 g/8 oz butter
1 dessertspoon Worcestershire sauce

Soak the rabbit joints in salted water for two hours and dry well. Put them into a casserole with a tightly-fitting lid, and add 50 g/2 oz butter, sugar, the onion stuck with cloves, allspice, peppercorns, and a good sprinkling of nutmeg. Put on the lid and cook at 300°F, 150°C, gas mark 2 for three hours. Cool and remove meat from the bones. Put the meat through the mincer twice and mix with the juices from the casserole, most of the 225 g/8 oz butter and the Worcestershire sauce. Put into small pots, and cover with a little extra melted butter.

Serves 4–6

Page 175: **Rosemary, thyme and bay are some of the most useful fresh herbs to give colour and flavour to savoury dishes.**
Left: **Hearty rabbit casserole and dumplings for a warming winter meal.**

POTTED PARTRIDGE

2 partridges
225 g/8 oz butter
300 ml/½ pint game stock

Season the birds inside and out and put a lump of butter in each. Put into a casserole with some good stock and the rest of the butter, cover with a double layer of cooking foil and a lid and cook at 325°F, 170°C, gas mark 3 for one and a half hours. Leave until cold, when the butter will form a seal on top. Do not uncover until they are to be eaten; they will keep for several days.

Serves 4–6

POTTED PIGEON

3 pigeons
Worcestershire sauce, if liked
Pepper and salt
Bone stock from pigeons
Melted butter

Skin and clean the pigeons. Place in a pan and cook till meat begins to leave the bones. Take off fire, remove bones and mince meat finely. Put bones back in pan and boil till water has reduced to one cupful. Add all seasonings, moisten with bone stock and a little melted butter. Boil or bake small heatproof pots or jars to sterilise. Press in the meat mixture, and knock out any air pockets. Cover with melted butter, preferably clarified.

Serves 4–6

POTTED GROUSE

2 old grouse
1 carrot
1 onion
50 g/2 oz streaky bacon
Clarified butter, melted
Bunch of mixed herbs
Salt and pepper

Slice the carrots and onions, and cut the bacon in neat pieces and fry in butter until golden. Put into a casserole with the herbs and plenty of salt and pepper, and put the grouse on top. Cover with stock and cook at 300°F, 150°C, gas mark 2 for two and a half hours. Remove the carrot. Remove all the bones of the grouse, and put the meat through a mincer, then pound, sieve or process it in a liquidiser. Press into a shallow dish and cover with melted, clarified butter.

Serves 4–6

POTTED CHEESE

225 g/8 oz butter
900 g/2 lb mature cheese
Salt
Powdered mace
Port as required
Clarified butter

Pound the butter and cheese in a mortar. Season with salt and mace, moisten with a very little port and press down well in little pots. Cover with clarified butter.

Serves 4

CHAPTER TWELVE

STORING, SALTING

AND SMOKING

STORING VEGETABLES AND FRUITS

Root vegetables can be stored in trenches or under straw or sand on a dry floor. Potatoes and turnips take up a lot of space indoors, so they are best stored outside in trenches about 1 m/3 ft wide and 15 cm/6 in deep. The roots should be piled in triangular heaps about three feet high, covered with straw or earth, leaving a little straw at the top so that moisture escapes. Turnips can also be stored in a heap, simply covered with straw or stand, and so can beetroot. Parsnips can be stored under straw in a cool place, or they can be left in the ground. Carrots are best lifted and stored in a cool place in boxes raised above ground level.

Marrows and pumpkins can be stored in a cool dry place away from frost, or they can be hung in nets. Plenty of stalk should be left on, and it is wise to seal the stalk end with wax.

Let onions dry outside for a week or two, and then store them in an old stocking, or plait them together.

Storing fruit and nuts Apples, pears and quinces are best left in an airy place to cool and sweat for a few days before storing permanently. The apple store should be a cool, dark and very slightly moist place such as a shed, cellar or attic which is frost-proof. Store the fruit on trays; inspect it frequently and remove unsound fruit. Pears ripen quickly and need extra care. Special eating apples can be wrapped in waxed paper or in sheets of newspaper before storing in boxes.

Nuts should be removed from their outer husks, and walnuts and almonds need scrubbing. Chestnuts and walnuts can be packed in a crock with salt or dry sand between each layer. Nuts to be used for cooking can be shelled, dried off in a cool oven, and packed into clean glass jars.

DRYING FRUIT AND VEGETABLES

Drying is the oldest method of preservation. Apples, dessert pears, grapes, sweet plums, peas, beans, onions, leeks and mushrooms are all suited to it. They can be dried in the oven, a warm cupboard or a rack over the stove, in a constant gentle heat with a current of air to carry away moisture (this is best obtained by leaving a cupboard or oven door slightly open). Fruit and vegetables should be spread on oven racks or wire cake trays spread with muslin; this should be scalded before use, or it may scorch during drying. The ideal heat for drying is between 60°C–75°C, 120°F–150°F, as the fruit or vegetables should be dried, *not* cooked or scorched.

Apple Rings Apples should be ripe but not over-ripe. Using a silver or stainless steel knife, peel and core the apples and cut into rings about quarter of an inch thick. Put into a basin of salt water immediately (use 15 g/$\frac{1}{2}$ oz salt to 1.1 litre/2 pints water) and leave for ten minutes. The rings should be threaded on a stick which can rest on the runners of an oven, and the rings should not touch each other. Dry at 150°F, 75°C, for some hours. Apples should be like dry chamois leather, moist and pliable. Cool in the air before packing tightly in paper bags, or in dry jars or tins. Store in a dry, dark place.

It is best to soak dried fruit for twenty-four hours before cooking, and to use the water used to soak them for cooking too; flavour it with a little lemon or vanilla, a clove or a piece of ginger.

Dried Plums Plums must be ripe. Halve and stone them, or dry them whole. Stretch muslin on sticks to replace oven shelves, and dry plums on these. Dry slowly like apples.

Dried Beans Leave haricot beans on the plants until dry and withered. Pull up plants and hang in an airy shed. Shell the peas and store as for seed. Young French and runner beans can be sliced, blanched for five minutres, drained, and dried in a thin layer.

Dried Mushrooms Cut the stalks short and peel the mushrooms. Lay them on the oven racks and when they are dried quite stiff, store them away. When preparing them for use, soak them in water and simmer them in a little stock.

Dried Onions and Leeks Peel onions and take away any bad parts, and slice them; lay on muslin on oven racks. Leeks may be cut in strips lengthwise if preferred. Keep them moving about occasionally to help the drying, and when they are quite crisp take them out, and after a little while store them away.

Dried Peas Leave marrowfat varieties on the plants until dry and withered. Pull up plants and hang in an airy shed. Shell the peas and store as for seed. For young, sugary peas, blanch them for five minutes, drain them and shake off excess

moisture. Spread out in a thin layer and dry very carefully, without scorching.

SALTING AND SMOKING

While it is comparatively easy to salt food at home, smoking is a more complicated business and involves the preparation of a smoke-box. Salting preserves food quite well, but smoking had additional preservative qualities as well as giving the food a special flavour. Food which can be smoked include eel, salmon, trout, cod's roe, ham and bacon, tongue, turkey, goose, duck and chicken, beef, mutton and home-made sausages; some items need brining before smoking.

The simplest form of smokehouse can be constructed in a ten-gallon drum with the bottom cut out and a replaceable top which has a few holes punched in. This is mostly useful for smoking trout or haddock, suspended over the concentrated source of heat and smoke. Haddock should be split, cleaned and beheaded, rubbed inside and out with salt, and left overnight, then dried in the open air for three days.

Trout need not be split or beheaded, but the gut should be removed. The fish should then be suspended by the tail on a rod across the top of the drum, and tied with a piece of wire at least one foot from the fire. The drum should then be up-ended over the fire – best made between bricks on which the drum stands. The heat must be evenly maintained during smoking – which will take from nine to twelve hours.

In addition to the basic smokehouse, keep a good supply of wood handy. The object of creating the smoke is to make fumes which solidify the albumen in the meat. This halts decomposition; any special flavour is a bonus. The best smoke is produced by slow combustion by hardwood shavings; oak, beech, and hornbeam are excellent, especially with additional flavour provided by juniper and bay. The addition of thyme, sage or heather makes a good variation. Resinous wood should be avoided because they can give an unpleasant flavour to some products.

A slightly more elaborate smokehouse can be constructed for permanent use. This can be a drum or a packing-case which has been made smoke-proof at the joints, standing across a trench. The trench should be about 3 meters/10 feet long, 30 cm one foot deep and 30 cm/1 foot wide, dug in the direction of the prevailing wind, with old paving stones or sheet iron to roof it over. If the lid of the house is hinged, it will be easier to use, and it should have small holes or a tube inserted as a vent.

To use this type of smokehouse, light a fire at the end furthest from the box, cover with stones or iron sheets, and open the lid of the box. When the fire is red hot, draw it to the end of the trench and put a load of hardwood sawdust between the fire and the box. Leave a little flue space, cover the trench and seal all spaces with earth. The food can be hung across the box and the lid closed and not opened for forty-eight hours.

The idea is to build up a progressively denser smoke which dries and flavours the food gradually; if the first smoke is too dense, it will form a dry coating on the food which will not then be penetrated by the later smoking. For this type of smoking, the food should be brined first in a strong brine (with enough salt to float a potato). A small fish need only be brined for twenty minutes, but a salmon needs several days, and more elaborate preparation.

The smoking method which is most likely to appeal today is the one using an old-fashioned farmhouse chimney with equipment which can still be used for hams, sausages and other meats. These must be cured first, and are then best left to dry for two or three days before smoking. The food to be smoked can also be hung above the opening of an old bread oven so that the smoke gently enfolds it.

In the latter case, the temperature should never rise above 145°C (90°F), at which point the fat melts and the meat is spoiled. The fire should only be smouldering, not flaming. On the first day, the meat should be smoked for thirty minutes, then rubbed down with pepper, thyme and chopped bay leaves, which will cling to the fat. After cooling and drying for forty-eight hours, the meat should be smoked again for one hour. After further drying for forty-eight hours, and one hour's smoking, a light flavour will be obtained. The meat should then be hung in the chimney for two or three weeks before being stored in a cool dry place. The meat will lose about one-quarter of its weight in smoking.

The wide chimney can be used for the complete smoking, simply with the exposed meat suspended high up on a bar or on hooks on wire, but the fire will need careful attention throughout. Smoke the meat for about an hour a day, allowing a total of at least three weeks for complete smoking.

A better method of smoking is by regulating the smoke-flow; construct a smoking-box for the fireplace, to fit on a wall above the fire. To do this, a sheet of metal has to be fitted across the whole chimney with a piece of piping going through it and the wall into the smoking-box. A second piece of piping should then go out of the top of the box and back into the chimney. Meat in the box needs about two hours a day for eight consecutive days.

SALT CURES FOR HAM AND BACON

Sweet Cure This is a sweet pickle for ham or bacon, using a carcass of about eight score lb. Split the carcass, and from each side cut a rounded ham and a round shoulder (fore-ham). De-bone the middle except for the chump end of the loin, which can be used fresh or lightly salted. To make packing easier, the middle may be sub-divided into back and belly. Rub the knuckles with salt, and sprinkle salt on the joints, then pack into a crock. Pour over a pickle (for 7 kg/15 lb ham or fore-ham) consisting of 225 g/½ lb block salt, 450 g/1 lb black treacle, 220 g/½ lb brown sugar, 600 ml/1 pint malt vinegar and 1.1 litre/2 pints old ale, with 1 tablespoon saltpetre. Turn the joints over in the pickle twice daily for the first week, then once daily for four weeks. Hang the meat to drain for twenty-four hours, then encase in clean cotton bags and suspend from hooks. The hams are ready for use in six months and do not need soaking before cooking. For 7 kg/15 lb bacon, use a pickle of 225 g/8 oz salt, 225 g/8 oz brown sugar, 50 g/2 oz black treacle, 150 ml/¼ pint vinegar and no saltpetre. Pack in crocks and pour over pickle, and turn joints twice daily for three weeks. The bacon can be used immediately after curing, or it can be soaked for one week with several changes of water before cooking as required.

Dry Cure This is a dry-cure method for a carcass of 16–20 score, using 12.5 kg/28 lb salt and 225 g/8 oz saltpetre. Singe the flesh to remove hair and cut the carcass, removing the head, the chine with some of the back meat, and the ribs with a coating of lean meat.

Clean by sprinkling the flesh side with salt, and rubbing salt into the skin. Leave the sides, flesh side down, to drain for twenty-four hours, then wipe with a clean cloth. Sprinkle saltpetre on the flesh side of the shoulders and hams. Sprinkle half the salt over the sides, which are placed one on top of the other. After seven days, sprinkle half the remaining salt on, and put the top side at the bottom. After seven more days, add remaining salt, and reverse positions of sides. The sides are in cure for about four weeks in all.

Wipe off sides after curing, and hang up to dry for seven days. Store sides whole, or for convenience cut into hams, middles and shoulders before hanging them in clean cotton bags.

Heavy Carcass Cure This is most suitable for a heavy carcass, which may be cut in three different ways. One method involves removing a chine of six inches to eight inches wide and salting the 'long side'; the carcass can be simply split; or it may be cut into hams, fore-hams and middles. The ingredients for curing are 12.5 kg/28 lb salt, 225 g/$\frac{1}{2}$ lb saltpetre and 450 g/1 lb demerara sugar. Rub saltpetre in first, spreading most thickly on blood patches. Sprinkle meat with salt and pack on a layer of salt in a trough. Place hams on top and every day for a fortnight, sprinkle on salt. When meat is cured, wipe salt off and sprinkle with flour. After being dry for three months, pack in a bin containing slaked line.

CHAPTER THIRTEEN

THE HERB GARDEN

Most cottages and farm gardens have various herbs growing among the flowers or vegetables, where they can be quickly and easily picked for cooking. A specially-planned herb garden is pleasant, but by no means necessary for the cook; a large tub or a series of pots can provide nearly all the herbs needed in the kitchen. The taller and more decorative herbs can be used in flower borders in the time-honoured country way.

Herbs are easy to grow and not fussy about soil on the whole. The many types of mint, and angelica, like moist soil, and parsley needs a rich soil, while fennel prefers open ground. Many others prefer poor, dry land, but they do like sunshine. Most of the herbs can be grown from seed, but others are best grown from the division of older plants. Where a plant can be grown by both methods, it will be found that root division gives quicker results.

A selection of the following herbs will be found very useful in the kitchen. These herbs are of course best used fresh, as they have a much stronger, fresher flavour; but they can usefully be dried or frozen for winter use.

Drying Herbs Herbs for drying should be picked just before they come into flower. They are best picked on a dry day before the sun is hot. Remove leaves from the stalks of large varieties, and tie small herbs into sprays. Put on shallow trays in thin layers and leave in a cool oven (125°F, 60°C) or an airing cupboard, or on a cooker rack, until dry. This gives clean freshly-coloured herbs with good flavour. Parsley is not very easy to dry; it should be placed in a hot oven (400°F, 200°C) for one minute, and then be finished off in the cool oven or airing cupboard; then it will retain its bright green colour. When the herbs are dry, remove the stems and rub the herbs down with a rolling pin. Put into small tins or jars, and store in a cool, dry place. Dried herbs should be used within a year, sooner if possible.

Freezing Herbs Wash herbs and pack them in foil or polythene to freeze. Herbs can also be chopped and frozen in ice-cube trays, and then the cubes can be taken out and packed into bags for storage.

GROWING AND USING
HERBS

ANGELICA
Growing   Seeds germinate slowly and should be kept in moist sand before sowing in August, or should be used straight from the plant.
Main Uses   Candy the stems for decoration and flavouring. Good as a flavour with rhubarb.

BASIL
Growing   Sow the seeds in gentle heat in March, prick off into boxes and then plant in a rich warm border in June. Plants also grow well in pots. This is a tender plant which does not care for cold.
Main Uses   Use with turtle soup, tomatoes, liver.

CARAWAY
Growing   Sow the seeds in autumn or spring. This plant is a hardy biennial. Harvest in July and remove seeds at once.
Main Uses   In cakes and biscuits, and on cabbage.

CHEVRIL
Growing   Sow small successions of seed from early spring until autumn, watering carefully in dry weather.
Main Uses   In salads, egg and fish dishes.

CHIVES
Growing   Divide clumps every spring or autumn, and lift and re-plant every two years. Don't let the plant run to flower.
Main Uses   For salads, egg dishes, cream cheese, soups, flavoured vinegar.

CORIANDER
Growing   Sow seeds of this annual plant in April. Cut down the plant when the seeds begin to ripen, leave in a warm place to dry and remove the seeds.
Main Uses   With sweets, curries. Use the leaves in soups and stews.

DILL
Growing Sow seeds in March and thin out plants.
Main Uses Leaves – new potatoes, fish. Seeds – flavoured vinegar, cucumber dishes.

FENNEL
Growing Sow seeds in April or May, but germination is uncertain.
Main Uses Use leaves for fish, salads, vinegar, pickles.

HORSERADISH
Growing Plant single crowns with young roots 15 cm/6 in long in well-prepared soil trenched with a dressing of rotten manure. Spring plants will give good roots in autumn, which should be lifted and stored in sand.
Main Uses In sauce, flavoured vinegar.

LOVAGE
Growing A large plant which likes a lot of water. Sow plants in the spring (they will need about 1 meter/3 ft growing space, and are also tall). Will also grow from fresh seed.
Main Uses The flavour of the leaves which is like hot-spiced celery is good in soups, casseroles, stews.

MARJORAM
Growing Pot and Sweet-Knotted Marjorams are the types most commonly grown; grow from seed. The plant is tender and best grown as an annual.
Main Uses In forcemeats, soups, stews.

MINT
Growing There are dozens of different mints, but round-leaved (Lamb Mint) is best for sauce. Plant in early spring by division of roots in a moist place. Mint roots spread rapidly.
Main Uses In mint sauce, and on new potatoes, jelly.

PARSLEY
Growing Grow from seed in the open ground or in pots. Germination is slow. Plants like a well-drained soil in a semi-shady position.
Main Uses Immensely varied. Our most commonly used garnishing and flavouring herb.

ROSEMARY
Growing Grow from cuttings in well-drained sheltered soil.
Main Uses With lamb, pork.

SAGE

Growing   Grow from seed or root division. There are many varieties, but Narrow Silver Leaved and Red Sage make very beautiful plants.

Main Uses   Use with pork, goose, duck, sausages, broad beans.

SAVORY

Growing   Winter Savory is a perennial, evergreen in winter; but Summer Savory which is an annual raised from seed, has a more subtle flavour.

Main Uses   With broad beans.

SWEET BAY

Growing   A bush which grows best in dryish half-shady conditions. Bay trees are difficult to get started; they are best propagated by layering.

Plants do not like frost, but young plants in pots can be kept in a greenhouse in winter.

Main Uses   In soups, stews, fish dishes, egg custards, milk puddings.

TARRAGON

Growing   Choose French tarragon which has a better flavour then the Russian variety. Grow from cuttings or root division. The plant does not dry well and is best used fresh.

Main Uses   With many foods; a favourite mild seasoning for chicken, fish, sauces, flavoured vinegar.

THYME

Growing   There are many varieties of thyme, which may be grown from seed or from root division. Lemon thyme is deliciously refreshing.

Main Uses   In forcemeats and stuffings, soups.

DISHES USING HERBS

Herb Vinegar Flavoured vinegars can be made which are delicious for cooking. Place 225 g/8 oz herbs in 600 ml/1 pint of wine vinegar for four days to infuse. Tarragon and fennel make particularly good vinegars.

Herb Jelly Mint jelly is often made, but the same recipe is less often used (though it can be) to produce parsley, sage, thyme or bay leaf jelly. These are delicious with pork, ham and poultry.

SAGE AND ONION STUFFING

450 g/1 lb onions
Salt and pepper
100 g/4 oz soft white breadcrumbs
2 teaspoons finely-chopped sage
25 g/1 oz butter

Chop the onions and simmer with just enough water to cover them for ten minutes. Strain and keep the cooking water. Mix the onions with the breadcrumbs, sage, butter, salt and pepper and add just enough water to bind the stuffing. Use for fat meats such as pork, goose and duck.

Serves 4–5

PARSLEY AND THYME STUFFING

75 g/3 oz soft white breadcrumbs
50 g/2 oz butter
1 tablespoon chopped onion
Grated rind and juice of 1 lemon
Salt and pepper
1 tablespoon chopped fresh thyme
½ tablespoon chopped fresh parsley
1 tablespoon chopped fresh marjoram
1 egg

Melt the butter, and soften the onion in it until golden. Mix with all the other ingredients and use for stuffing chicken, turkey or veal.

Serves

HERB SEASONING

Dried orange peel
Dried thyme
Dried marjoram
Dried hyssop

Pound the orange peel to powder. Mix two parts orange peel with one part of each of the herbs. Keep in a well-stoppered jar to use for stuffings, forcemeats and meat loaves.

SWEET HERB SEASONING

50 g/2 oz parsley
50 g/2 oz marjoram
50 g/2 oz chervil
25 g/1 oz thyme
25 g/1 oz lemon thyme
25 g/1 oz basil
25 g/1 oz savory
15 g/½ oz tarragon

Dry the herbs when they are in season and weigh them when they are dried. Rub each one to a fine powder, and sift through a strainer. Mix together and keep in a tightly-stoppered bottle for seasoning.

SEASONING SALT, HOME-MADE

1 teaspoon, mixed dried herbs
15 g/½ oz mixed ground cloves, mace
   and ginger
25 g/1 oz pepper
25 g/1 oz salt

Mix well together and rub through a sieve. Put into an airtight tin or bottle and keep near the stove. Use sparingly in soups and stews.

ROSEMARY OR LAVENDER SUGAR

Sprigs of fresh rosemary or lavender
Caster sugar

Clean and dry the rosemary or lavender. Put into a screw-topped jar and fill with sugar. Shake well and leave for twenty-four hours. Shake again and leave for a week before use. Use the sugar in milk puddings of all kinds, or spinkle on cakes or biscuits.

MIXED HERB BUTTER

100 g/4 oz butter
1 teaspoon chopped fresh parsley
½ teaspoon chopped fresh mint
½ teaspoon chopped fresh chives
¼ teaspoon chopped fresh tarragon
¼ teaspoon chopped fresh marjoram
Lemon juice

Soften the butter at room temperature until it can be creamed. Blend in the herbs, and add as much lemon juice as the butter will absorb easily. Put into tightly-covered jars and keep in a cool place. Use on bread, toast or sandwiches, or on hot meat or fish.

Makes 100 g/4 oz

PARSLEY SAUCE

1 tablespoon butter
1 tablespoon flour
300 ml/½ pint milk or stock
3 tablespoons chopped fresh parsley

Melt the butter and work in the flour. Add the milk slowly, and cook gently for five minutes. Just before serving, add the chopped parsley.

This is a good standard sauce with fish and ham, and the stock from cooking the fish or ham can be used as all or part of the liquid.

Serves 2–3

FENNEL SAUCE

40 g/1½ oz butter
1 heaped tablespoon chopped fennel
25 g/1 oz plain flour
450 ml/¾ pint water
Salt and pepper

Melt 25 g/1 oz butter and cook the fennel in it for half-a-minute. Blend in the flour and gradually add the water, beating smoothly over a low heat. Cook gently until the sauce is creamy, season to taste and add the remaining butter. Serve with grilled mackerel and other fish. (It does wonders for frozen fillets.)

Serves 3–4

HERB CHEESE

2 tablespoons fresh mixed herbs
2 tablespoons double cream
3 tablespoons dry sherry
100 g/4 oz grated sharp-flavoured
  cheese
Salt and pepper

Choose a good mixture of herbs, such as parsley, sage, thyme, chives and tarragon. Put them with the cream, sherry, cheese, salt and pepper into a thick pan over a low heat, and heat very gently until the mixture is creamy and very pale green in colour. Put into small hot jars and cover with jam pot covers. Keep in a cool place, and use fairly quickly.

Serves 4

HERBED SAVOURY BALLS

75 g/3 oz plain flour
25 g/1 oz shredded suet
½ teaspoon baking powder
1 small onion, finely-chopped
Salt and pepper
1 heaped tablespoon chopped mixed
    herbs

Mix together the flour, suet and baking powder. Add the very finely-chopped onion, salt and pepper and chopped herbs. Mix to a light dough with cold water. Form into small balls and roll them lightly in flour. Put into soup or stew and simmer for twenty minutes.

Serves 4

HERB PIE WITH HAM

225 g/8 oz shortcrust pastry
25 g/1 oz grated cheese
100 g/4 oz cooked ham or rindless
    bacon
2 eggs
300 ml/½ pint milk
1 tablespoon chopped onion
1 teaspoon chopped chives
1 teaspoon chopped parsley
1 teaspoon chopped tarragon
1 teaspoon chopped lovage
1 teaspoon chopped chervil
1 teaspoon chopped marjoram
Salt and pepper

This combination of herbs is a very good one, but of course you can vary the selection to suit what you have to hand. Mix the pastry, including the cheese in it; line a 20 cm/8 in flan ring or pie plate with the pastry. Chop the ham or bacon finely and sprinkle on the pastry base of the pie. Beat together the eggs and milk lightly and add the finely-chopped onions and herbs. Season with salt and pepper and pour into the pastry case. Bake at 400°F, 200°C, gas mark 6 for thirty-five minutes.

Serves 4

SAGE AND ONION TART

225 g/8 oz shortcrust pastry
3 medium-sized onions
25 g/1 oz butter
150 ml/¼ pint creamy milk
1 egg
1 tablespoon chopped fresh sage
1 teaspoon chopped fresh parsley
100 g/4 oz rindless bacon, chopped
Salt and pepper

Line a 20 cm/8 in pie plate with the pastry. Chop the onions and toss them in the hot butter until soft. Mix with the milk, egg, herbs, chopped bacon and seasoning, and pour into the pastry case. Bake at 400°F, 200°C, gas mark 6 for thirty-five minutes.

Serves 4

POTATO POT PIE WITH ROSEMARY

900 g/2 lb potatoes
450 g/1 lb onions
Salt and pepper
Rosemary sprigs
50 g/2 oz butter
300 ml/½ pint milk

Peel the potatoes and onions and slice them thinly. Put into a greased casserole in alternate layer, seasoning well with salt and pepper and with very finely-chopped rosemary leaves. Dot with the butter and finish with a layer of potatoes. Pour in the milk. Put on a lid and bake at 350°F, 180°C, gas mark 4 for one and a half hours until the milk has been absorbed. The lid should be removed for the last fifteen minutes to brown the top of the potatoes. This pot pie is good with all kinds of meat or poultry.

Serves 4

HERBED MEAT LOAF

450 g/1 lb spinach
450 g/1 lb lean pork
100 g/4 oz cooked ham
1 heaped tablespoon chopped mixed
    herbs
50 g/2 oz onion
½ garlic clove
1 teaspoon salt
Pinch of black pepper
¼ teaspoon ground nutmeg
1 egg

Cook the spinach in as little liquid as possible, drain it and press it dry. Mince the pork finely, and chop the ham in small pieces. Grate the onion and crush the garlic clove. Mix together the spinach, pork, ham, herbs, onion and garlic and season with salt, pepper and nutmeg. Mix well with the egg. Put into a 900 g/2 lb loaf tin, and cover. Put into a baking tin containing hot water which comes halfway up the dish. Bake at 350°F, 190°C, gas mark 4 for one hour. Cool for twenty-four hours before using.

Serves 4

FISH IN CIDER AND HERB SAUCE

450 g/1 lb fish fillets
Seasoned flour
Butter
Mixed fresh herbs, chopped
Squeeze of lemon juice
5 tablespoons dry cider
2 tablespoons cream

Use any filleted fish you like for this dish. Bream, sole, hake and John Dory are all good cooked this way. Dry the fillets and dip them in seasoned flour, using plenty of freshly-ground pepper. Heat a good knob of butter in a flameproof oven-to-table pan and add about a tablespoon of finely-chopped mixed fresh herbs (fennel, parsley, marjoram and basil are good for this). Fry the fish, skin side down, for three minutes, then turn the fish and cook for a further three minutes. Squeeze on lemon juice, and add the cider. Cover the pan and simmer over very low heat for ten minutes. Just before serving, take the skin off the fish, and pour on the cream. Serve straight from the hot dish.

Serves 4

PICKLED NASTURTIUMS (MOCK CAPERS)

Nasturtium seeds
1.1 litre/2 pints vinegar
50 g/2 oz salt
12 peppercorns
Piece of horseradish root
2 cloves
4 tarragon leaves

Wash the seeds and leave them to soak overnight in cold water. Mix the vinegar with salt, peppercorns, horseradish, cloves and tarragon. Drain the seeds and put them into jars. Cover with the cold spiced vinegar. Cover tightly and keep for twelve months before using.

CHAPTER FOURTEEN

GOOD CHEER

Home-made wines, beers and soft drinks used to be part of every country household's stores. These drinks were made from flowers, fruit, roots, grains and herbs. The normal equipment for the brewing or wine-making consisted of a stoneware crock with a lid; and fermentation was usually started by the old method of spreading yeast on a piece of toasted bread. After fermentation, the liquid was put into wooden casks, and, later, into bottles.

In winter, the home-made beer, cider or wine was often used heated and spiced, to ward off colds and chills. But for children, the treatment for colds was more usually a dose of a fruit or flower-flavoured syrup, diluted with water; this served to soothe a rough throat, and induce sleep, and it unintentionally gave a child the much-needed vitamins stored in the summer fruit.

Lighter drinks, such as barley water and lemonade, were usually made as thirst-quenchers. The same use was made of the wines, beer and cider drunk (often in the form of syllabubs) by the men working in the harvest and hay fields in summer. They were, however, used even more for social occasions of all kinds, as were whey and buttermilk drinks.

BEERS, CIDER AND WINES

HOP BEER

450 g/1 lb malt extract
25 g/1 oz hops
4.5 litres/8 pints water
25 g/1 oz yeast

Boil the malt, hops and water for one and a half hours, adding water to make up the original quantity. Strain through muslin. When the liquid is cool, add the yeast and leave covered for three days. Syphon off and bottle. Put one lump of sugar in each bottle and cork. This is ready in seven days.

Makes 4.5 litres (8 pints)

GINGER BEER FROM A 'PLANT'

15 g/½ oz fresh yeast
2 teaspoons ground ginger
2 teaspoons sugaer
450 ml/¾ pint water
For ingredients added later, see the
   recipe

Mix all these ingredients. Leave for twenty-four hours, then feed daily with one teaspoon ground ginger and one teaspoon sugar. After seven days, strain through a cloth. Reserve both the liquid and the solid matter in the cloth (which is the 'plant').

To finish the ginger beer, mix the strained liquid with 3 litres/5 pints cold water, the juice of two lemons and 675 g/1½ lb sugar dissolved in two pints hot water. Mix well, pour into screw-topped (beer or cider) bottles, and leave for a week before using. This makes one gallon ginger beer.

Halve the remaining solid (the 'plant') and mix with 450 ml/¾ pint water; add another 15 g/½ oz

fresh yeast, two teaspoons ground ginger and 2 teaspoons sugar. Leave for twenty-four hours, then feed daily with 1 teaspoon ground ginger and 1 teaspoon sugar for seven days as before. Strain as before. Repeat the whole process every two weeks to keep up a supply of ginger beer.

Makes 4.5 litres (8 pints)

QUICK GINGER BEER

25 g/1 oz root ginger
450 g/1 lb sugar
25 g/1 oz cream of tartar
Juice and rind of one lemon
25 g/1 oz yeast

Put the bruised ginger, sugar, cream of tartar and lemon rind into a bowl. Pour on 4.5 litre/8 pints boiling water, stir well, and leave to stand until cold. Add the lemon juice. Mix the yeast with a good 5 tablespoons cold water and add to the other ingredients. Leave overnight, then bottle in screw-topped bottles. This ginger beer can be used after forty-eight hours.

Makes 4.5 litres (8 pints)

SIMPLE CIDER

1.4 kg/3 lb cooking apples
6.8 litres/12 pints water
900 g/2 lb granulated sugar
3 lemons

Clean the apples, cut them up and mince them with the cores and skins, Place in an (for preference) earthenware bowl and add cold unboiled water. Leave for one week, stirring night and morning. Strain the liquid. Stir in the sugar and add the grated rind and juice of the lemons. Set aside for twenty-four hours, then strain and bottle tightly in screw-topped bottles. This still cider can be drunk within a few days of making, but tastes even finer if left for a few months.

Makes 6 litres (10 pints)

CIDER

3.5 kg/8 lb apples
9 litres/16 pints boiling water
25 g/1 oz root ginger
Juice of three large lemons
3.5 kg/8 lb sugar
Scand 150 ml/¼ pint boiling water

Do not use any metal when making this drink. Do not peel the apples, but cut them up roughly. Cover with boiling water and leave for two weeks, pressing and crushing the apples well from time to time. Strain the liquid. Add the bruised root ginger, lemon juice and sugar, and stir to dissolve the sugar. Add 150 ml/¼ pint boiling water, and then leave to stand for fourteen days, removing the scrum as it rises. Strain into screw-topped bottles and screw on the tops lightly for two days. Tighten the stoppers and keep in a cool, dark, dry place for two months.

Makes 9 litres (16 pints)

NETTLE BEER

900 g/2 lb young nettles
4.5 litres/8 pints water
2 lemons, rind and juice
450 g/1 lb Demerara sugar
25 g/1 oz cream of tartar
25 g/1 oz yeast

Cut off the nettle roots and discard them. Rinse the tops, drain and boil in the water for fifteen minutes. Strain into a bowl containing the lemon peel (remove all white pith) and juice, sugar and cream of tartar. Stir vigorously and cool. Add the yeast and keep the bowl covered with a thick cloth in a warm room for three days. Strain, bottle and cork, and keep a week before drinking. This is supposed to be a good drink for cleansing the system in spring and early summer.

Makes 4.5 litres (8 pints)

HERB BEER

Small bunch of mixed herbs
25 g/1 oz hops
9 litres/16 pints water
900 g/2 lb sugar
15 g/½ oz yeast

Make a good selection of herbs, including parsley, thyme, sage and mint. Put the hops and herbs into water and boil for one hour. Strain on to the sugar and stir until it is dissolved. When the mixture is cool, add the yeast. Leave the liquid to stand for twelve hours, and put it into bottles.

Makes 9 litres (16 pints)

BEETROOT BEER

450 g/1 lb beetroot
225 g/8 oz sugar
600 ml/1 pint stout

Wash the beetroot and slice into a bowl. Sprinkle on the sugar and leave for twenty-four hours. Strain, add the stout, bottle and cork. This is ready in 7–14 days.

Makes 750 ml (1¼ pints)

TREACLE ALE

450 g/1 lb golden syrup
225 g/8 oz black treacle
4.5 litres/8 pints water
25 g/1 oz yeast
15 g/½ oz ground ginger (optional)
Rind of one lemon (optional)

Melt the syrup and treacle in the boiling water. Cool and add yeast. Cover the bowl with a thick cloth and keep in a warm room for three days. Syphon off the liquid without disturbing the yeast deposit, bottle and cork. Keep several days before drinking. If ginger and lemon rind are used, add with the boiling water.

Makes 4.5 litres (8 pints)

BARLEY WINE

450 g/1 lb barley
450 g/1 lb raisins
450 g/1 lb potatoes
1.75 kg/4 lb sugar
25 g/1 oz yeast

Put the barley and chopped raisins into an earthenware jar. Do not peel the potatoes but cut them into very small pieces or grate them. Add them to the barley and raisins, with the sugar. Pour on one gallon of hot, but not boiling, water and stir until the sugar has dissolved. Add the yeast and leave for twenty-one days, stirring every day. Strain and bottle, leaving the corks loose for a week or two. Cork firmly and leave at least six months before use.

Makes 4.5 litres (8 pints)

HONEY BOTCHARD

25 g/1 oz hops
4.5 litres/8 pints water
1.5 kg/3½ lb honey
25 g/1 oz yeast
1 slice toast

Put the hops into the water and boil them for thirty minutes. Strain the liquid and then stir in the honey. Spread the yeast on both sides of the toast and let it float in the wine. Let it start fermenting, and leave it for twenty-one days after fermentation has begun. Then skim the wine and pour into bottles. It is ready to drink within a few weeks after bottling.

Makes 4.5 litres (8 pints)

EASY APPLE WINE

2.75 kg/6 lb apples
4.5 litres/8 pints water
900 g/2 lb sugar

Cut up the apples, including the skins and cores. Cover with one gallon of water, and mash and

stir frequently for two days. Strain the liquid and heat up 600 ml/1 pint of it. Pour this over the sugar. Stir well to dissolve, and then add the rest of the liquid. Leave to stand for three days. Skim, strain and bottle, corking lightly at first. Push corks in firmly later.

Makes 4.5 litres (8 pints)

BEE WINE

1.4 kg/3 lb honey
Peel of two lemons
4.5 litres/8 pints cold water
15 g/½ oz yeast
7 g/¼ oz phosphate of ammonia
7 g/¼ oz cream of tartar

Add the honey and lemon peel to cold water and boil for thirty minutes. Pour into a container and when the mixture has become tepid, add the yeast creamed with a little cold water. Add the phosphate of ammonia and the cream of tartar. Cover the container with a piece of muslin and let it ferment. When the liquid has ceased 'working', cover the container closely. After six months, pour into bottles and cork down.

Makes 4.5 litres (8 pints)

NETTLE WINE

4.5 litres/8 pints young nettles
50 g/2 oz root ginger
3 lemons, rind and juice
4.5 litres/8 pints water
1.4 kg/3 lb white sugar
15 g/½ oz yeast
1 slice toast

Boil the nettles, bruised ginger root, lemon rinds and juice together in the water until a dark green, then strain and add the sugar. Put the yeast on toast, and put it on the wine when it is at blood heat. Allow to ferment. When fermentation has ceased, put into bottles with a few raisins in each one.

Makes 4.5 litres (8 pints)

ORANGE WINE

12 large juicy oranges
4.5 litres/8 pints boiling water
1.4 kg/3 lb sugar

Wash the oranges and slice them thinly, including the peel. Put into a china basin and pour over boiling water. Cover with a cloth and leave for a week, stirring two or three times a day. Strain the liquid. Heat up 600 ml/1 pint and stir in the sugar until dissolved. Add to the remaining liquid. Pour into bottles and cork lightly. Allow to ferment. Leave until fermentation has ceased, and then seal. This will be ready in four months.

Makes 4.5 litres (8 pints)

POTATO WINE

900 g/2 lb raisins
1.75 kg/4 lb granulated sugar
600 ml/1 pint clean wheat
2 large potatoes, grated
4.5 litres/8 pints hot water
25 g/1 oz yeast

Mix the raisins, sugar, wheat and grated potato with the hot water. When cooled to just warm, add the yeast. Set aside in a warm place and allow it to ferment for three weeks. Stir it every day. Carefully strain off through a jelly bag into bottles but do not squeeze the bag as this will make the wine cloudy. Seal and store. The wine will clear itself in about four weeks and should be fit to use soon afterwards but it will improve with longer keeping.

Makes 4.5 litres (8 pints)

SLOE WINE

4.5 litres/8 pints sloes
4.5 litres/8 pints boiling water
50 g/2 oz root ginger
Sugar

The sloes are best picked after a frost. Put them into a bowl and pour on boiling water. Add the bruised ginger and cover with a piece of muslin. Leave for three days, stirring each day. Strain and allow 450 g/1 lb sugar to each 1.1 litre/2 pints of liquid. Stir well, and then bottle and cork lightly. Fermentation will soon start. Leave alone until fermentation ceases. This wine can be drunk after four months, but improves with keeping longer.

Makes 4.5 litres (8 pints)

MEAD

25 g/1 oz dried hops
900 g/2 lb honey
9 litres/16 pints water
25 g/1 oz yeast
1 slice toast

Put the hops and honey into the water and boil slowly for one hour. Cool, and when lukewarm add the yeast spread on a piece of toast. Cover and leave for four days. Strain through muslin, and bottle. Allow to ferment. Only cork loosely until fermentation has ceased, then cork tightly. Keep for one year before using.

Makes 9 litres (16 pints)

ELDERFLOWER CHAMPAGNE

4 heads of elderflowers
675 g/1½ lb sugar
2 tablespoons white wine vinegar
4.5 litres/8 pints cold water
2 lemons

Put elderflowers, sugar, vinegar and water into a bowl. Squeeze the lemons and add the juice to the mixture. Cut the lemon skins in quarters and add to the liquid. Leave to stand for twenty-four hours, stirring occasionally. Strain and bottle into screw-topped bottles. Ready to drink within a few days.

Makes 4.5 litres (8 pints)

MARROW RUM

1 large firm ripe marrow
Demerara sugar

The marrow should be very, very firm and too tough for cooking or cutting with a kitchen knife. Saw through the stalk end, and scoop out the seeds and pulp. Fill the marrow completely with sugar. Put the top back and tape it tightly in place. Put into a bag made of strong cloth and hang it in a cool, dry place. After two weeks, fill the marrow again with sugar. Seal the top again and hang up the marrow. After about a month, the sugar will begin to drip. Take the marrow from the bag and make a hole in it where the sugar is starting to drip. Let the liquid run through a muslin-covered funnel into bottles. Cork them lightly. Fermentation will soon start. When it has ceased (in a few weeks) cork firmly. Keep for at least a year before using.

SOFT DRINKS, CORDIALS AND SYRUPS

THRIFTY APPLE DRINK

Peelings and cores from 1.75 kg/4 lb
apples
2.25 litres/4 pints boiling water
1 lemon
12 lumps sugar

Put the peelings and cores in a bowl and pour on boiling water. Rub the sugar lumps over the rind of the lemon to extract the flavour, and add these to the liquid. Cut the lemon in thin slices and add. Cover and leave overnight. Strain and sweeten. Do not keep.

Makes 2.25 litres (4 pints)

RHUBARB DRINK

3 sticks rhubarb
1 lemon
225 g/8 oz sugar

Cut the rhubarb in very small pieces and pour on 4.5 litres/8 pints boiling water. Add the lemon cut in thin slices and the sugar. Stir until the sugar has dissolved, and then leave until cold. This is a very refreshing drink on a hot day, but not for keeping.

Makes 4.5 litres (8 pints)

LEMON BARLEY WATER

100 g/4 oz pearl barley
2 lemons
50 g/2 oz loaf sugar
1.1 litre/2 pints boiling water

Wash the barley and put into a saucepan. Just cover with cold water and bring to the boil. Boil for four minutes and strain off the water. Put the barley into a large jug. Rub off the yellow part of the lemon rind on to the sugar and add this to the barley. Pour on boiling water. Stir to dissolve the sugar and leave until cold. Stir in the juice of the lemons. Strain into a jug, and chill.

Makes 1.1 litre (2 pints)

FRESH LEMONADE

4 lemons
900 g/2 lb sugar
1 teaspoon oil of lemon
1 dessertspoon tartaric acid
1.1 litre/2 pints boiling water

Squeeze the lemons over the sugar in a basin. Add the oil and acid. Pour on the boiling water. Stir well to dissolve the sugar and leave until cold. Pour into bottles and cork firmly. Store in a cool place, and dilute with water to taste.

Makes 1.1 litre (2 pints)

SPICED CIDER DRINK

1.1 litre/2 pints cider
2 tablespoons honey
2 tablespoons lemon juice
1 teaspoon ground nutmeg
1 teaspoon ground cinnamon

Place all the ingredients in a saucepan and bring gently to the boil. Simmer for ten minutes. Strain through muslin before pouring into glasses. Garnish with apple slices and lemon slices.

Makes 1.1 litre (2 pints)

KENTISH CORDIAL

1.1 litre/2 pints damsons
1.1 litre/2 pints water
600 ml/1 pint elderberries
1.75 kg/4 lb sugar
5 drops essence of cloves
A little clear honey

Remove the stones from the damsons, and crack twelve of them. Pour water over the damsons and cracked stones and leave for twenty-four hours. Boil for fifteen minutes, then strain the liquid over the elderberries. Leave again for twenty-four hours and bring to boiling point. Add the sugar and simmer for ten minutes. Take off the heat and add the essence of cloves. Bottle when cold, adding one teaspoon clear honey to each pint. Good for a cold, diluted with hot water.

Makes 1.8 litre (3 pints)

SUFFOLK BLACKBERRY CORDIAL

1.1 litre/2 pints ripe blackberries
600 ml/1 pint white vinegar
450 g/1 lb loaf sugar
225 g/8 oz honey

Put the blackberries into an earthenware jar and pour on the vinegar. Leave them to stand for a week, stirring and pressing the blackberries two or three times a day to squeeze out the juices. Strain the liquid into a saucepan and add the sugar and honey, and boil for five minutes. Cool completely and pour into dark bottles. Cork well and store in a cool place. Use one tablespoon of cordial in a glass of hot water as a good bedtime drink; again, it is very good for relieving a cold.

Makes 1.1 litre (2 pints)

ELDERBERRY SYRUP

2.25 kg/5 lb ripe elderberries, weighted
  after stripping
600 ml/1 pint water
1 small egg white, lightly whipped
Loaf sugar
Brandy

The berries should be weighed when they have been stripped from their stalks. Wash them and put them into an earthenware jar with the water. Cover and leave in a very low oven until the fruit is pulpy. Strain through a jelly bag and measure the juice. Allow 450 g/1 lb sugar to each 600 ml/1 pint of liquid. Put the juice in a pan and add the egg white which has been whipped to a light froth. Bring to the boil and remove the scum. Warm the sugar and add to the liquid. Bring to the boil, skimming often, and leave to simmer for five minutes. Put into bottles and add one teaspoon brandy to each bottle. Seal tightly. Dilute with hot or cold water when used. Another drink very good for colds.

Makes 1.1 litre (2 pints)

LEMON SYRUP

2 lemons
800 g/1¾ lb cube sugar
600 ml/1 pint boiling water
25 g/1 oz tartaric acid

Peel the lemons very thinly. Add the peel to the loaf sugar and pour on the boiling water. Squeeze the juice of the lemons into a basin. Mix the tartaric acid with it, then stir all together. Strain and bottle. Use about 2 tablespoonsful to a tumbler of water.

Makes 1.1 litre (2 pints)

RASPBERRY VINEGAR

900 g/2 lb raspberries
1.1 litre/2 pints white vinegar
900 g/2 lb sugar

Put the raspberries into a bowl and crush well. Put them into a jar with the vinegar, cover with muslin, and leave for a week. Strain the liquid into a saucepan and add the sugar. Heat gently until the sugar has dissolved, then boil rapidly, removing the scum as it rises. Pour into warm bottles and cork well. Dilute with hot or cold water to drink.

Makes 1.1 litre (2 pints)

HOT MIXED DRINKS

MULLED ALE

3 eggs
1.1 litre/2 pints milk
600 ml/1 pint ale
400 g/4 oz caster sugar
A little grated nutmeg

Bring the ale to the boil in a saucepan, then set aside. Beat the eggs, and stir in the milk, pour

this mixture into the ale. Add the sugar and nutmeg, and heat slowly, but do not boil. Let it thicken, stirring meanwhile. Serve very hot.

Serves 6

OATMEAL CAUDLE

2 tablespoons oatmeal
600 ml/1 pint hot water
Lemon rind
Pinch of cinnamon
Light soft brown sugar
Blade of mace
600 ml/1 pint ale, heated

Boil the oatmeal in the water with the lemon rind and spices and enough brown sugar to taste. When thick, pour into the heated ale, stirring meanwhile.

Serves 5

MILK POSSET

600 ml/1 pint milk
75 ml/3 fl oz white wine or sherry
A squeeze of lemon
A little sugar
Pinch of ground ginger
Pinch of nutmeg

Heat the milk; when it froths add the wine or sherry. Strain and add lemon juice, and sugar to taste. Stir in ginger and nutmeg. Serve hot.

Serves 3

CORNISH EGGY'OT

2 eggs
2 tablespoons sugar
1.1 litre/2 pints beer

Beat the eggs and sugar together and pour on hot beer. Stir briskly and drink while hot. *Sampson* is made the same way but substituting cider for beer.

Serves 4

TREACLE POSSET

300 ml/½ pint milk
1 tablespoon golden syrup, or dark
   treacle

Bring the milk to the boil and pour it over the syrup or treacle in a jug; stir well and serve very hot.

Serves 2

HOT CHRISTMAS PUNCH

12 lumps sugar
2 oranges
8 cloves
1 level teaspoon ground nutmeg
1 stick cinnamon
4 tablespoons water
2 lemons
1 litre/1¾ pints cider
75 ml/3 fl oz rum
75 ml/3 fl oz brandy

Rub the sugar over the rind of one of the oranges to remove the zest. Cut this orange in halves, squeeze out the juice and put into a pan with the sugar. Cut the other orange into eight sections, stick a clove into the skin of each section and then sprinkle with the nutmeg. Add to the pan with the cinnamon, water and rind of the lemons, cut into strips. Heat gently until the sugar dissolves and then simmer for five minutes. Leave to cool until needed. Remove the cinnamon, pour in the cider and heat until really hot, but not boiling. Add the rum and then the brandy and heat again for a minute. Divide the orange sections and lemon rind between eight glasses, add the hot cider and serve at once.

Serves 8

COLD MIXED DRINKS

HIPPOCRAS

225 g/8 oz light soft brown sugar
25 g/1 oz cinnamon
15 g/½ oz ginger
7 g/¼ oz cardamom
Pinch of Cayenne pepper
1.1 litre/2 pints red wine

Stir the sugar and spices into the wine and leave it to stand until it clears completely. Pour off the clear liquid into a bottle. This is a good drink after a rather heavy meal. The spicy dregs can be used to add savour to stews and soups.

Serves 8

CORNISH SPICED ALE

1.1 litre/2 pints ale
4 cloves
Pinch of mixed spice
½ teaspoon ground nutmeg
1 teaspoon sugar
2 large apples

Heat the ale slowly but do not boil. Add the cloves and other spices, and the sugar. Peel and slice the apples and add them to the ale. Leave in a warm place to infuse for ten minutes and strain. Serve with a piece of apple in each tankard.

Serves 4

CHAPTER FIFTEEN

FESTIVAL FOOD

The country year's labour has always been broken from time to time by festivals noted for special seasonal dishes. Many of these feast days have their origins far back in history, in ancient pagan worship of the changing seasons and weather. These were later taken over by the early Christian church, and their feast-day foods with them. For instance, in Lancashire, a cake now associated with All Souls' Day on November 2nd used also to be known as a 'Har Cake', so named for the Norse god Odin or 'Har'.

Other feasts with their special suppers or cakes, marked the times when vital seasonal tasks were completed; sheep-shearing was one; the in-gathering of the harvest was another, when the annual Michaelmas goose was roasted.

Many of the favourite old buns and cakes were originally specially baked for these occasions, but the association is now forgotten. Such cakes include Sally Lunns, which were baked for Good Friday.

Shrewsbury Cakes, Tansy Cakes, Johnny Cakes, Popovers and Pikelets were all served during Lent or at Easter. So were fruit-filled pastries such as Cumberland Cakes, Banbury Cakes and Eccles Cakes.

Sometimes, however, our cakes, gingerbreads and pies record, by their names or shapes, the reason why they are made on special days. Some gingerbread moulds, for instance, record the story of an old event long past or of an act of charity; in both cases, money was left in trust long ago to provide the annual hand-out, and is still used for the same purpose.

FRITTERS, CAKES AND PIES

PATELEY FRITTERS

20 g/¾ oz yeast
600 ml/1 pint milk
350 g/12 oz plain flour
25 g/1 oz lard
75 g/3 oz currants
40 g/1½ oz raisins
½ teaspoon grated lemon rind
1 tablespoon sugar
Pinch of salt
Pinch of ground cinnamon
1 large apple

These fritters come from Yorkshire and were traditionally eaten on Ash Wednesday. The first four days of the week which signalled Lent or Shrovetide all had their own names and special foods. Collop Monday was celebrated with eggs and collops (thick slices of meat); this was followed by Shrove or Pancake Tuesday, Fritter or Frutas Wednesday, and Bloody Thursday (when black puddings were eaten).

Mix the yeast with a little warm milk and leave it to start working. Put the flour into a warm bowl. Melt the lard in the remaining milk, heated to lukewarm. Put the yeast into the centre of the flour, and add the lard and milk mixture. Leave for five minutes, and then add the currants, raisins, lemon peel, sugar, salt and cinnamon. Peel the apple and chop it finely. Add to the mixture and beat all the ingredients to a stiff batter. Leave in a warm place for one hour to rise. Put large spoonfuls of the batter into hot dripping or lard and fry for 3 minutes each side, until golden.

Makes 20

KENTISH LENTEN PIES

450 g/1 lb plain flour
2 teaspoons baking powder
100 g/4 oz butter
175 g/6 oz lard

Filling
1.1 litre/2 pints milk
2 bay leaves
4 tablespoons ground rice
100 g/4 oz sugar
100 g/4 oz butter
Pinch of mixed spice
2 eggs
1 tablespoon currants

Make a pastry with the flour, baking powder, butter and lard, and enough cold water to make a firm dough. Line large patty tins with this pastry. Reserve 150 ml/¼ pint milk, and boil the rest with the bay leaves. Mix the remaining milk with the ground rice, and add this mixture to the boiling milk. Cook for three minutes. Add the sugar, butter and spice and leave to cool to lukewarm. Add the beaten eggs and pour the mixture into the pastry-lined tins. Sprinkle with currants and bake at 375°F, 190°C, gas mark 5 for thirty minutes. Eat hot or cold.

Makes 20

PALM SUNDAY FIG CAKE

175 g/6 oz dried figs
175 g/6 oz plain flour
½ teaspoon baking powder
Pinch of salt
65 g/2½ oz caster sugar
65 g/2½ oz butter

Chop the figs roughly and simmer in just enough water to cover them until they are tender. Leave to cool. Mix together the flour, baking powder, salt and sugar, and rub in the butter. Mix to a batter with the cooled figs and cooking water. Pour into a greased and floured 18 cm/7 in cake tin, and bake at 375°F, 190°C, gas mark 5 for forty-five minutes.

Makes one 18 cm/7 in cake

SEDGEMOOR EASTER CAKES

225 g/8 oz plain flour
100 g/4 oz butter
100 g/4 oz caster sugar
100 g/4 oz currants
½ teaspoon mixed spice
½ teaspoon ground cinnamon
1 egg
2 tablespoons brandy

Rub the butter into the flour and stir in the sugar, currants, spice and cinnamon. Beat the egg with the brandy and mix with the dry ingredients. Roll out to 1.25 cm/½ in thick, cut into rounds and bake at 350°F, 180°C, gas mark 4 for twenty minutes.

Makes 24

SIMNEL CAKE

Marzipan
450 g/1 lb ground almonds
450 g/1 lb icing sugar
½ teaspoon almond essence
1 tablespoon lemon juice
4 egg yolks

Cake
175 g/6 oz butter
175 g/6 oz demerara sugar
3 eggs
225 g/8 oz self-raising flour
1 level teaspoon nutmeg
1 level teaspoon cinnamon
1 level teaspoon mixed spice
Pinch of salt
450 g/1 lb currants
225 g/8 oz sultanas
100 g/4 oz mixed peel
Milk to mix
Jam
Beaten egg to glaze
Glacé icing

Mix the marzipan ingredients to a stiff paste and knead well; divide into three and roll out two of the pieces into circles 20 cm/8 in in diameter. Put aside with the rest of the marzipan. To make the cake, cream butter and sugar together until light and fluffy, then beat in the eggs one at a time. Sieve the flour, spices and salt together and add to the mixture; finally add the dried fruit. If the mixture is a little stiff, add enough milk to give a dropping consistency. Put half the cake mixture into a greased and lined 20 cm/8 in cake tin, then put in one circle of marzipan and cover with remaining cake mixture. Bake at 300°F, 150°C, gas mark 2 for three and a half hours. Allow to cool. Brush the top of the cake with a little warm jam, and put on the second circle of marzipan; press down well. Make eleven small balls from the remaining marzipan, and arrange these round the edge. Brush lightly with a little egg and put the cake into a hot oven or under the grill for a few seconds to glaze lightly. Fill the centre with a little white glacé icing and decorate.

Makes one 20 cm/8 in cake

Originally, the Simnel cake was taken home by servant girls on 'Mothering Sunday' (the fourth Sunday in Lent) as a present for their mothers. It was made with figs, the fruit symbolising 'fruitfulness in offspring'.

Only later did it become a traditional Easter-time cake. The balls of marzipan symbolise the number of Christ's disciples.

GOOD FRIDAY HOT CROSS BUNS

225 g/8 oz plain flour
Pinch of salt
¼ teaspoon mixed spice
150 ml/¼ pint milk
15 g/½ oz yeast
50 g/2 oz butter
40 g/1½ oz caster sugar
1 egg
75 g/3 oz currants
15 g/½ oz finely-chopped peel

Sieve the flour, salt and spice in a mixing bowl. Warm milk to blood heat. Add yeast and butter, stir until dissolved, mix in sugar and beaten egg. Pour on to the flour, and beat until smooth. Turn on to a floured board, work in the currants and peel, and knead well. Put in a buttered bowl, sprinkle with flour, cover with a clean cloth, and put in a warm place to rise for one and a half hours or until the mixture has doubled its bulk. Knock down with the hand and leave to rise as before for thirty minutes. Knead the dough and shape into eight rounds. Put on two greased baking sheets and on each bun put a paste cross made with flour and water dough. Prove in a warm place until nearly doubled in size (about fifteen minutes). Bake at 425°F, 220°C, gas mark 7 for fifteen minutes. While still hot, brush with a glaze made by boiling one tablespoon sugar in one tablespoon milk.

Makes 8

EASTER BISCUITS

75 g/3 oz butter
75 g/3 oz caster sugar
1 egg yolk
Pinch of mixed spice
175 g/6 oz plain flour
50 g/2 oz currants
15 g/½ oz candied chopped peel
Milk to mix

Glaze
1 egg white
Caster sugar

Cream the butter and the sugar until light and fluffy. Add the egg yolk and work into the spice and flour. Add the fruit and peel and enough milk to give a stiff dough. Roll out thinly on a floured board and cut into shapes with a cutter. Put on to a greased baking sheet and bake at 400°F, 200°C, gas mark 6 for fifteen minutes. After ten minutes, brush with egg white and sprinkle with caster sugar.

Makes 15

GLOUCESTERSHIRE WHITE POT

1.1 litre/2 pints milk
2 eggs
1 tablespoon plain flour
1 tablespoon dark soft brown sugar
2 tablespoons black treacle or golden syrup
15 g/½ oz butter
100 ml/4 fl oz water

Mix the eggs, flour, sugar and treacle together with a little cold milk. Bring the rest of the milk to the boil and pour it on to the mixture, stirring well. Put in oven dish and dot with butter. Pour the cold water in the middle without stirring. Bake at 325°F, 170°C, gas mark 3 for two hours. This is a traditional dish for Whitsun, but is used for other festivals too.

Serves 6

FIDGET PIE

450 g/1 lb potatoes
450 g/1 lb apples
225 g/8 oz bacon
Salt and pepper
Stock
225 g/8 oz shortcrust pastry

Peel and slice the potatoes and apples. Cut the bacon into small pieces. In an ovenware dish, put a layer of potato slices, then a layer of bacon and a layer of apples. Season the layers with salt and pepper. Repeat the layers until the dish is full, and then moisten with a little stock. Cover with pastry. Bake at 400°F, 200°C, gas mark 6 for one hour. This pie was often eaten at harvest suppers. Neck of lamb can be substituted for the bacon.

Serves 4–6

SHEARING CAKE

225 g/8 oz plain flour
100 g/4 oz butter
175 g/6 oz light soft brown sugar
Rind of half lemon
1 teaspoon baking powder
2 teaspoons caraway seeds
Ground nutmeg
150 ml/¼ pint milk
1 egg

Rub butter into the flour until the mixture is like fine breadcrumbs. Stir in the sugar, lemon, baking powder, caraway seeds and a good pinch of nutmeg. Mix in the milk and lightly-beaten egg. Line a greased 18 cm/7 in cake tin with buttered paper, and put in the mixture. Bake at 350°F, 180°C, gas mark 4 for one hour. This was served to celebrate sheep-shearing time.

Makes one 18 cm/7 in cake

CREED WHEAT AND FRUMENTY

225 g/8 oz wheat grains
Pinch of salt
1.75 litres/3 pints water
1.1 litre/2 pints milk
50 g/2 oz raisins
50 g/2 oz currants
Pinch of nutmeg
50 g/2 oz sugar
2 eggs, beaten (optional)
Garnish (see recipe)

Put the wheat and salt into water in a casserole. Put into a very low oven and leave overnight to simmer until there is no water left. The wheat will then be 'creed'. Leave until needed. Then add the milk and dried fruit, together with the nutmeg and sugar, and cook gently on the hob or in the oven for two hours. Some recipes also include two beaten eggs just before the frumenty is ready. Serve with sweetened whey, chopped fresh fruit, or with rum or brandy and cream.

Serves 8

In Wiltshire, this used to be eaten on Mothering Sunday in Lent, and the 'creed' wheat could be bought ready for the dish. In Lincolnshire, it was served hot or cold at sheep-shearing time, and at harvest suppers. In Yorkshire, it was a traditional Christmas Eve or Twelfth Night dish. It is also known as Furmenty and Firmity, and a 'firmity tea' was often served to Lincolnshire children to celebrate sheep clipping.

HEREFORD BRANDY SNAP

75 g/3 oz butter
100 g/4 oz sugar
100 g/4 oz black treacle
100 g/4 oz plain flour
½ teaspoon ground ginger
1 teaspoon brandy (optional)
Squeeze of lemon juice

Melt the butter, sugar and treacle together, and leave them until cold. Stir in the flour, ginger and lemon juice and mix very thoroughly. Drop in teaspoonsful on to a well-greased tin. Bake at 350°F, 180°C, gas mark 4 for ten minutes until golden. Cool briefly, then roll quickly round the handle of a wooden spoon before they 'set'.

Makes 20

Brandy snaps used to be known as 'jumbles', and even earlier as 'gaufres' or wafers. They were traditionally sold at fairs. This recipe was used for the brandy snaps sold at the Hereford Annual May Fair.

KATT PIES (MUTTON OR LAMB)

450 g/1 lb flour
225 g/8 oz shredded suet
Pinch of salt
225 g/8 oz minced mutton or lamb
225 g/8 oz brown sugar
Salt and pepper

The pastry for this dish is made like hot-water pastry for raised pies. Put the suet into 150 ml/¼ pint of water and bring to the boil. Boil for two minutes and mix into the flour with a good pinch of salt. Cool slightly and mould into pies about 10 cm/4 in in diameter, leaving enough for lids. Arrange layers of meat, currants and sugar in the pastry cases, seasoning them well. Top with thin rounds of pastry and bake at 425°F, 220°C, gas mark 7 for thirty minutes. Eat the pies hot.

Makes 4

This is a Welsh dish, made for November 12th, Templeton Fair Day, for the past two hundred years.

HARVEST BETSY CAKE

225 g/8 oz barley flour
225 g/8 oz plain flour
1½ teaspoons baking powder
½ teaspoon salt
100 g/4 oz butter
100 g/4 oz caster sugar
1 dessertspoon golden syrup
300 ml/½ pint milk
225 g/8 oz sultanas

Sift the two kinds of flour together with baking powder and salt. Cream butter and sugar, and add syrup. Add the flour mixture and milk alternately, then fold in the sultanas. Put into a buttered 18 cm/7 in cake tin, and bake at 350°F, 180°C, gas mark 4 for one and a half hours.

Makes one 18 cm/7 in cake

SHROPSHIRE SOUL CAKES

1.4 kg/3 lb plain flour
225 g/8 oz butter, softened
225 g/8 oz sugar
25 g/1 oz yeast
2 eggs
1 teaspoon ground allspice
Milk

Sift the flour and rub in the slightly softened butter. Work the yeast with a teaspoon of sugar until it is creamy. Mix the flour with the eggs, yeast and enough milk to make a light dough. Leave to rise in a warm place for thirty minutes. Work in the sugar and spice and form into flat buns. Leave in a warm place for fifteen minutes, and then bake at 425°F, 220°C, gas mark 7 for fifteen minutes.

Makes 24

These were distributed on All Souls' Day (November 2nd) until about 1850. In parts of Cheshire and Shropshire, children still go 'souling' at the end of October, singing from house to house and collecting money.

SHROPSHIRE SPECIAL CAKES

100 g/4 oz ground rice
100 g/4 oz plain flour
Pinch of caraway seeds
100 g/4 oz butter
100 g/4 oz caster sugar
2 eggs

Mix together the ground rice, flour and caraway seeds. Cream the butter and sugar, and work in the flour mixture. Beat the eggs well and gradually add them to the mixture to make a firm dough. Roll out like pastry and cut in circles about 12.5 cm/5 in across. Bake at 375°F, 190°C, gas mark 5 for fifteen minutes.

Makes 12

This is another version of the cakes distributed on All Soul's Day.

SPECIAL PARKIN FOR GUY FAWKES NIGHT

450 g/1 lb fine oatmeal
225 g/8 oz plain flour
100 g/4 oz dark brown sugar
2 teaspoons ground ginger
1 teaspoon baking powder
225 g/8 oz black treacle
75 g/3 oz melted butter or dripping

This is a rich dark gingerbread which should be soft and sticky, and is very good eaten with a piece of cheese. Keep it for several weeks to mellow before eating, if possible in an old-fashioned bread crock. Mix all the dry ingredients together, make a well in the centre and pour in the treacle and melted butter. Heat thoroughly and bake in a buttered 18 × 28 cm/ 7 × 11 in tin at 325°F, 170°C, gas mark 3 for one and a half hours.

Makes one 18 × 28 cm/7 × 11 in cake

NORTH COUNTRY PARKIN

175 g/6 oz plain flour
1 teaspoon salt
1 teaspoon ground ginger
2 teaspoons ground cinnamon
1 teaspoon bicarbonate of soda
275 g/10 oz medium oatmeal
175 g/6 oz black treacle
150 g/5 oz butter or dripping
100 g/4 oz dark soft brown sugar
150 ml/¼ pint milk
1 egg

Sift together the flour, salt, spices and soda. Add the oatmeal and toss lightly, to mix. Warm the treacle, butter, sugar and milk together until the butter has melted. Cool slightly, add egg and beat well. Pour into the centre of the dry ingredients and stir rapidly until smooth. Turn into a greased and lined 18 cm/7 in square tin. Bake at 350°F, 180°C, gas mark 4 for one hour. Store in an airtight tin for at least two weeks before using.

Makes one 18 cm/7 in square cake

Every part of the North Country makes its own special parkin. Some are quite dry, others very moist and sticky. Parkin is still eaten on Bonfire or Guy Fawkes Night, November 5th. But it is much more ancient than the Guy Fawkes plot; in fact it is associated with old pagan fire-worship and the feast marking the beginning of winter on November 2nd. Because of this, Lancashire parkin used to be called 'Harcake' or 'Soul Hars Cake' when that date came to commemorate the Feast of All Souls.

BEDFORDSHIRE WIGS

450 g/1 lb black treacle
100 g/4 oz butter
200 ml/7 fl oz milk
450 g/1 lb plain flour
100 g/4 oz sugar
1 teaspoon bicarbonate of soda
2 teaspoons ground ginger
15 g/½ oz caraway seeds

Melt the treacle and butter together in a thick saucepan. When the mixture is hot, stir in the mix. Put all the other ingredients into a bowl and make a well in the centre. Stir in the syrup mixture and blend thoroughly together. Pour into 7.5 cm/3 in shallow round tins or one large tin, and bake at 350°F, 180°C, gas mark 4 for thirty minutes. The mixture will rise over the edge of the tins so that the thick rim looks like the curl of a wig.

Makes 24

These were eaten on St Katherine's Day, November 25th. St Katherine was the patron saint of lacemakers, and her day was considered in the country to herald the beginning of winter. Her feast was observed in many parts of the country. Somerset had Cattern Cakes, which were wheels of spiced pastry with currants. (St Katherine was martyred on a wheel, so she is also commemorated by firework Catherine wheels.)

CAROL-SINGING OR PEPPER CAKE

675 g/1½ lb plain flour
225 g/8 oz butter
225 g/8 oz dark soft brown sugar
25 g/1 oz ground cloves
675 g/1½ lb black treacle
4 eggs
1 teaspoon bicarbonate of soda
A little milk

Rub the butter into the flour until the mixture is like fine breadcrumbs. Stir in the sugar and cloves. Add the treacle and well-beaten eggs, and the bicarbonate of soda mixed with a little milk. Pour into a well-greased roasting tin and bake at 325°F, 170°C, gas mark 3 for one and three quarter hours.

Makes

This Yorkshire cake was often called 'Pepper Cake' and was given to Carol singers at Christmastide.

SPECIAL CHRISTMAS CAKE

275 g/10 oz butter
150 g/5 oz caster sugar
150 g/5 oz light soft brown sugar
5 eggs
350 g/12 oz plain flour, sifted
Pinch of salt
½ teaspoon ground nutmeg
¾ teaspoon ground cinnamon
225 g/8 oz currants
225 g/8 oz sultanas
225 g/8 oz seedless raisins
100 g/4 oz glacé cherries (quartered)
100 g/4 oz chopped candied peel
1 lemon
100 g/4 oz chopped walnuts
2 tablespoons brandy or sherry

Grease and line a 20 cm/8 in cake tin, and tie a band of brown paper round the outside. Cream together the butter and sugars till light and fluffy. Beat the eggs well and add gradually to the butter and sugar, together with a little of the sifted flour and spices. Fold in the rest of the flour, salt, fruit, peel, nuts, grated rind and juice of the lemon, brandy or sherry. When evenly mixed, turn into the prepared tin and make a slight hollow in the centre. Bake at 300°F, 150°C, gas mark 2 for two hours, then reduce heat to 275°F, 140°C, gas mark 1 for two hours. Cover top with a sheet of paper if getting too brown. Keep for three weeks before cutting. This makes a lovely moist cake.

Makes one 20 cm/8 in cake

MISS PEDELTY'S CHRISTMAS CAKE

225 g/8 oz butter
225 g/8 oz Demerara sugar
5 eggs
275 g/10 oz plain flour
50 g/2 oz ground almonds
225 g/8 oz sultanas
225 g/8 oz currants
100 g/4 oz peel
100 g/4 oz glacé cherries
50 g/2 oz chopped almonds
1 teaspoon mixed spice
1 grated orange rind
1 grated lemon rind
40 ml/1½ fl oz rum
150 ml/¼ pint milk

Mix like the previous cake and bake for 2½–3 hours at 325°F, 170°C, gas mark 3. This makes a nice Christmas cake which will keep moist for a long time.

Makes one 20 cm/8 in cake

RICH CHRISTMAS PUDDING

100 g/4 oz flour
50 g/2 oz soft white breadcrumbs
2 large eggs
1 teaspoon mixed spice
1 teaspoon ground nutmeg
1 teaspoon ground cinnamon
100 g/4 oz shredded suet
100 g/4 oz light soft brown sugar
100 g/4 oz grated apple
1 small grated carrot
100 g/4 oz mixed candied peel
100 g/4 oz chopped blanched almonds
150 ml/¼ pint beer, ale or milk
100 g/4 oz currants
225 g/8 oz raisins
100 g/4 oz sultanas
50 g/2 oz chopped prunes or dried
   apricots
Grated rind and juice of half lemon
Grated rind and juice of half orange
1 tablespoon black treacle

Mix all the ingredients together, stir well and leave overnight if possible. Place in two 1.1 litre/2 pint basins and cover with greaseproof paper and a floured cloth. Steam or boil for eight hours. Wrap very securely and store until required. Then re-boil for two hours. Serve with brandy butter or Cumberland Rum Butter.

Each pudding serves 8

MOIST CHRISTMAS PUDDING

100 g/4 oz carrots (after peeling)
100 g/4 oz potatoes (after peeling)
100 g/4 oz finely-chopped suet
100 g/4 oz currants
100 g/4 oz sultanas
50 g/2 oz candied peel
50 g/2 oz flour
50 g/2 oz soft white breadcrumbs
50 g/2 oz brown sugar
1 tablespoon black treacle

Boil the carrots and potatoes until tender. Drain and mash them well while still hot. Add all dry ingredients and treacle, and mix well. Put in a buttered 1.1 litre/2 pint basin, cover with greaseproof paper and cloth. Boil for six hours. Re-boil for two hours just before using, if stored. But eat within 2–3 weeks of making.

Serves 8

CHRISTMAS EVE WIGS

75 g/3 oz butter
225 g/8 oz self-raising flour
25 g/1 oz caster sugar
25 g/1 oz chopped mixed peel
2 teaspoons caraway seeds
1 egg
A little milk

Rub butter into flour, add sugar, peel and caraway seeds. Mix to a soft dough with egg and a little milk. Put into greased patty-pans and bake at 425°F, 220°C, gas mark 7 for twenty minutes. The mixture rises and curls over to resemble a wig. Eat with mulled elderberry wine, or dip in ale.

Makes 15

WELSH CHRISTMAS FRUIT LOAF

225 g/8 oz mixed dried fruit
25 g/1 oz chopped peel
50 g/2 oz glacé cherries
100 g/4 oz light soft brown sugar
Grated rind of one lemon
Grated rind of one orange
200 ml/7 fl oz hot strained tea
225 g/8 oz flour
½ teaspoon baking powder
50 g/2 oz butter
1 egg

Steep the fruit, chopped peel, quartered cherries, orange and lemon peel and sugar overnight in the hot tea. Sieve flour and baking powder. Rub in the butter. Beat the egg; add egg and the steeped mixture to the dry ingredients. Turn the mixture into a greased and lined 900 g/2 lb loaf tin. Bake at 350°F, 180°C, gas mark 4 for one hour. Keep for one day before cutting.

Makes 900 g (2 lb) loaf

GOD'S KITCHELS

450 g/1 lb puff pastry
225 g/8 oz currants
75 g/3 oz chopped candied peel
½ teaspoon cinnamon
1 teaspoon ground nutmeg
50 g/2 oz ground almonds
50 g/2 oz butter

These cakes were made in Suffolk during the twelve days of Christmas, from December 25th to January 6th, and were specially kept for visiting god-children, as this was the one time of the year when they were certain to pay a visit to their godparents. There used to be a saying 'Ask me a blessing and I will give you a kitchel.'

Divide the pastry into two pieces and roll out each piece to a thin square. Mix the currants, peel, spices and almonds and stir into the melted butter. Spread this filling evenly on to one piece of pastry to within 1.25 cm/½ in of the edge. Moisten the edge with water and press on the second piece of pastry. Press the edges together well. With the back of a knife, mark the top of the pastry into 5 cm/2 in squares without cutting through the filling. Bake at 425°F, 220°C, gas mark 7 for twenty-five minutes. Sprinkle with caster sugar and divide into small cakes, where marked, while still warm.

Makes 16 pieces

OTHER DISHES

Most of the cakes mentioned at the beginning of this chapter are not included in this book because they are so familiar. But recipes for many others are given in various parts of the book as well as in this chapter. The Berwick May Day tarts are one example, and the Harvest Betsy Cake is another.

Other dishes besides breads and cakes are associated with some of our festivals. Boar's Head was originally served on Twelfth Night, for instance. Hare Pie is still eaten at Hallerton in Leicestershire on Easter Monday. A Cockle and Mussel Feast is held at Clitheroe in Lancashire to mark the election of the Mayor each year: and grilled trout is the traditional dish served to commemorate Sir Francis Drake's bringing water to Plymouth. In some areas, flummery is put outside the back door on Midsummer Eve 'for the fairies'.

CHAPTER SIXTEEN

LOCAL DISHES

Local dishes originated in very early times, among tribes and groups of invaders with different customs. They developed individual features because communications were poor and very few people could travel away from their immediate neighbourhood. The raw materials available to country people were very similar, however, so that almost (but not quite) identical dishes appear in different parts of the country.

They developed almost identical traits, too, because even when the ingredients did differ, the cooking methods were similar. For instance, the West Country mackerel and pilchards were cooked in cider or vinegar with spices in the same way as the East Anglian herrings. In the same way, the plain baked goods made of flour and fat with a few currants or a little spice were cooked on a heated griddle over the fire every-

where before ovens came into common use. Because Britain had plenty of timber, stews and boiled puddings were the commonest cooked foods everywhere, for many centuries.

None the less, almost every region has developed its own recipes, and these are still treasured by countrywomen and are held with pride to be the best.

Local recipes from many different areas are included in every part of this book. But it is not always easy to track down their regional homes since cooking methods and the pace of life have changed in modern times. For one thing, people are more mobile now, and are not restricted to local dishes, so they tend to forget them. The local cakes, pies, biscuits and sweetmeats have kept their identity longest.

They still have their own marked features and, more than most other foods, are still made at home and appear in local shops. The following recipes show how countrywomen in different parts still use flour, sugar, fat, dried fruit and spices, and the local meat, to produce their own local specialties.

SWEET BAKED GOODS AND SWEETMEATS

CUMBERLAND CURRANT PASTY

225 g/8 oz plain flour
50 g/2 oz lard
75 g/3 oz butter
Pinch of salt

Filling
175 g/6 oz currants
¼ teaspoon cinnamon
½ teaspoon allspice
Pinch of ground mace
50 g/2 oz butter
50 g/2 oz light soft brown sugar
Grated rind of one lemon

Make pastry with the flour, fats and salt, but do not rub in the fat too much as the pastry should be rather flaky. Roll half the pastry to fit a 20 cm/8 in square baking tin. Mix all the filling ingredients and heat them over a gentle heat until the butter has melted and the ingredients can be well mixed together. Spread this filling on the pastry. Damp the edges of the pastry and cover with the remaining piece. Prick the top. Bake at 400°F, 200°C, gas mark 6 for ten minutes. Reduce the heat to 350°F, 180°C, gas mark 4 for thirty minutes. Cut in squares to serve.

Makes 12 squares

CORNISH HEAVY CAKE

675 g/1½ lb plain flour
100 g/4 oz butter or cream
100 g/4 oz beef dripping
350 g/12 oz currants
1 tablespoon sugar
1 teaspoon salt
½ teaspoon grated lemon peel

Mix the butter or cream and the dripping in to the flour without breaking it up too finely. Add the other ingredients and mix to a stiff dough with a little water. Roll out on a board and then roll up the dough again. Leave for an hour and roll out the dough into a circle about 1 cm/½ in thick. Cut across with a knife very lightly into fair-sized squares. Bake at 400°F, 200°C, gas mark 6 for twenty-five minutes.

Makes 12 squares

CORNISH FAIRINGS

450 g/1 lb plain flour
225 g/8 oz Demerara sugar
175 g/5 oz butter
50 g/2 oz lard
100 g/4 oz candied lemon peel
Pinch of mixed spice
225 g/8 oz golden syrup
25 g/1 oz bicarbonate of soda
Pinch of tartaric acid
1 teaspoon ground ginger

Rub the butter and lard into the flour. Mix the spices and sugar. Put the syrup into a bowl. Bring the soda to the boil in two tablespoons water in a saucepan and add this to the syrup. Do the same with the tartaric acid until it froths and then mix all the ingredients into the flour, together with the lemon peel cut very finely. Mix to a soft paste and roll out into 2.5 cm/1 in thick strips. Cut these in pieces 2.5 cm/1 in long. Put on to a greased tin, leaving room for the biscuits to spread. Bake at 350°F, 180°C, gas mark 4 for thirty minutes.

Makes 36

CUMBERLAND RUM BUTTER

100 g/4 oz butter
¼ teaspoon ground nutmeg
225 g/8 oz dark soft brown sugar
5 tablespoons rum

Cream the butter and work in the nutmeg and the sugar, gradually adding a few drops of rum at a time until it is all finished. The mixture should be smooth and creamy.

Makes 350 g (12 oz)

This sweet butter was made in Cumberland and Westmorland and put into a bowl to use at Christenings. It was eaten by everyone who visited the new baby, traditionally spread on oatcakes, but sometimes on biscuits or bread. The woman who first cut into the bowl was supposed to be the next one who would prepare a similar dish, and butter made for a boy's birth was said to be more infectious that that made for a girl. Sometimes, the bowl was hidden, and young people came to the house to search for it and eat the contents. The empty bowl was then used for a collection of money for the baby.

DERBYSHIRE BAKEWELL PUDDING

225 g/8 oz plain flour
225 g/8 oz butter
½ teaspoon lemon juice
4 egg yolks
2 egg whites
100 g/4 oz butter
100 g/4 oz sugar
5 drops almond essence
4 tablespoons raspberry jam

Make puff pastry using the flour, 225 g/8 oz butter, lemon juice and cold water to mix. Line a 20 cm/8 in pie plate with the pastry and spread with raspberry jam. Beat the egg yolks and white together. Melt with 100 g/4 oz butter and mix this with the eggs, adding the sugar. Beat for ten minutes and add the essence. Pour into the pastry case and bake at 400°F, 200°C, gas mark 6 for thirty minutes.

Serves 6

DEVONSHIRE FLATS

225 g/8 oz Devonshire cream
450 g/1 lb plain flour
1 egg
225 g/8 oz sugar
Milk

Rub the cream into the flour. Beat the egg into the mixture and add the sugar. Mix thoroughly with a little milk to make a smooth dough. Roll out very thinly and cut into 7.5 cm/3 in rounds. Sprinkle with a little sugar and bake at 375°F, 190°C, gas mark 5 for ten minutes.

Makes 36

DURHAM PIKELETS

225 g/8 oz plain flour
40 g/1½ oz sugar
Pinch of salt
Pinch of bicarbonate of soda
Buttermilk or sour milk

Mix the flour, sugar and salt. Make a well in the centre and pour in enough milk to make a batter with the consistency of thick cream. Dissolve the bicarbonate of soda in a little water and add to the batter. Beat well and fry on a griddle or in a frying pan with lard for 3 minutes each side until golden brown. Spread with butter and serve hot.

Makes 12

LANCASHIRE GOOSENARGH CAKES

450 g/1 lb plain flour
Pinch of salt
350 g/12 oz butter
1 teaspoon caraway seeds
1 teaspoon ground coriander
50 g/2 oz sugar

Mix the flour and the salt and rub in the butter. Mix to a smooth dough and roll out about 5 mm/¼ in thick. Cut into 5 cm/2 in rounds and sprinkle with the spices and sugar. Leave overnight. Bake at 300°F, 150°C, gas mark 2 for forty-five minutes until firm but still pale. Sift on a little more sugar as they cool.

Makes 30

GRANTHAM GINGERBREAD (LINCOLNSHIRE)

225 g/8 oz plain flour
1 teaspoon baking powder
100 g/4 oz butter
100 g/4 oz sugar
1 egg, separated
25 g/1 oz ground ginger

Cream the butter and sugar and beat in the egg yolk. Sift together the flour, baking powder and ginger and add to the butter mixture. Whip the egg white stiffly and fold into the mixture. Put into a 17.5 cm/7 in square tin lined with greased paper and bake at 350°F, 180°C, gas mark 4 for forty minutes. This is a white gingerbread and should remain pale.

Makes one 17.5 cm/7 in square

NORFOLK BIFFINS

Biffins are red-cheeked apples which are dried out very slowly. Choose apples which have no blemishes and put them on clean straw on a wire cake rack. Cover them well with more straw. Put into a very low oven for five hours. Take them out and press them very gently to flatten them slightly without breaking the skins. Return them to the oven for one hour and take them out and press them again. When they are cold, coat them lightly with sugar which has been melted over a low heat without colouring.

NORFOLK DUMPLINGS

If the sugar is left out of the recipe, these dumplings can be served with meat and gravy.

15 g/½ oz fresh yeast
1 teaspoon caster sugar
150 ml/¼ pint hot water
2 tablespoons milk
450 g/1 lb plain flour

Cream the yeast and the sugar. Pour the milk and water over the yeast. Put the flour into a basin and pour in the liquid. Mix well and leave to rise in a warm place for two hours. Knead the dough well and form into dumplings. Leave them to stand for ten minutes. Put into a saucepan of boiling water and boil for twenty minutes. Serve hot with melted butter and sugar.

Makes 10

WESTMORLAND THREE-DECKERS

450 g/1 lb shortcrust pastry
450 g/1 lb plums, apples or blackberries
Demerara sugar to taste

Line a 20 cm/8 in round flat tin with a layer of shortcrust pastry. Put half the fruit on this and sprinkle with sugar. Cover with another layer of pastry, then more fruit and sugar and then top with pastry. Bake at 375°F, 190°C, gas mark 5 for one hour; serve topped with sugar.

Serves 6

YORKSHIRE FAT RASCALS

450 g/1 lb plain flour
225 g/8 oz butter
25 g/1 oz light soft brown sugar
Pinch of salt
100 g/4 oz currants
Milk and water mixed

Rub the butter into the flour. Add the sugar, salt and currants and mix to a firm dough with a little milk and water mixed. Roll out to 1.25 cm/½ in thick and cut into 6.25 cm/2½ in rounds. Dust with a little caster sugar and bake at 350°F, 180°C, gas mark 4 for twenty minutes.

Makes 24

DONCASTER BUTTERSCOTCH (YORKSHIRE)

450 g/1 lb brown sugar
300 ml/½ pint milk
175 g/6 oz butter
Pinch of cream of tartar

Melt the sugar in the milk over a low heat. Add the butter and cream of tartar and boil until a little dropped into cold water forms a hard ball. Pour into a 17.5 × 27.5 cm/7 × 11 in greased tin and mark into squares with a knife just before the toffee hardens.

Makes 675 g (1½ lb)

FOCHABERS GINGERBREAD (SCOTLAND)

225 g/8 oz butter
100 g/4 oz sugar
225 g/8 oz black treacle
2 eggs
450 g/1 lb plain flour
15 g/½ oz ground ginger
25 g/1 oz mixed spice
Pinch of ground cloves
Pinch of ground cinnamon
100 g/4 oz currants
100 g/4 oz sultanas
75 g/3 oz chopped candied peel
75 g/3 oz ground almonds
1 teaspoon bicarbonate of soda
300 ml/½ pint beer

Cream the butter and sugar. Add the slightly warmed treacle. Add the lightly beaten eggs and beat the mixture well. Mix the flour with the spices, dried fruit and almonds. Dissolve the bicarbonate of soda in the beer and gradually mix all the ingredients together. Put into a 23 cm/9 in cake tin and bake at 325°F, 170°C, gas mark 3 for two hours.

Makes one 23 cm/9 in cake

EDINBURGH ROCK (SCOTLAND)

450 g/1 lb loaf sugar
Pinch of cream of tartar
300 ml/½ pint water
Flavouring and colouring (lemon, vanilla, raspberry, rose, ginger or orange)

Crush the sugar and put it into a saucepan with the water. Bring to the boil and add the cream of tartar. Continue boiling without stirring until a little dropped in cold water forms a hard lump. Put in the required flavouring and colouring and pour on to a marble slab. As the mixture cools, push the edges to the middle with a buttered knife. Dust with a little icing sugar and pull until the sugar looks dull. Cut it into pieces with a pair of scissors. Leave it to stand in a warm place for a day until it is powdery and soft.

Makes 450 g (1 lb)

PLAIN AND SAVOURY DISHES

CHESHIRE PORK PIE

675 g/1½ lb pork
450 g/1 lb apples
Salt and pepper
Ground nutmeg
25 g/1 oz sugar
150 ml/¼ pint cider
25 g/1 oz butter
225 g/8 oz shortcrust pastry

Cut the pork into small pieces. Peel and core the apples and cut them into slices. Arrange the pork and apple in layers in a 1.1 litre/2 pint pie dish, seasoning well with salt and pepper, nutmeg and sugar. Pour in the cider and top with the butter. Cover with pastry and bake at 400°F, 200°C, gas mark 6 for fifteen minutes. Reduce the heat to 375°F, 190°C, gas mark 5 and cook for forty-five minutes.

Serves 4

WELSH HOT POT

450 g/1 lb potatoes
225 g/8 oz onions
225 g/8 oz bacon
300 ml/½ pint stock
Salt and pepper

Peel the potatoes and slice them thickly. Peel and slice the onions. Cut the bacon into neat pieces. Put one-third potatoes into a casserole and top with half the onions and half the bacon. Put on a second layer of potatoes, then the remaining onions, bacon and top with potatoes. Season each layer well as the dish is assembled. Pour in the stock. Cover and bake at 325°F, 160°C, gas mark 3 for 2 hours. Remove the lid and continue cooking for 20 minutes.

CORNISH UNDERROAST

900 g/2 lb shin beef
225 g/8 oz ox kidney
450 g/1 lb onions
25 g/1 oz plain flour
Salt and pepper
600 ml/1 pint stock
Potatoes

Cut the beef and kidney into very small pieces. Slice the onions. Toss the meat in flour and season well. Fry the meat and onions in a meat tin with a little dripping until the meat has changed colour. Pour on the stock and leave to simmer while the potatoes are prepared. Peel the potatoes and cut them into pieces about the size of an egg. Put them all over the meat, half below and half above the gravy line like icebergs. Cook at 325°F, 170°C, gas mark 3 for two hours until the potato tops are brown and the bottoms soaked in gravy.

Serves 6

DEVONSHIRE LEEK PIE

225 g/8 oz shortcrust pastry
6 large leeks
300 ml/½ pint milk
Salt and pepper
75 ml/3 fl oz single cream

Roll out the pastry to make a 'lid' for a 1.1 litre/2 pint pie dish. Wash and trim the leeks and cut the white part (and a little of the green) into 2.5 cm/1 in pieces. Put into the milk with salt and pepper, and simmer gently until the leeks are just tender. Pour into the pie dish and add the cream. Cover with the pastry, and bake at 400°F, 200°C, gas mark 6 for thirty minutes. Serve with cold meat.

Variation

For Devonshire Turnip Pie, substitute 450 g/1 lb young turnips for the leeks. Make as above.

Serves 4

MELTON MOWBRAY PIE
(LEICESTERSHIRE)

675 g/1½ lb flour
Pinch of salt
450 g/1 lb lard
150 ml/¼ pint milk and water mixed
1 egg
900 g/2 lb pork
Salt and pepper
Stock from meat trimmings and bones

Sift the flour and salt and rub in half the lard. Boil the remaining lard with the milk and water. When it is boiling, pour half of the liquid into the flour and stir well. Add the beaten egg and then the remaining hot liquid. Knead the dough and leave to stand for a few minutes. Line a 15 cm/6 in mould or tin, or raise the pastry with the hands over a wooden mould or jam jar and tie a double piece of greaseproof paper round it. Cut the meat into small dice and fill the pastry case seasoning the meat well with salt and pepper. Cover with the remaining pastry and brush well with beaten egg which contains a pinch of salt. Bake at 400°F, 200°C, gas mark 6 for twenty minutes. Lower the heat to 350°F, 180°C, gas mark 4 and continue cooking for one and a half hours. It is best to make the stock from the meat trimmings and bones the night before and let it set into a jelly. The addition of a pig's trotter will make the jelly set more firmly. When the pie is lukewarm, heat the stock until melted and pour it carefully into the pie through a hole in the lid. Leave until cold and firm before eating.

Serves 6

NORFOLK BEEF PUDDING

225 g/8 oz self-raising flour
75 g/3 oz shredded suet
Pinch of salt
350 g/12 oz stewing steak
1 shallot
Salt and pepper

Make up a suet crust with the flour, suet, salt and enough water to make a firm dough. Roll it out 17.5 × 27.5 cm/7 × 11 in and put on a piece of greased foil or greaseproof paper. Cut up the meat and shallot finely and put them on to the suet pastry. Sprinkle with water and season with salt and pepper. Roll up the pastry and tie up in a cloth and steam for three and a half hours.

Serves 4

SCOTCH MUTTON PIES

100 g/4 oz beef dripping
300 ml/½ pint water
450 g/1 lb plain flour
1 teaspoon salt
350 g/12 oz lean mutton
Salt and pepper
Grated nutmeg
Gravy

Put the dripping into a pan with the water and bring it to the boil. Sieve the flour and salt together and stir in the hot liquid. Mix well to form a firm dough. Put one-third of the pastry on one side and use the rest to line six pie dishes. Cut the meat into very small pieces and season with salt and pepper and nutmeg. Put the meat into the pastry cases and cover with the remaining pastry. Wet the edges and press them down firmly. Cut a small hole in the centre of each lid. Bake at 375°F, 190°C, gas mark 5 for forty minutes. Pour a little hot gravy into the pies and serve hot.

Serves 6

NORTHUMBERLAND SINGIN' HINNIES

450 g/1 lb plain flour
½ teaspoon cream of tartar
¼ teaspoon bicarbonate of soda
Pinch of salt
175 g/6 oz currants
100 g/4 oz lard
100 g/4 oz butter
A little milk

Sift the flour with the cream of tartar, bicarbonate of soda and salt. Rub in the lard and butter and stir in the currants. Make into a stiff dough with a little milk. Shape into a round and roll out to 1.25 cm/½ in thickness. Rub a girdle or frying pan with a little fat. Put on the dough and cook until brown underneath. Turn the cake carefully to brown the other side. Turn once again to make sure it is hot right through. Cut into pieces, split and butter and serve hot.

Serves 8

NORTHUMBERLAND BACON CAKE

450 g/1 lb plain flour
225 g/8 oz lard
1 teaspoon baking powder
225 g/8 oz cold boiled streaky bacon

Put the flour into a bowl and rub in the lard until the mixture is like fine breadcrumbs. Add the baking powder and mix well, and then add enough cold water to make a firm pastry. Roll and pastry out into a circle. Cut the bacon into thin slices and cover half the pastry completely. Fold over the other half of the pastry and roll it gently to exclude all air. Prick the pastry all over with a fork and pinch the edges together. Put on a baking sheet and bake at 375°F, 190°C, gas mark 5 for forty minutes. This is a favourite mid-morning snack for hungry workers. The cold bacon was often used for breakfast and the remains made into a bacon cake.

Serves 4

NORTHUMBERLAND PAN HAGGERTY

450 g/1 lb potatoes
225 g/8 oz onions
A little dripping
100 g/4 oz grated cheese
Salt and pepper

Peel the potatoes and the onions. Cut them in very thin slices and dry the potatoes in a cloth. Heat the dripping and put in a layer of potatoes, then onions, then cheese and another layer of potatoes. Season the layers with salt and pepper. Fry gently until nearly cooked through. Turn in the pan to brown the other side, or brown the top under a grill.

Serves 4

YORKSHIRE PAN PIE (BEEF)

1 tablespoon dripping
1 large onion
225 g/8 oz stewing steak
3 carrots
2 tomatoes
2 leeks
Salt and pepper
75 g/3 oz self-raising flour
40 g/1½ oz shredded suet

Melt the fat in a saucepan. Chop the onion finely and cut the meat into cubes. Fry the onion and the meat until golden. Slice the carrots, tomatoes and leeks, and add them to the saucepan. Add just enough water to cover and simmer for thirty minutes. Season well with salt and pepper and continue cooking gently for fifteen minutes. Mix together the flour and suet with a pinch of salt and enough cold water to make a firm dough. Form this dough into a circle slightly smaller than the saucepan. Put this on top of the meat and vegetables. Put on the lid and cook gently for one hour.

Serves 4

CHAPTER SEVENTEEN

FARM COOKING FROM FURTHER AFIELD

Traditional farmhouse recipes have travelled widely. The families who left Europe to settle in America, Africa and Australia took with them centuries-old recipes and cooking methods, and adapted them to the conditions and the raw materials they found in their new homes. Sometimes they kept to the old ways and the old recipes long after we did. So not only do similar dishes appear in dozens of countries, but the cooking methods used by our ancestors are still used elsewhere. Thus we can re-create some of our favourite dishes of the past.

In nearly every northern country, there are thick soups which make complete meals, concocted from root vegetables which were quickly and easily grown. Salt pork and bacon appear in very many of them, reminding us of the old, hard days when each family had to kill its pig and preserve the flesh for winter use. This salt meat was particularly good with cabbage, and everywhere in northern climates we find pork and cabbage dishes. Bacon, salt or fresh pork, or chicken fat was cooked or 'tryed out' slowly in a thick pan to produce fat for baking and for frying, and the deliciously crisp remains, the 'scratchings', were used in many dishes, including cakes. Dried peas and beans were another invaluable stand-by in cold winter northern days, and apples were treasured as a fruit because they could be stored and enjoyed in cakes, pies and puddings. Where corn was grown, plain cakes and pancakes were prepared, traditionally baked on the hearthstone or bakestone before ovens were invented. Milk and sour milk were used for this baking, or for cheese-making, or for puddings flavoured with spices. Spices were also popular in cakes, and much used for many centuries.

The following recipes are but a small selection of the many dishes with a common ancestry which are still popular in so many parts of the world.

SOUPS AND STEWS WITH PORK OR BACON

POTTAGE

(La Potée. France)

12 small carrots
6 small turnips
6 small onions
12 small potatoes
900 g/2 lb broad beans
900 g/2 lb peas
1 small cabbage
450 g/1 lb bacon

Clean the carrots, turnips, onions and potatoes and put them into a heavy saucepan with the bacon in a whole piece. Cover with water and simmer for thirty minutes. Add the beans and peas and continue simmering for thirty minutes. Cut the cabbage into small pieces and simmer for five minutes. To serve, cut the bacon into small pieces and put into a tureen. Pour over the soup and vegetables.

Serves 6

TUESDAY SOUP

(Tisdagssoppa. Sweden)

2 tablespoons barley
1.1 litre/2 pints pork stock, with bits of pork in it
2 carrots
1 parsnip
1 stick celery
1 small turnip
3 medium-sized potatoes
Salt and pepper
350 ml/12 fl oz milk

Rinse the barley in cold water, and then cook it in the stock for one hour. Clean the vegetables and cut them in cubes. Add to the stock and barley and simmer for thirty minutes, seasoning with salt and pepper to taste. Stir in the milk, heat gently and serve at once.

Serves 6

PEAS AND PORK

(Ärter Med Fläsk. Sweden)

225 g/8 oz dried yellow peas
3 litres/5 pints water
450 g/1 lb salt pork
2 medium-sized onions
½ teaspoon ground ginger
1 teaspoon marjoram
Salt and pepper

Rinse the peas and put them into a saucepan. Cover with the water and leave overnight. Do not change the water, but cover the saucepan and bring the peas quickly to boiling point. Remove the outer casings of the peas floating on top of the water. Simmer for two hours. Add the pork, sliced onions, ginger and marjoram. Cover again and simmer for one hour. Season with salt and pepper to taste. Take out the pork and cut it into slices to serve separately with mustard.

Serves 6–8

This soup and meat dish is traditionally served on Thursdays in Sweden, followed by pancakes with jam or berries.

MIXED VEGETABLE SOUP

(Minestrone. Italy)

100 g/4 oz haricot beans
2 carrots
2 small potatoes
1 small turnip
2 medium-sized onions
1 stick celery
4 tomatoes
½ small cabbage
2 tablespoons olive oil
50 g/2 oz bacon
2 garlic cloves
2 sprigs parsley
5 tablespoons red wine
1.75 litre/3 pints water or stock
50 g/2 oz broken macaroni or spaghetti
2 teaspoons fresh basil
1 tablespoon fresh parsley
Salt and pepper
50 g/2 oz Parmesan cheese

There are many versions of this soup. Vegetables such as spinach, small marrows, leeks, peas and beans are often used; sage, thyme and marjoram can be added; rice is sometimes used instead of pasta.

Soak the beans overnight. Slice the carrots, potatoes, turnip, onions and celery, the chop the tomatoes and cabbage. Heat the olive oil and cook the onions until soft and golden. Add the bacon cut in pieces, the garlic and the sprigs of parsley. Add the tomatoes and the wine, and leave to simmer for three minutes. Add the drained beans, cover with water or stock, season with salt and pepper and simmer for two hours. Add carrots and cook for fifteen minutes. Add turnip and potatoes. About fifteen minutes before serving time, add celery, cabbage and macaroni or spaghetti. Just before serving, remove the sprigs of parsley, and stir in the chopped basil and parsley. Serve with grated cheese.

Serves 6

MIXED VEGETABLE SOUP

(La Garbure. France)

1 cabbage
450 g/1 lb salt pork
175 g/6 oz haricot beans
3 large potatoes
2 large carrots
1 large turnip
2 leeks
2 onions
1 garlic clove
Sprig of thyme
Salt and pepper

The haricot beans are best soaked overnight before the soup is made. Cut the cabbage in quarters. Cut the potatoes in half, and slice the other vegetables and the garlic. Put all the vegetables into a large pan and cover them with cold water. Season well with salt and pepper, and simmer for one and a half hours. Add the pork and simmer for one hour until the meat is tender. Remove the pork to serve separately. To serve the soup, fry a slice of bread for each person in butter until golden. Put the bread into bowls and pour on the vegetable soup.

Serves 6

CHICKEN AND PORK CHOWDER

(United States)

2.25 kg/5 lb chicken
100 g/4 oz fat salt pork
225 g/8 oz onions
8 cloves
½ teaspoon dried marjoram
1 bay leaf
Salt and pepper
4 large potatoes
450 ml/¾ pint milk

Cut up the chicken. Remove any yellow chicken fat and put it in a frying pan, together with the pork cut in small pieces. Heat the fat gently, and then brown the pieces of chicken in this fat. Put the chicken pieces in a large saucepan. Slice the onion and brown the slices in the same fat. Put the onion slices into the saucepan together with the cloves, marjoram, bay leaf, salt and pepper. Add the pan juices from the frying pan which has been lightly rinsed with boiling water. Cover the chicken with warm water, and simmer until the flesh leaves the bones. Take out the bones. Dice the potatoes and add these to the chowder, and simmer until they are tender. Add the milk, and bring to the boil, but do not boil. Add seasoning if required.

Serves 6

CABBAGE AND SAUSAGE CASSEROLE

(Chou Provençal. France)

450 g/1 lb pork sausages
6 rashers streaky bacon
1 green cabbage
2 medium onions
225 g/8 oz tomatoes
150 ml/¼ pint red wine
300 ml/½ pint stock
Salt and pepper
1 tablespoon tomato purée
1 garlic clove
1 tablespoon brown sugar

Separate the sausages. Chop the bacon finely. Shred the cabbage thinly and slice the onions into thin rings. Remove skins from tomatoes and chop the flesh roughly. Mix the bacon, cabbage, onion and tomatoes together and arrange in layers with the sausages in a casserole. Mix the wine, stock, salt, pepper, tomato purée, crushed garlic and sugar and pour into the casserole. Cover and cook at 325°F, 170°C, gas mark 3 for 1½ hours. Serve with plenty of crusty French bread.

Serves 4

HAM AND KALE SOUP

(United States)

1 ham bone with some meat on it
Bunch of fresh herbs
1.75–2 litres/3–3½ pints water
675 g/1½ lb kale
10 tablespoons quick-cooking rolled oats
Salt and black pepper

Place the ham bone, herbs and water in a large pan and bring to the boil. Skim off the froth, lower the heat, cover, and simmer for two hours. Remove the ham bone and chop the meat. Mince the kale and add to the stock. Cover and boil gently for twenty minutes. Add the oats and chopped ham, and boil for ten minutes more. Adjust the seasoning and serve very hot.

Serves 6

PEA SOUP

(Zupa Grochowka. Poland)

2.25 litre/4 pints stock
450 g/1 lb dried peas
1 small onion
50 g/2 oz potato flour
Salt and pepper
2 sprigs marjoram
100 g/4 oz cooked lean bacon
100 g/4 oz frankfurter sausages
Sour cream

The stock may be made from meat or vegetables. Soak the peas for twelve hours in cold water, and then drain them. Put them into a saucepan with the cold stock and bring to the boil. Add the onion and simmer until the peas are soft. Put through a sieve, and mix the purée and stock with the potato flour. Season with salt and pepper and chopped marjoram. Add pieces of the bacon and sliced sausages, and simmer for ten minutes. Stir in a little sour cream just before serving.

Serves 6–8

PORK WITH CABBAGE

(Flaesk I Kaal. Denmark)

900 g/2 lb salt pork or bacon
1 large white cabbage

Keep the meat in one piece, and put it into a heavy saucepan. Just cover with water and bring to the boil. Simmer for thirty minutes. Drain off the cooking liquid, leaving about quarter of a pint in the bottom of the pan. Cut the cabbage into eight sections and place it round and on top of the meat. Cover and simmer for three hours, until the meat and cabbage are tender. Stir the cabbage from time to time so that it does not burn and add a little of the original cooking liquid from time to time if necessary. Serve the pork or bacon in slices with the cabbage.

Serves 4–6

PORK AND BEANS

(United States)

450 g/1 lb dried kidney beans
1 teaspoon mustard powder
1 dessertspoon salt
1 dessertspoon brown sugar
2 tablespoons black treacle
450 g/1 lb salt streaky pork

Soak the beans overnight, and then cook them until the outer shell comes off. Put the beans into an earthenware pot after draining them. Mix the mustard, salt, sugar and treacle and stir into the liquid from the beans. Pour this mixture over the beans. Put the salt pork into a bowl and pour boiling water over it. Dry the meat and fry it lightly on both sides. Cut the meat into strips and place them on top of the beans. Cover the bean pot and bake at 275°F, 140°C, gas mark 1 for six hours, removing the lid for the last hour so that the pork becomes brown and crisp.

Serves 4

POTATOES FRIED WITH SALT PORK

(United States)

225 g/8 oz coarse ends of salt pork,
*   sliced or chopped*
3 tablespoons vegetable oil
900 g/2 lb boiled potatoes, sliced
1 tablespoon chopped fresh sage or 1
*   teaspoon powdered sage*

Wipe the salt pork with a damp cloth and fry it in the oil. Discard the meat, season the potato with the sage, and fry in the drippings in the pan. Turn once.

Serves 4

BACON-SPICED CABBAGE

(United States)

4 rashers rindless bacon, minced
1 large head cabbage
25 g/1 oz flour
1 tablespoon granulated sugar, to taste
¾ teaspoon salt
450 ml/¾ pint milk
3 tablespoons white vinegar

Fry the bacon until crisp. Remove with a perforated spoon and reserve. Remove the tough outer leaves and hard core of the cabbage and chop into medium-fine shreds. Add the cabbage to the bacon fat and fry over medium heat, stirring occasionally until the cabbage is tender and brown-flecked in about fifteen minutes.

Stir the flour, sugar, and salt into the cooked cabbage. Mix the milk and vinegar and stir it into the cabbage. Stir constantly over medium heat until thick and smooth. Sprinkle with bacon bits and serve hot.

Serves 4

POTATO AND BACON OMELET

(Bauernomelette. Austria)

450 g/1 lb cooked potatoes
150 g/5 oz rindless streaky bacon
75 g/75 oz onions
8 eggs

Cut the potatoes in slices. Dice the bacon and chop the onions finely. Put the bacon and onions into a heavy frying pan and cook them gently so that the fat runs from the bacon to cook the onions. When they are golden, drain off any surplus fat. Add the sliced potatoes to the pan and stir them occasionally until they are hot and slightly browned. Beat the eggs lightly until yolks and whites are blended. Pour over the potato mixture and leave to set, stirring several times. Serve with salad.

Serves 4

FARMER'S CABBAGE

(United States)

1 small cabbage
225 g/8 oz salt pork or bacon
Salt and pepper
Dash of cayenne pepper

Take the outer leaves and core from the cabbage, and cut the cabbage in thin strips. Cut the salt pork or bacon in strips, and put them into a heavy frying pan. Heat gently until the fat starts to run. Add the cabbage and stir the meat and cabbage together until the cabbage separates. Season with salt, pepper and cayenne, and cover with boiling water. Do not put on a lid, but simmer until the liquid has disappeared. Stir the cabbage from time to time until it is tender and lightly browned.

Serves 2–3

FARMHOUSE HAM HOCK, BEANS AND POTATOES

(United States)

1 ham hock
1.75–2.25 litre/3–4 pints water
450 g/1 lb green beans
6 medium-sized potatoes
Salt and black pepper
Cider vinegar

Place the ham hock in a large pan, cover with water, and bring to the boil. Reduce the heat, cover the pan, and simmer the ham for one and a half hours.

Rinse the beans, snap off the ends, and place in the pan with the ham. Cook over medium heat for fifteen minutes. Peel and quarter the potatoes, and add them. Continue to cook for a further 20–25 minutes or until the potatoes are tender.

Remove the ham hock, cut off the meat, and chop finely. Place the vegetables in a serving bowl, cover with one cup cooking liquid, and the chopped (or minced) ham. Season to taste and serve immediately with a cruet of vinegar to sprinkle over the vegetables if desired.

Serves 4

SAGE SAUSAGE

(United States)

1.4 kg/3 lb pork
1 tablespoon salt
2 tablespoons sage
1 dessertspoon marjoram
¼ teaspoon ground cloves
¼ teaspoon black pepper
1 dash of Cayenne pepper

Use pork which has a mixture of fat and lean. The loin cut is best for this, but shoulder pork can be used. Cut the meat into cubes and put through the fine plate of the mincer. Spread the meat out thinly on a board and sprinkle on the salt, sage, marjoram, cloves, pepper and Cayenne pepper. Work in the seasoning thoroughly with the hands. Mince the meat twice more. Leave in a refrigerator for at least twenty-four hours, but if possible for forty-eight hours. Form the mixture into three-inch rounds, about half an inch thick. Brown them on both sides in a hot thick frying pan. Drain off most of the fat, and continue cooking gently until thoroughly cooked.

Serves 6

NEW ENGLAND BOILED DINNER

(United States)

2.25 kg/5 lb salt beef
225 g/8 oz salt pork
1 cabbage
1 medium-sized turnip
6 carrots
4 parsnips
6 potatoes

If the beef is very salt, soak it overnight; if it has not been in pickle for more than a week, it need only be soaked for an hour or two. Put the beef

into fresh water and simmer for one hour. Pour off this water and cover the meat with fresh water. Add the pork and continue simmering for three hours. Cut the cabbage in quarters. Cut the turnip, carrots and parsnips into chunks. Leave the potatoes in their skins. Simmer for one hour. Put the beef and pork in the centre of the serving dish, surrounded with the vegetables.

Serves 6–8

OTHER MEAT DISHES

FLEMISH BEEF AND VEGETABLE STEW

(Carbonnade à la Flamande. Belgium)

675 g/1½ lb lean stewing steak
Salt and pepper
100 g/4 oz butter or lard
450 g/1 lb onions
3 carrots
150 g/5 oz button mushrooms
2 bay leaves
300 ml/½ pint stock or beef bouillon
300 ml/½ pint beer
50 g/2 oz flour
1 tablespoon soft brown sugar

Cut the beef into thick slices. Season with salt and pepper. Brown the slices quickly in the butter or lard, turning them to brown them on all sides. Remove the meat from the heat. Skin the onions, slice and brown in the fat remaining in the pan. Remove them. Slice the carrots.

Place the beef, onions, carrots, mushrooms and bay leaves in an ovenproof dish. Pour in most of the stock or bouillon, and the beer. Add the flour to the fat in the pan. Fry it until brown, and mix it with the reserved stock or bouillon. Simmer to thicken. Stir the thickened liquid into the liquid in the casserole. Season with the sugar. Cover the casserole, and cook at 170°C/ 325°F/gas mark 3 for two and a half hours.

Serves 4

LAMB WITH PEPPERED CABBAGE

(Fár I Kal. Norway)

1.75 kg/4 lb breast of lamb
40 g/1½ oz plain flour
900 g/2 lb firm white cabbage
3 sticks celery
Salt
600 ml/1 pint stock
2 tablespoons whole black peppercorns

Trim any excess fat from the meat and cut the meat into 5 cm/2 in squares. Cook the meat in a little hot oil until evenly browned. Toss the meat cubes in flour until evenly coated. Arrange a layer of meat in a heavy saucepan or a large casserole. Top with a layer of cabbage cut into 2.5 cm/1 in wedges, and then with chopped celery. Sprinkle with salt. Continue in layers twice more, and end with a layer of cabbage. Pour in stock. Bruise the peppercorns lightly with a rolling pin and tie in muslin. Add the peppercorns to the pan and cover the dish tightly. Cook on gentle heat, or in the oven set at 350°F, 180°C, gas mark 4 for one and a half hours. Serve with boiled potatoes.

Serves 6

MEAT AND APPLE CASSEROLE

(Jachtschotel. Holland)

1.25 kg/2½ lb cooked potatoes
350 g/12 oz cooked meat
100 g/4 oz onions
225 g/8 oz sour apples
300 ml/½ pint white stock
40 g/1½ oz butter
Salt and pepper
Ground nutmeg

Slice the cooked potatoes and the meat. Peel and slice the onions. Peel, core and slice the apples. Melt the butter and fry the onions and apples until golden-brown. Arrange layers of potatoes, meat, apples and onions in an ovenproof dish, seasoning the layers with salt and pepper and nutmeg. Pour on the stock and dot the top with a little butter. Bake at 350°F, 180°C, gas mark 4 for about forty-five minutes until golden brown.

Serves 4

CHICKEN, GHENT STYLE

(Waterzooi de Poulet Gantoise. Belgium)

1 tender 1.4 kg/3 lb chicken
1 carrot
50 g/2 oz mushrooms
2 leeks
2 sticks white celery
25 g/1 oz butter
40 g/1½ oz flour
150 ml/¼ pint single cream
2 egg yolks, beaten

Prepare the chicken for poaching. Make a julienne of the vegetables by trimming, scraping and washing the carrot, leeks and celery, and cutting all the vegetables into matchsticks. Put the chicken and julienne into a saucepan, cover with 2.2 litres/4 pts boiling water, and poach for forty-five minutes. Drain but reserve the liquid. Make a roux by melting the butter, adding the flour and cooking them together for a few moments without browning. Add enough cooking liquor gradually to make a pouring sauce. Add the cream and then the egg yolks. Remove the sauce from the heat at once, and stir to incorporate the cream and eggs and thicken it. If necessary, return to the heat for a moment or two, but on no account let the sauce boil. When it thickens, keep it warm by standing the pan in a dish of hot water. Cut the chicken into neat pieces, removing the bones and skin. Put the chicken pieces, vegetables and sauce into a deep dish for serving. Serve with boiled potatoes.

Serves 6

HEAVEN AND EARTH

(Himmel und Erde. Germany)

900 g/2 lb potatoes
350 g/12 oz apples
Sugar
225 g/8 oz black pudding
40 g/1½ oz butter
2 medium-sized onions, sliced
Salt, pepper and nutmeg to season

Wash the potatoes, boil them in their skins. Peel the apples, core, quarter and stew them until soft with a little sugar and water. Meanwhile, slice the black pudding and fry with the onions in half the butter until both are crisp. Keep hot. Pass the apple through a sieve, then blend into the potato with the remaining butter. Season well with salt, pepper and nutmeg. Arrange the slices of black pudding round a warmed serving dish, pile the potato in the centre and sprinkle the onion over all. Serve with home-baked bread and a glass of Dutch gin.

Serves 4

NORMANDY RABBIT

(Lapin en Cidre. France)

1 young rabbit
75 g/3 oz butter
4 garlic cloves
1 tablespoon tomato purée
Salt and pepper
300 ml/½ pint cider
Chopped parsley

Cut the rabbit into joints and leave it to soak in cold salted water for an hour. Drain well. Put into fresh water with a little salt and pepper and boil gently for thirty minutes. Drain the rabbit joints and take the meat from the bones in large pieces. Fry these in the butter with the chopped garlic cloves until well brown. Add the tomato purée with salt and pepper and cook gently for five minutes. Pour in the cider, and simmer for five minutes. Serve sprinkled with chopped parsley.

Serves 4

SALTED SPICED GOOSE

(Sprängd Gås. Sweden)

1 goose, 10–12 lb (4.5–5.5 kg)
150 g/5 oz salt
100 g/4 oz sugar
2 black peppercorns
2 white peppercorns
1 bay leaf
1 small carrot
1 small onion
Sprig of parsley

Wash and dry the goose, and rub it inside and out with the salt and the sugar. Keep the goose in a cold place for twenty-four hours. Mix a brine by adding 75 g/3 oz salt and 75 g/3 oz sugar to each 1.1 litre/2 pints water, and bring this to boiling point. Cool and pour over the goose to cover the bird. Leave in a cold place for three days, turning the bird occasionally. Drain the bird and truss it neatly, and put breast up into fresh boiling water. Bring to boiling point and strain the liquid. Add the peppercorns, bayleaf, carrot, onion and parsley and cover the saucepan. Simmer for two and a half hours until the bird is tender. Serve hot with boiled potatoes, Brussels sprouts, red cabbage and a hot tomato sauce. The goose can also be served cold with potato salad.

Serves 6–8

SWEET DISHES AND CAKES

APPLES IN CIDER

(Pommes en Cidre. France)

900 g/2 lb apples
175 g/6 oz soft brown sugar
300 ml/½ pint cider

Peel and slice the apples and put into a oven-proof dish sprinkled with brown sugar. Pour on the cider. Cover the dish and cook at 350°F, 180°C, gas mark 4 for thirty minutes. Remove the lid and continue cooking for ten minutes. Serve hot or cold.

Serves 4–6

WHITE CHEESE TART

(Tarte au Fromage Blanc. Belgium)

175 g/6 oz flaky pastry
450 g/1 lb unsalted white curd cheese
50 g/2 oz caster sugar
Pinch of salt
15 g/½ oz flour
2 egg yolks
2 tablespoons melted butter
2 egg whites, whipped
Crushed loaf or granulated sugar to
*   glaze*

Line a shallow 20 cm/8 in flan ring or pie plate with the pastry. Crumble the cheese into a basin and work in the sugar, salt, flour, egg yolks and butter. Stir in one tablespoon of whipped egg white, then fold in the rest. Fill the tart with this mixture. Bake at 425°F, 220°C, gas mark 7 until firm in the centre. Shortly before the end of the cooking time, sprinkle with the extra sugar and raise the heat to 450°F, 230°C, gas mark 8 to glaze the tart.

Serves 6

'THICK MILK'

(Dikkemelk. Holland)

Fresh milk
Sugar
Ground cinnamon

Skim the cream from the milk and keep it in a cool place. Leave the milk in a warm place until it becomes sour and solid. Put the solid milk into a cloth or a piece of butter muslin, and hang it up for about twelve hours to drain off liquid. Serve the curd with the reserved, skimmed cream, sugar and cinnamon.

FRUIT DUMPLINGS

(Früchteknödel. Austria)

40 g/1½ oz butter
300 ml/½ pint milk
Salt
250 g/9 oz plain flour
1 egg
Fruit (apricots, cherries, or plums)

Put the butter and milk into a saucepan and bring to the boil. Add the salt and the flour and continue to stir over a low heat until the mixture forms a lump which comes away from the side of the saucepan. Stir in the egg. Put the dough on to a floured board and roll out about 75 mm/¼ in thick. Cut into 6.75 cm/2½ in squares. In the centre of each square, put the fruit. Use (1) a small fresh apricot without a stone, with a little sugar in the cavity (2) three or four cherries (3) a large plum without a stone. Form the pastry squares into dumplings round the fruit. Cook them in lightly salted water which has been brought to the boil. Let the dumplings simmer for ten minutes when they will rise to the surface. Drain the dumplings and roll in golden, fried breadcrumbs. Serve with sugar.

Makes 12

CIDER PIE

(Canada)

150 ml/¼ pint cider
150 ml/¼ pint water
100 g/4 oz black treacle or 3 oz dark
soft brown sugar
15 g/½ oz butter
2 eggs
75 g/3 oz seedless raisins
½ teaspoon lemon juice
Pinch of ground nutmeg
225 g/8 oz shortcrust pastry

Mix the cider with the water and add the black treacle or sugar. Simmer until the mixture forms a syrup. Cool, and stir in the butter, beaten eggs and chopped raisins. Add the lemon juice and nutmeg. Line a 20 cm/8 in pie plate with the pastry. Pour in the filling. Bake at 300°F, 150°C, gas mark 2 for forty-five minutes. Raise the heat to 350°F, 180°C, gas mark 4 and continue cooking for five minutes.

Serves 6

APPLE-TOPPED CINNAMON SQUARES

(United States)

75 g/3 oz butter
175 g/6 oz granulated sugar
200 g/7 oz flour
1 teaspoon ground cinnamon
1 good teaspoon baking powder
5 tablespoons milk
75 g/3 oz chopped nuts
3 tablespoons tart apple, finely-chopped
1 egg yolk

Preheat the oven to 375°F, 190°C, gas mark 5. Whip 50 g/2 oz of the butter with an electric mixer. Add 100 g/4 oz of the sugar, and cream together. Sift the flour with the cinnamon and baking powder. Add the flour mixture and milk alternately to the butter and sugar, a little at a time, stirring well after each addition. Add more flour if necessary to form a fairly stiff dough. Roll out on a floured board and cut into 5 cm/2 in squares.

Make a topping: cream the remaining butter with the sugar, then mix in the nuts and apple. Beat the egg yolk lightly, and brush it over the tops of the squares. Place half a teaspoon topping in the centre of each cinnamon square. Arrange on well-buttered baking sheets and bake for 10–12 minutes. Remove from baking sheets immediately and cool on a wire rack.

Makes 12

GRANDMOTHER'S GINGERBREAD

(United States)

350 g/12 oz plain flour
½ teaspoon salt
½ teaspoon mixed ground ginger,
nutmeg and cinnamon
½ teaspoon bicarbonate of soda
1 dessertspoon warm water
225 g/8 oz black treacle
1 tablespoon melted butter
5 tablespoons milk
1 egg

Sift together the flour, salt and spices. Dissolve the soda in the water and add this to the dry ingredients. Mix together the black treacle, butter, milk and beaten egg. Pour this mixture into the other ingredients and beat very thoroughly. Put into a well-greased 20 × 27.5 cm/ 8 × 11 in tin. Bake at the bottom of the oven set at 350°F, 180°C, gas mark 4 for forty-five minutes.

Makes one 20 × 27.5 cm/8 × 11 in cake

GRANDMOTHER'S RASPBERRY JAM CAKE

(United States)

175 g/6 oz butter
250 g/9 oz dark brown sugar
6 eggs
350 g/12 oz sifted flour
1½ teaspoons bicarbonate of soda
1 teaspoon ground allspice
½ teaspoon ground cinnamon
½ teaspoon grated nutmeg
¼ teaspoon ground cloves
½ teaspoon lemon juice
4 tablespoons double cream
450 g/1 lb sieved raspberry jam
175 g/6 oz currants
Lemon glacé icing

Preheat the oven to 375°F, 190°C, gas mark 5. Beat the butter until light and fluffy, and cream with the sugar. Separate the eggs, reserving the whites. Beat the yolks until lemon-coloured and beat them into the butter and sugar. Combine the sifted flour with the bicarbonate of soda and spices, and sift again. Stir the lemon juice into the cream, and set the mixture in the oven for a few minutes to allow the cream to curdle. Remove and blend with 350 g/12 oz jam.

Add the dry ingredients and the jam mixture alternately to the creamed mixture, stirring well after each addition. Sprinkle the currants with a little flour and mix them into the batter. Beat the reserved egg whites until they are stiff but not dry, then gently fold them into the batter.

Grease two 20 cm/8 in cake tins lightly. Divide the mixture between them and bake for about thirty minutes, or until the layers are springy and brown. Cool in the pans for fifteen minutes, then turn out to cool further on a wire rack. Spread the reserved jam between the layers before covering with the icing.

Makes one 20 cm/8 in cake

THANKSGIVING MARBLED CAKE

(United States)

Dark mixture
275 g/10 oz plain flour
¾ teaspoon baking powder
¼ teaspoon salt
¼ teaspoon ground cinnamon
¼ teaspoon ground cloves
¼ teaspoon ground nutmeg
¼ teaspoon ground allspice
175 g/6 oz dark soft brown sugar
100 g/4 oz butter
4 egg yolks
100 g/4 oz black treacle
Scant 150 ml/¼ pint sour milk

Light mixture
100 g/4 oz butter
350 g/12 oz sugar
275 g/10 oz plain flour
½ teaspoon baking powder
Scant 150 ml/¼ pint milk
4 egg whites

The two cake mixtures are prepared separately, and then put into the baking tin so that 'marbling' occurs, and the cake is a mixture of golden-brown and white. Make the *dark mixture* by sifting the flour with the baking powder, salt and spices. Cream together the sugar and butter until light and fluffy. Beat the egg yolks and mix them with the black treacle, and with the butter and sugar mixture. Put in the flour and milk alternately, a little at a time, beating until well blended. Make the *light mixture* by creaming the sugar and butter. Sift the flour and baking powder and work into the butter mixture alternately with the milk. Beat the egg whites stiffly and fold into the mixture. Grease a 900 g/2 lb loaf tin and drop in large spoonfuls of the two mixtures alternately. Bake at 325°F, 170°C, gas mark 3 for one hour.

Makes one 900 g/2 lb loaf

SAXON CHEESECAKE

(Sächsischer Käsekuchen. Germany)

225 g/8 oz strong plain flour
½ teaspoon sugar
7 oz/¼ oz fresh yeast
150 ml/¼ pint warm milk
½ teaspoon salt
25 g/1 oz butter
3 eggs, separated
115 g/4½ oz caster sugar
800 g/1¾ lb curd cheese
Salt
50 g/2 oz plain flour
65 g/2½ oz butter, melted
90 g/3½ oz raisins
Icing sugar

Make a dough first. Blend together 65 g/2½ oz strong flour, the half teaspoon sugar, and the yeast and milk to make a thick batter. Leave the batter in a warm place until frothy, for about twenty minutes. Sift the remaining strong flour and salt, and rub in 25 g/1 oz butter. Add this flour mixture to the batter, and mix well to give a fairly soft dough. Knead for about ten minutes. Place in a lightly oiled polythene bag and allow to rise until double in size. Turn the dough on to a lightly floured surface and knead. Butter a 20 cm/8 in loose-bottomed, springform tin. Line with the dough.

For the filling, whisk the egg whites stiffly, gradually adding the caster sugar. Sieve the cheese and add a little of the egg white to it. Fold the mixture into the bulk of the egg whites with a pinch of salt, the flour added a spoonful at a time, the egg yolks, melted butter and raisins. Turn into the tin and bake in the bottom of the oven heated to 350°F, 180°C, gas mark 4 for about three quarters of an hour. Allow to cool, remove from the tin, and dust heavily with icing sugar.

Serves 8

SPICED GINGER BISCUITS

(Pepparkakor. Sweden)

150 g/5 oz dark soft brown sugar
150 g/5 oz black treacle
1 teaspoon ground ginger
1 teaspoon ground cinnamon
½ teaspoon ground cloves
2 teaspoons bicarbonate of soda
165 g/5½ oz butter
1 egg
550 g/1¼ lb plain flour
Glace icing, for decoration

Put the sugar, black treacle and spices into a saucepan and bring to boiling point. Add the bicarbonate of soda and pour the mixture over the butter in a bowl. Stir until the butter melts. Work in the egg and sifted flour and mix thoroughly. Knead on a floured board and then chill for thirty minutes. Roll out thinly and cut into shapes. Put on greased baking tins and bake at 325°F, 170°C, gas mark 3 for ten minutes. Cool on a wire rack, and decorate with icing.

Makes 48

These are particularly popular at Christmas time cut into special shapes such as angels, Christmas trees, stars, hearts and animals.

RELISHES, PRESERVES AND DRINKS

APPLE AND ONION RELISH

(United States)

3 slices fat salt pork
1 large onion
¼ teaspoon black pepper
225 g/8 oz sour apples
1 dessertspoon sugar

Fry the pork slices until they are crisp. Remove them, and cook the onion cut in thin slices in the fat. Turn the slices often to avoid burning. Season with pepper and then put a layer of peeled sliced apples on top of the onions. Dust with the sugar and put on a lid. Bake at 400°F, 200°C, gas mark 6 for fifteen minutes. Serve with fat meat or poultry, such as pork, ham, goose or duck.

Serves 4

SWITCHEL

(United States)

Black treacle
Cider
Ground ginger

Sweeten water to taste with some black treacle. Add enough cider to make the drink tart and refreshing. Stir ½ teaspoon ginger into each 1.1 litre/2 pints liquid. This is the traditional drink for haymakers in New England.

PENNSYLVANIA PLUM CONSERVE

(United States)

2 oranges
1.4 kg/3 lb stoned plums
1.4 kg/3 lb sugar
450 g/1 lb seeded raisins
150 ml/¼ pint water
100 g/4 oz chopped walnuts

Wash the oranges but do not peel them. Cut them in small pieces and mince them. Cut the plums in small pieces. Mix together the oranges, plums, sugar, raisins and water. Simmer together for one and a half hours. Add the walnuts and continue cooking for fifteen minutes. Pour into hot jars and seal.

Makes 2.7 kg (6 lb)

MUSHROOM PICKLE

(Salenyia Gribi. Russia)

450 g/1 lb small mushrooms
600 ml/1 pint wine vinegar
2 tablespoons salad oil
4 cloves
12 peppercorns
1 tablespoon salt

Wash the mushrooms and dry them thoroughly, and remove the stalks. Boil in a little salted water until tender, and drain completely. Simmer the vinegar for ten minutes with the cloves, peppercorns and salt, and then leave until cold. When the mushrooms are cold, put them into preserving jars. Pour over the cold vinegar and top with the oil. Cover tightly and leave in a cold place for a few days before eating.

Makes 450 g (1 lb)

IN THE KITCHEN

The farmer's wife was traditionally a very busy person. As well as cooking for the family, any casual visitors who might arrive, perhaps then staying for months, and looking after indoor and outdoor staff, she would help in the fields, rear calves, take charge of the poultry, and grow vegetables, fruit and herbs. She would also brew beer, prepare butter and cheese, and make wines, cordials, medicines, ointments and beauty preparations. There were daughters and young village girls to help, but they needed close supervision.

Some farmhouses were little more than cottages, while others could be large comfortable dwellings, or even manor houses. All of them conformed to a similar kitchen pattern, however, with one large room containing a huge fire on one wall. Poorer families would use this room for preparing food, eating, general living, and even sometimes sleeping. More prosperous kitchens would feature additional side-rooms for storage and special food preparation, and the best houses had a separate dining room.

The main room was simply furnished, usually with a large solid table in the centre, and possibly benches or simple chairs (in poorer houses, meal were eaten standing). At the side, there might be a long narrow table for 'dressing' meat, game, and fish, with shelves above for ingredients and implements. Later the dresser table and shelves were joined to make the dressers we know today. Precious ingredients such as spices, sugar, tea and coffee were often stored in locked cupboards, and carefully distributed by the lady of the house who held the lock and key.

The huge fire, which also warmed the house and heated water, limited the style of cooking. There were no ovens, except in the grander houses, and meat had to be spit-roasted in front of the fire over a dripping pan. Smaller pieces of meat, poultry and even fruit were cooked on small dangling spits, or on rigid screens fitted with rows of small hooks. Iron grids were used for toasting bread or grilling small food items.

Because of the difficulty of cooking meat, it was common to cook a large joint on Sunday, the only rest day for the family, and this was then eaten cold or in made-up dishes during the rest of the week. Naturally, the cook became hot and cross, as she handled the spit as well as heavy cauldrons suspended over the fire, and awkward long-handled pans for grilling and frying, made of cast iron. The cauldrons of boiling water were used for simmering meat and vegetables, and for cooking puddings wrapped in cloths.

Lucky housewives had a small domed 'beehive' oven at the back or side of her big fire. The oven would be filled with small pieces of wood known as faggots. When these had burned through and been reduced to hot ash, the ashes were swept out and the oven filled with the coarse household bread. When this was removed, finer white bread and cakes would be put into the cooler oven. These were followed by small cakes and fine biscuits, and finally an overnight 'oven bottom' cake would be put in to take advantage of the last vestiges of heat. Traditionally, the bread, which formed the bulk of the baking, was made on Monday which was also washday, because the kitchen was then warm and damp and provided ideal conditions for proving (or rising) the bread.

It was not until the end of the eighteenth century that the vast fires began to be enclosed with bricks, and most homes did not enjoy an enclosed cooking fire and oven until well into the nineteenth century. Gas was introduced in the middle of the century, but was not available to country families until the turn of the century, while electric stoves were not available until the first quarter of this century, with many country houses not being connected to the electric grid until the 1950s.

Men worked from dawn to dusk, mainly sustained by dark, heavy bread, fat bacon and beer. They needed large quantities of bread and pastry to eke out expensive meat, for most of the good beef and lamb was sold to the towns. The pig was the most commonly used animal, along with poultry and game and the odd rabbit and pigeon. To save precious fodder, livestock were killed during the autumn and winter. The meat was salted to preserve it and cooked later with dried pulses and grains, root vegetables which had been stored, and fruit which had been preserved.

Not all the food was heavy, for big farmhouses were social centres and there were many guests and much entertaining.

Many better farmhouses had a stillroom, which was actually designed to be a distillery for the preparation of fine liqueurs, medicines and toilet waters. In this room, the farmer's wife had a charcoal stove and lighter equipment (often the pans were of silver) in which she made her jellies, delicate puddings and sweetmeats. She set her clear fruit jellies in pretty moulds, shaped gingerbread and shortbread in wooden moulds with intricate pictures, and made ices in pretty shapes like flowers or bowls of fruit. These ices and other chilly foods were finished in icehouses or caves filled with straw as an insulating material, and great blocks of ice cut from a local lake. By the middle of the nineteenth century, there were tin- or zinc-lined boxes which held ice blocks. These could be kept in the house and used as primitive refrigerators.

The only other method of preservation apart from salting was by pickling in vinegar or by bottling or jamming with sugar, and the farmer's wife was proud of her larder full of preserves which gave zest to heavy winter meals. Simple country cooks could not read and even had to be instructed by their mistresses on the use of elementary equipment (twigs or feathers were used as whisks and eggs had to be beaten for hours to get the desired results). The housewives who had some education were able to record their favourite recipes and to exchange them with their friends and families. Many of these old recipes have been used as the basis of the authentic recipes in this book.

INDEX